Praise for 100

"I've heard a lot of stories in 30 years as a Hollywood producer but I've rarely found one as beautifully bizarre, deeply touching and as uplifting as Shant Kenderian's story."

—Robert Cort, Executive Film Producer

"Shant Kenderian invites us into a privileged place rarely visited by outsiders in Baghdad, the perspective of an accidental Iraqi soldier. With him, we take a jagged road to the front lines of Saddam Hussein's impetuous war against Kuwait. He takes us on an emotional journey that is both tormented and complex and, in the process, establishes an important context through which we can view today's Iraqi conflicts. What a ride!"

—Liz Balmaseda, two-time Pulitzer Prize–winning journalist

"Authentic, uplifting, and above all human—this is a moving story of success against the odds."

—Robert Lacey, bestselling author of *The Kingdom*

"The story of an innocent man hurled into a maelstrom of seemingly endless perils and predicaments, Shant Kenderian's *1001 Nights in Iraq* rivals anything in the fantastic tales narrated by Scheherazade. But Kenderian's story is true, making it all the more astonishing and unforgettable. Only a man of great courage and resilience could have survived such a harrowing ordeal. And only a storyteller of extraordinary talent could have related it with such humanity, grace, and humor."

—Andrew Carroll, *New York Times* bestselling editor
of *War Letters* and *Behind the Lines*

"Shant is a modern-day Odysseus—yet the nymphs and monsters he faced were far from mythological. His book is proof that truth is sometimes not just stranger, but also more beautiful than fiction. Life is good after all."

—Scarlett Lacey, film producer

"Shant has written a fast-paced, riveting story that allows the reader to peek into the beautiful mind and heart of a man who manages to stay away from the traps of bitterness and despair; and who against all odds, survives a satanic hell with dignity intact. This real-life story underscores the correctness of my great-granduncle Alfred Nobel when he said: 'War is the horror of horrors and the crime of crimes.'"

—Claes Nobel

"Few true life adventures are as filled with hard-to-believe events as those recorded in Shant's *1001 Nights in Iraq*. As a participant in Desert Shield/Desert Storm, this remarkable account brought me back to key events but from a human, personal perspective that spans life-threatening as well as humorous, heartwarming events. This story proves that even in the most dire circumstances, Providence can intervene in a most profound way and that this impact continues in the lives of many of the key characters in this story."

—Patrick P. Caruana Lt. Gen. (Ret), USAF

1001 NIGHTS
IN IRAQ

1001 NIGHTS
IN IRAQ

The Shocking Story of an American Forced to
Fight for Saddam Against the Country He Loves

SHANT KENDERIAN

ATRIA BOOKS

NEW YORK   LONDON   TORONTO   SYDNEY

ATRIA BOOKS

1230 Avenue of the Americas
New York, NY 10020

This work is a memoir. It reflects the author's present
recollections of his experiences over a period of years.

Copyright © 2007 by Shant Kenderian

ISBN-13: 978-1-4165-4019-9
ISBN-10: 1-4165-4019-9

First Atria Books trade paperback edition June 2007

1   3   5   7   9   10   8   6   4   2

ATRIA BOOKS is a trademark of Simon & Schuster, Inc.

Manufactured in the United States of America

For information regarding special discounts for bulk purchases,
please contact Simon & Schuster Special Sales at 1-800-456-6798
or business@simonandschuster.com.

Manufactured in the United States of America

To my Guardian Angel,
who took part in the events of this book, no less than I did,
and without whom this story would have never been told.

1001 Nights in Iraq *tells the story of Iraqis forced to soldier in the Arabian Desert, sailors forced to go to sea, and of miraculous escapes from death, time and again. While an army of one million marches through the desert and mysterious events take place in the sea,* 1001 Nights in Iraq *resembles the world-renown classic known in the West by the title,* 1001 Arabian Nights.

Both stories tell of travel and adventure in an increasingly bizarre world. But unlike its namesake, 1001 Nights in Iraq *tells a story true to the last word.*

—Shant Kenderian

1. Land of Mirrors

The door to my father's house was open, but I could not step inside. My cousin stood in the doorway, blocking my path. Her eyes warned me to take pause. If only it wasn't too late. I had traveled an unfathomable distance to make things right with my father. I had ventured beyond boundaries of family, culture, and convention. I had no map, no compass, no tangible itinerary. A little more than two years after moving to the United States with my mother and brother, after embracing a new life and a new language, I had returned to my native Iraq to bid my father a proper farewell. On the heels of my parents' contentious breakup, we had left too abruptly for good-byes. No amount of American food, adventure, and distraction could chase away the deep regret I felt for dishonoring my father by leaving without a word. A simple good-bye, that's all I sought to bring him. At seventeen, I decided I would travel home, embrace him, make myself whole again, then return to my new world in America.

But nothing back home is that easy. My beloved Iraq is a land of mirrors and trick doors. By the time I learned this, just days after my return in 1980, it was too late. I was trapped. On September 22 of that year, only seven days after I arrived and made peace with my father, Saddam Hussein launched an attack against the neighboring country of Iran, marking the beginning of what would be an eight-year war. Saddam closed the borders and forbade all males of military age, myself included, from leaving the country. In one impetuous stroke, Saddam's edict tossed me into a holding pattern that would endure not one war, but two. I would be stranded there for more than ten years and forced to take an unimaginable route back to America.

Now, nearly two years into my Iraqi limbo, I stood outside my father's house, at yet another door deceptively open. I glared at my cousin and she stepped aside, revealing a living room full of mourners. I bowed in prayer. *Our Father, who art in heaven, hallowed be Thy name . . .*

I made my way past the mourners until I reached my father's coffin. Two months earlier, my father, Hagop Kenderian, was struck as he drove on a one-lane road through the mountainous regions of northern Iraq. Two reckless Turkish cargo truck drivers were passing each other on an uphill segment of the road and collided with my father atop the hill. He was taken to a hospital in Mosul, but he never regained consciousness.

I draped my arms across the casket and I gave him the longest embrace I could ever remember. As I did this, I could hear through my sobs the chatter of strangers, relatives of my father's wife.

"Who is he?"

"This is his son who came back from America."

America. It no longer seemed a real place to me, certainly not one that could be accessed via Baghdad. It all seemed a memory: landing in Chicago, Illinois, as a grateful green card holder and permanent resident. I was fifteen years old. I eagerly took in the novelties of American life and the notion that in the United States democracy and freedom are God-given rights. Granted, I felt like an outsider at first. But then again, I've always felt like an outsider. As an Iraqi Christian of Armenian descent, I often felt like an interloper in my own country. I was raised in a tight Armenian community, attended a private Armenian school, and worshipped within the ornate walls of the St. Gregory the Illuminator Armenian Apostolic Church in Baghdad's ancient city. Since our great-grandparents settled in Iraq, fleeing rampant massacres in Ottoman Turkey in the early 1900s, we've shared a precarious existence as tolerated foreign infidels in a land of Muslim dominance.

By comparison, my entry into the United States was a breeze. I plunged into school and soaked up every bit of knowledge I could. It was exciting to experience new things, to speak a new language, shop at the supermarket and get lost in the aisles of infinite candies. I loved donuts at first bite and cafeteria-style mashed potatoes with gravy. I saw a squirrel for the first time and was shocked to learn that skunks can stink up a few neighborhood blocks when angered. I loved the American traditions of Halloween and Thanksgiving—the former for its weird and colorful costumes and the latter for the cozy family feeling it brought me.

My brother became rebellious and difficult. I dealt with life by burying myself in my studies. I borrowed books from the library and devoured them long before the due date. I always finished my math and science homework, then solved the remaining chapter problems that were not included in the assignment. When I could not exchange my PE class in favor of another science class, I convinced my advisor to sign me up for a German-language class during lunch period. Each day, I'd grab a bag of Cheetos from the vending machine on my way to class.

The pages of my German book gradually turned an odd shade of orange. By the time I reached my junior year, I was taking advanced courses in physics, chemistry, and math. I didn't know what a "GPA" was, nor did I understand what value it possessed. From a letter sent to my mother from school, I know now that my GPA was somewhere above 4.5, but I barely had a clue whether that meant I was successful.

Not only was school a great adventure, it was a safe harbor from the pain of a broken family. I missed my father. At first, my mother forbade me from writing letters to him. Then, she allowed me as long as I did not include a return address. I obeyed her for about six months, then told her I was going to break the rule. My mother's anger only intensified as letters filled with venomous references to her began to arrive from Baghdad. Caught in the volley of harsh words between my parents, I began to dread the arrival of mail from Iraq.

As if our new life weren't jarring enough, my mother announced abruptly that she would remarry soon. She gave us no warning, no tactful preamble, just a nonnegotiable declaration. My brother and I stepped out onto the balcony and cried. A few months later, my mother and her fiancé, Bob, went to the courthouse and said their vows. From one day to the next, there was a man in our house with a new set of rules. Just a few weeks after that, my aunt telephoned from Iraq to tell me my father also had remarried. He never called to break the news. I sensed he was too hurt to do so. So far away, I felt powerless. I desperately wanted to mend my family's wounds. I felt I needed to do so before I could resume my new life.

Shortly before what would have been my senior year in high school, I set off for Iraq on a solo mission to set things straight. For the first time, I felt grown-up, responsible, in control of my life. But it was only an illusion. Just one week later, I was no longer a high school student trapped in an annoying family drama. I was a prisoner of Saddam Hussein, a pawn in his ludicrous war against Iran.

I managed to evade military service for a while by enrolling in a college program. I took solace in my Christian-Armenian community and tried to make the best of my predicament. I continued my schooling in Baghdad and enrolled in engineering courses at the University of Technology. But I only managed to delay the inevitable. As soon as I graduated with a bachelors of science degree in engineering in 1985, I was forced into the military service, drafted into the Iraqi Navy. I had no choice. In Saddam's Iraq, the only option to enlistment was execution. I spent the next three and a half years fighting the Iranians on the front lines, in and near the city of Basra.

During that eight-year conflict, which played out almost unnoticed on the world stage, it was not unusual for one country to suffer losses in a single night that were equal in magnitude to all of those suffered by the American troops during their years in Vietnam. It was an unpopular war, one that left the Iraqi people grasping for feeble justifications. Within months of the beginning of the war, the only justification they could find to continue Saddam's fight was to defend their land from the country that they themselves had invaded.

During that time, the United States opened an embassy in Baghdad, which gave me tremendous hope that I might find a way to get inside and claim asylum. However, as an enlisted soldier I was forbidden from approaching any foreign embassy. It also was a crime punishable by death. On a visit to Baghdad in 1986, my mother pled my case before U.S. embassy officials. They transferred the paperwork to the embassy in London, so that the front-office Iraqi clerks, almost certainly agents for Saddam, would not see my name. But nothing came of it. I was forced to wait until after the Iraqi government lifted the travel ban in 1990 to contact the embassy in Baghdad. By then, the Iran-Iraq War had been over for more than a year. The most treasured pieces of my world had been rearranged. My mother and brother had moved to Los Angeles, California. In Baghdad, my father had died, as had my grandparents. Most of my close relatives in Iraq had departed. There were nothing but ghosts and childhood memories to fill the ample boulevards I once found so stunning in my Baghdad neighborhood. Although I had never been to California, it seemed more like home than the decaying city around me. I couldn't wait to get there.

But once again, Saddam Hussein's ambitions intervened. Before my green card renewal process was complete, he lashed out at yet another neighboring country. On August 2, 1990, Iraqi forces invaded Kuwait, triggering a sequence of events that would culminate in war with the West during Operation Desert Storm.

On the day Saddam announced his military action against Kuwait, he gave all Iraqi males under the age of fifty-five three days to register for military service. The penalty for refusing to do so had a familiar ring: summary execution.

And I thought my military days were safely behind me. But those days were schoolboy outings compared to what lay ahead in my 1,001 nights in the Iraqi Army. Those nights would give me a front-line view of the abject corruption of Saddam's regime. They would take me across enemy lines. They would transform a misplaced engineer and melancholic painter—a science geek from Chicago's Wheeling High School, a guy with really bad timing—into a witness of history, a desperate schemer, and a prisoner of war, an Iraqi suspect in the hands of the U.S. Army. I spent more than a decade searching for an escape hatch out of Saddam's fright house. The funny thing is I found the door to freedom in the least-expected place—in prison. Only in Iraq.

Of course I hadn't yet heard the rumblings of war on the morning I set out to meet an artist friend for what I thought would be just another sweltering day in Baghdad.

2. Register Within Seventy-two Hours or Be Shot

Mohammed was late as usual. We were supposed to meet at 8:00 A.M. on August 2, 1990, near the Academy of Fine Arts, where he studied. But twenty minutes had passed and so had most of the morning's fair, more manageable temperatures. The summer heat crept into the heart of Baghdad's ancient city and I knew that soon it would reach the usual hundred and twenty degrees of a typical August day. I wasn't about to stand around and wait for another one of Mohammed's poor excuses for chronic tardiness.

It's not that I had anywhere pressing to go. I had finished school. I didn't have a job. In truth, I didn't want one, not in Baghdad anyway. I didn't see the point. I was financially stable, having inherited money from my wealthy grandfather. I had a family home and a car. Yes, I had job opportunities. In fact, from a pool of two hundred and fifty applicants for one coveted position, I got the offer. I turned it down because my only goal was to leave Iraq for the United States. So I had nowhere particularly important to go that day. But, I had better things to do than wait in the sun for Mohammed.

As I headed for my car, I bumped into an old friend and fellow engineering graduate from the University of Technology. Sardar was preoccupied, nervous. He skipped all the usual Iraqi formalities of public greetings. At a minimum, customs dictate that the person entering the presence of others should initiate the greeting with *"Al-Salamu Alaykum"* (Peace be upon you), while the other should respond with *"Wa Alaykum Al-Salam"* (And upon you be peace). Anything short of that is considered offensive. I was often criticized for trying to get by with "good morning" and "good afternoon" rather than abide by Arab traditions.

"Why aren't you in the United States?" Sardar demanded.

I was taken aback slightly, but I explained that I was in the process of renewing my green card.

"It should be ready in two or three weeks," I told him.

"Then you haven't heard?" Sardar asked.

The look on his face told me it wasn't good news.

"The entire Iraqi border is closed again," he announced.

His words drifted past me and melted into the summer heat. I shrugged in denial.

"No, it's not," I told him. "I just drove my aunts to the airport last night. I stood there and watched their plane take off, just before midnight."

Sardar gave a sarcastic grin.

"Your aunts are very lucky," he said. "They closed the borders this morning."

A sick dread seeped into my gut.

"I don't understand . . . Why?" I wanted to know.

"Because we invaded Kuwait."

"We."

"We. Us. You and me."

His words were all the more unsettling because he spoke with calm resignation.

"*We* invaded Kuwait," I persisted.

"Yes. Kuwait."

I refused to believe him. I needed a headline, a news account, something concrete and official. Instead, I got tardy Mohammed, who rushed up with his own news bulletin. Sadly, it was the same one I had heard from Sardar.

The three of us walked to the nearest café to find a radio. There were only a few people inside, all clustered around a small radio atop the counter. The waiter saw us come in, but only nodded before turning his attention back to the radio. The café scene was an eerie still life. The morning's *stikan*, those ubiquitous glass teacups in every café in Baghdad, sat untouched. And there was silence, none of the usual constant jingling of little spoons stirring excessive amounts of sugar into tea. The faceless radio announcer had the floor and his words reverberated across the room.

"Iraq has answered the call to help a group of faithful Kuwaiti men who overthrew the corrupt prince early this morning . . . This military action will only be a matter of a few days. Or maybe a few weeks."

In just six days, Saddam Hussein's regime could have celebrated two full years of peace for the first time in its eleven-year rule. It would have been a unique position for the strongman who muscled his way into the presidency and the leadership of Iraq's giant standing army with such blatant disregard for traditional government. With the borders finally open, thousands of Iraqis had been flocking to foreign embassies to apply for travel visas. And those who weren't intent on traveling seemed generally optimistic about the future. The war was fading into memory. People were publicly confident that Iraq's oil-rich economy would spring back. They had faith that the Iraqi dinar, worth thirty U.S. cents at the time, would return to its former trading value of three U.S. dollars.

Two years of peace.

But the world would see no such restraint from Saddam. He was busy crushing the civilian Kuwaiti population at that very moment.

We lingered at the café, waiting for the radio announcer to give a coherent explanation for the invasion. Instead, he delivered the words we all dreaded: Saddam had militarized the entire Iraqi nation—again. Every able-bodied male in the country, between the ages of eighteen and fifty-five, had three days to report to their local recruiting office. After that, if we were caught on the streets without our draft papers, we would be executed for "desertion."

The announcement left no room for doubt. But somehow I couldn't bring myself to believe it. It would be just my luck—strange things always seem to happen to me. The counterrevolution of November 1963 broke out right after I was born. The hospital's maternity ward rattled with the cross fire of soldiers and rebels. My parents hid me in a closet drawer, my first cradle, to protect me from stray bullets.

I wanted to cling to that sense of hope I had just a few hours earlier that my passage to America was only days away. That glimmer of hope had carried me through the daily inertia of life in Baghdad. I was afraid to let it go. I couldn't make sense of this new situation. For that matter, neither could other Iraqis I came across during the next couple of days. The word on the street was that this would be a short incident. Saddam's troops would soon withdraw. The budding sense of normalcy would be restored.

I avoided the recruiting office for as long as I could. I re-

ported on the third and final day. It was only a formality, I tried to
tell myself. Always a good student, I was simply playing by the
rule book. But deep inside I knew hope was quickly fading. As I
filled out the paperwork, I felt sick to my stomach. I felt powerless before the truth that, for the second time, Saddam's exploits
had jerked my life off course. He was the petulant child playing
out his dysfunction upon the world's stage. Meanwhile, the pop-
ulace had no choice but to dwell in the shadows of his war
games.

Four hours later, I was back in the Iraqi Navy. The previous
war remained ambiguous to the last day. In all, it was estimated
that 1.5 million soldiers were killed from both sides; several hundred thousand others were executed with or without reason and
billions of dollars were spent on the war. Most of the working
force was engaged on the front lines instead of on the production
floor, and the economy deteriorated at a phenomenal rate. Nothing was accomplished whatsoever by the Iran-Iraq War. When
asked the common question, "Who won the war?"—although
Iraq was considered the victor—most Iraqis would answer, "Both
sides lost." The only positive thing that the Iraqis thought came
out of the war was the belief that their generation would never
see war again. They were convinced that the Iran-Iraq War experience was so horrible that it would deter any man, even one like
Saddam Hussein, from engaging in another conflict during his
lifetime. In less than two years, Saddam proved them all wrong.

Iraq had not only suffered a severe decline in its economy
and the life expectancy of its male population, but also the
morals of the Iraqi people deteriorated a great extent. Up until
the early years of the Iran-Iraq War, the crime rate in Baghdad
was very low. I would visit a friend from college in the poorest
neighborhoods of Baghdad. I walked the darkest and narrowest

alleys past midnight without the slightest concern for my safety. But when all efforts to end the war were thwarted, the battles became more brutal. Thousands of soldiers deserted their military duty and became refugees from the government. Beginning with the second year of war, the desertion rate began to rise annually and became a serious national problem by the sixth year. With no other source of income, the deserters resorted to crime to provide for their families.

The lowest point and greatest confusion of ethics came when a father told the story of his son on Iraqi television. The married son lived with his own family on the second floor of his father's house. The father and the mother lived on the first floor. This arrangement was not uncommon in the Middle East. The son had been wounded in battle several times. Instead of showing the slightest concern toward his son's health, the father was proud of his son's scars because, as he put it, they decorated his son like medals. Each time the son was wounded, his wounds were quickly patched up and he was sent back to the front lines. The incident that the father was explaining on TV occurred when the son refused to return to the front lines. This time, he knew he would surely die. Having a son who is a deserter would destroy the father's hopes of climbing the ranks of the Ba'ath Party. But a martyred son (those killed in battle were called martyrs) would boost his promotion rate. When the son refused to return to his unit, the father was upset. He told his son to go back to the front lines and bring honor to the family with his martyrdom. The son refused to change his mind. The father brought his gun from downstairs and went back to the second floor. He gave his son an ultimatum: Either he would go to the front lines to fight and die like a hero or die like a coward right there and then. The son sat on the bedroom floor and called his father's bluff. The father shot and killed his son in the presence of his pleading wife, crying children, and elderly mother. The father was on Iraqi TV because of a special ceremony where he was awarded a medal of bravery pinned on his chest by the devil incarnate himself, Saddam Hussein. Needless to say, none of the other family members attended the ceremony.

Now, here I was, forced back onto Saddam's team. I, along with every draftee affiliated with the navy, was dispatched to the Naval Academy in the city of Basra, in southern Iraq. The academy served as a holding tank of sorts. It was not set up as a base or shelter of any kind, simply as a transfer station for thousands of men responding to the three-day draft notice. There were no beds, no food, and no semblance of comfort. We were expected to sit on the ground all day and all night and to avoid asking impertinent questions about meals or sleep. The school's staff was charged with processing and reassigning the draftees to different naval units headed to Kuwait. After a couple of days, the situation approached pandemonium. At times, it felt like the Mother of All Class Reunions as thousands of old comrades from the Iran-Iraq War met again on the academy campus.

I had studied here in 1985, when I first entered the navy. I was assigned to the Engineering Department of the Navy headquarters, which had been moved to the academy after Iranian bombs destroyed its original location. The move didn't help much—the Iraqi and Iranian shelling over the skies of Basra was so dense that projectiles collided midair by sheer coincidence on more than one occasion. The random bombings hit key targets within the academy grounds. The walls in our offices and living quarters were riddled with shrapnel holes. We learned to recognize the sound of falling bombs and the pattern of shrapnel scatter. At the end of our school day, we often found ourselves caught in the middle of Iranian shelling as we walked from our classroom back to the Engineering Department. The fifteen-minute walk felt like fifteen hours as we constantly dove for cover while shrapnel from enemy fire sprayed the walls and fell to the ground like rain.

This time around at the academy, the inflow of draftees was far greater than the capacity of the small academy staff, so errors were rampant. Names were shuffled around. Transfer papers were lost. In the chaos, I wound up stuck at the academy for an entire month. It seemed as though my transfer would never come. But, given that fighting in Kuwait was the alternative, I wasn't about to complain.

Soon enough, we discovered gaps in the academy's security. We found ways to sneak in and out to find food or even a place to spend the night. Officially, we weren't allowed to leave without a pass, and the academy refused to issue any. So we took to escaping out of the academy through a large hole in the fence. The military police guards were too overwhelmed to do anything about it. Conveniently, they always seemed to look the other way.

I noticed that some recruits were leaving the academy for several days at a time, and actually getting away with it. So I followed suit, giving myself several days off every week and returning periodically to check in. I'd change into civilian clothes, grab my bright-red Wilson duffel bag, and, once outside the campus, I'd show the guards my Iraqi Engineers Association membership card instead of a military pass.

During my extended escapes, I'd sometimes embark on a twelve-hour journey from Basra to Mosul to visit a childhood friend who was now a priest. Father Vahan was one of the few people left in Iraq in whom I could confide. We had known each other since the seventh grade. We were the same age, born four days apart in the same hospital. We went to school together. Later, he studied electrical engineering; I studied production engineering. We both loved the arts. I dabbled as a painter; he played the keyboards in a band. We also shared a desire to travel to America.

My friend had earned a master's degree at an Armenian seminary in New Rochelle, New York, and had returned to Iraq to be ordained. The church sent him on an assignment to the city of Mosul, two hundred and twenty miles north of Baghdad. He loved to talk of his plans to study for his doctorate degree in theology back in the United States. We made a pact: One day we'd celebrate Christmas together with two glasses of beer in New York City. Our visits were so enjoyable that I'd spend my monthly stipend on the trips to Mosul.

But soon enough, the staff at the Naval Academy managed to gain control over the chaotic scene there. The transfer process was picking up speed. Throughout Basra, military police were randomly stopping male passengers and pedestrians to check for proper ID and military passes. I had already spent a month in limbo at the academy. With tensions rising in the city around me, I was actually beginning to look forward to my transfer, still mysteriously delayed.

I finally learned from old friends at the Engineering Department of the Navy headquarters that my transfer had been issued weeks earlier. It turns out there was another draftee named Shant at the academy. Once they transferred him, they must have crossed the name off the list. That means I probably didn't exist on their rolls. But I was too frustrated to remain silent. I began to ask questions. The bureaucrats on the scene rebuked me for interfering with their business. Within an hour, they transferred me to the Second Naval Brigade in Umm Qasr.

Two days later, the Second Naval Brigade assigned me to the

Landing Craft Unit. Then, strangely enough, they issued me a three-day pass—with full permission to use it before reporting for duty. Such was their level of confidence in the fugitive-stopping power of their military border patrols. If they didn't get you, the vast stretches of lethal desert surely would.

To travel back to Baghdad from Umm Qasr, I had to change means of transportation at least four times and fight for seats at each leg of the journey. Bus seats were a precious few, so I had to try to outrun other soldiers and endure pushing and shoving matches to secure a spot.

My two duffel bags were too heavy. I had loaded them with snacks and clothes to last me a whole month, which was the time I expected to spend at my navy unit before I was allowed to go on leave again. I didn't want to carry them with me on a long and physically draining journey. I had a three-day pass, two of which would be spent on travel. Another draftee was given a three-day pass with me. He had just spent ten days in prison for reporting late and suggested that we leave our belongings with friends he made during his imprisonment. They were still in jail. But since we had no lockers, it seemed like a good idea, at the time, to lock up our belongings with the prisoners in jail. Three days later, when I returned, I came to one of those revealing moments when engineers are surprised to learn that they are not as street-smart as they might like to think they are. My possessions were all gone and I was too embarrassed to complain to anyone about it. My excuse was that I was an engineer, but the other guy . . .

Things began looking up slightly once I arrived at my Landing Craft Unit in mid-September 1990. The engineering officers, overwhelmed with the amount of work that needed to be done, were happy to have another engineer on board. For years, the Landing Craft Unit was comprised of three large landing craft boats that Iraq had originally purchased from Poland. During the Iran-Iraq War, they lost one of them. But they gained more than ten, virtually overnight, after the invasion of Kuwait. The Kuwaiti landing craft boats were much smaller in comparison to the original three. They seemed better suited to serving in a coastal guard unit than the navy. All of the Kuwaiti boats were now docked in single, double, and sometimes triple rows at the port in Um Qassr. Most of the boats seized from Kuwait during the invasion were in good operational condition, needing only simple repairs and maintenance. This was not true, however, for the floating wreck of a landing craft marked L-93.

The L-93 had sat abandoned for quite a while at the port, until some ambitious soul at headquarters decided it needed to be protected as diligently as her sister boats. I was the lucky draftee chosen for the task. One morning, late in September, my superiors ordered me to gather my belongings and go stay on the L-93. The problem was that the other crewman assigned to the boat was on leave, as we were given one week each month for home leave.

So I boarded the craft alone and ventured inside. I wasn't prepared for the stark scene: The cabin was charred so badly that its large wooden columns and bedposts seemed to be covered in black alligator skin. Pillows and mattresses were burned and ripped to shreds. The deck was strewn with debris. The engine room revealed a disaster zone of scattered mechanical parts.

The setting spoke to the sheer violence the poor craft had endured. The boat was uninhabitable, made worse by the fact that food and water were not readily available. But that didn't stop my superiors from sending me to live on the L-93. It was typical Iraqi military fashion to assign a man to a boat he could not leave, with little concern about how he might sustain himself.

So my first task was to establish a source of drinking water. After scavenging around on the deck, I found a glass globe from a lighting fixture that was hanging by a thin rope. Nearby, I found the boat's freshwater ventilation hole.

Dangling the globe on the rope, I lowered the round-bottom fixture down into the hole like a bucket into a well. It came back filled with rusty water—but thankfully no salt water. I held the bowl still for a few minutes until most of the rust particles settled at the bottom of the jar and only the tiniest bits remained suspended. The water remained a disturbing shade of brown. Even so, it became my drinking supply.

I discovered it took particular skill to retrieve my brown water from the ventilation hole without getting the bowl stuck inside the tank, and one time I must have miscalculated the maneuver. The jar got snagged. As I tugged on the rope, it tore off, sending the jar tumbling into the tank out of my reach. I scoured around the deck until I found another light fixture. Then I realized most of the light fixtures of the L-93 were missing. Apparently, I was not the first caveman to come aboard.

Life grew more surreal when the commander of the L-93 came aboard. Lieutenant Ahmed was the Inspector Clouseau of boat commanders. A strange fellow with an imagination to match, he arrived flinging about orders as if he had a staff of dozens. In fact, he had but one humble servant—me. The only other man assigned to the L-93, a guy named Haroon, remained out on leave. Still, Lieutenant Ahmed insisted that I repair the boat to operational condition before the rest of "the crew" reported for duty. He seemed convinced that at least twelve or thirteen other crewmen would show up within two or three days. Mind you, no one else back at the Landing Craft Unit headquarters knew anything about this crew. Every soldier and officer was accounted for and assigned to his respective boat. The crew of the L-93 existed only in Lieutenant Ahmed's mind. I confess, however, that after a few days aboard the wreckage of the L-93 with Lieutenant Ahmed, I could see a few wispy ghosts as well, but they were no help—I still got stuck with their chores. In all, with its lifeless condition and its phantom crew, the L-93 felt more like the *Titanic* than a looted war vessel.

Still, I tried to play along.

"So, when is the crew coming back, sir?" I asked the lieutenant.

"Three days."

"I can't fix this boat in three days."

"Why not? Aren't you an engineer?"

"I'm a mechanical engineer, but I can't do everything by myself. When the crew returns, I'll need the electricians to help me with the electrical work."

Lieutenant Ahmed walked away in a huff. But after gathering his thoughts he came back with a brilliant conclusion: If indeed I was an engineer, then I should be able to do all the repairs by myself.

I glared at him in disbelief.

"Sir, you need a miracle worker, not an engineer. The engine is busted and its parts are missing. We have no tools, not so much as a single screwdriver. And we have no spare parts, not even a screw. The cables are cut up and burned. We have no water, no electricity, no engine power, no food, and nowhere to sleep or go to the bathroom. But, yes, the boat still floats. So I suggest they make it an office for paperwork during the day. Use the parts as spares for the other boats."

Lieutenant Ahmed's eyes narrowed into a mean squint. From that day forward, he held a grudge against me. After our exchange, he vented to the fleet commander and other officers while they ate together. And a funny thing happened: Within two weeks, the superiors declared that the L-93 would become a day-office and also would be stripped for spare parts.

But until the craft was officially converted, I remained under the watchful command of one angry lieutenant.

One day he came to me with a curious assignment. He had seen a rug somewhere in the cabin but could no longer find it. He wanted me to go search for it. I suspected that my boss, like many other Iraqis, was in the postinvasion looting spirit. Since nothing of Kuwaiti origin was accounted for, it was considered fair game. I imagined he wanted to take the rug home with him. The problem was that I couldn't find it. I told him I had searched the cabin to no avail. But he didn't believe me. He grilled me and accused me of stealing the rug. He made me search the entire boat several times. I cringed each time I saw him approach. I knew what was coming—either he was going to ask me about the rug, or demand to know when the boat would be operational for his blasted crew.

Finally, Haroon showed up. From the start, he displayed a pious lack of concern for his surroundings. He was aloof, lost in a world of his own. Certainly he was no help on the day Lieutenant Ahmed ordered both of us to be on the pier at 6:00 P.M. in full uniform. The boss had an urgent matter to question us about.

Precisely at six, I stood on the pier, ready as ordered. Haroon, however, was in his pajamas, praying on the deck of the L-93 nearby. Even so, Lieutenant Ahmed barreled into his inquiry.

"Where's the rug?"

He leaned into me with an accusatory stare. I was beside myself.

"Sir, I live more than five hundred kilometers away. I've been on this boat day and night. If I had stolen the rug, it would have to be somewhere on this boat. But this boat is only thirty meters long, and both you and I have looked everywhere. Sir, I think there never was a rug on this boat."

He reddened at my words.

"Are you accusing me of lying?"

"No, no. I didn't say that. All I'm saying is that from the minute I set foot aboard until right now, I have not seen this rug you describe."

"What happened to it, then?"

"I don't know."

"Maybe you stole it."

"Sir, even if I wanted a rug, I wouldn't be able to carry it with me all the way to Baghdad whenever it is that I go home. I can barely manage with my duffel bag."

"I'm going to tell the commander you stole it."

"You know, I'm beginning to think that *you* took it and you're trying to cover it up by accusing me."

Lieutenant Ahmed was outraged at my accusation. He ordered me to drop to the floor and do push-ups. He hovered over me for a while, then walked away. Exhausted, I stopped. But as soon as I got up, he stormed back over.

"Get down right now!"

But I was growing weary of his tantrums. I decided I wasn't going to take any more of his accusations.

"I refuse to take punishment for something I did not do. You asked both of us to be on the pier and in uniform. I am here but what about Haroon? He is praying in his pajamas. And *I* get the punishment. Do you think that we Christians don't have prayers? I'd rather be in my pajamas, too, next to Haroon, bowing down to

God. But you had your mind set on punishing me from the moment you gave us the order to be out here at six o'clock. Haroon knew it, too. You're just trying to humiliate me."

The fleet commander and a few other officers came to see what the fuss was all about. One of the warrant officers, Abu Wissam, offered to go back to the boat with me and help me look for the rug. When we got aboard, he disappeared into the cabin and pretended to look around. Within moments, he emerged with an odd-shaped scrap of material. I had imagined we were talking about some lush, Persian rug, but there he stood, holding a filthy remnant, smaller than a doormat, snipped from an old fitted carpet. The famous "rug" was not a real rug by any stretch of the imagination.

As it turned out, Abu Wissam had stashed the rug in the cabin days earlier, intending to take it home with him at the end of his shift. But as his luck would have it, I was assigned to guard the L-93 before he could finalize his scheme.

"See, there was a rug on the boat after all!" Lieutenant Ahmed gloated when he saw the dirty scrap.

I looked at him in disbelief.

"Yes, and good thing Abu Wissam found it before I threw it in the trash."

I don't know if I was more offended by the accusation that I stole something or the implication that I would steal something so laughable. Not too many times can a soldier defy an officer's order and escape punishment. But in my case, the fleet commander and remaining officers recognized the situation for what it was: two grown men fighting over a scrap of dirty carpet. They walked away and took Lieutenant Ahmed with them. I was left standing on the pier in shock.

A week later, I was given a seven-day pass. I decided to go

visit Father Vahan in Mosul. Back aboard the L-93, the surreal happenings continued, as Haroon remained alone on the boat. He must have been bored one night because he roamed onto the cargo deck, where we had stored a shipment of ammunition. Haroon took one of the ammunition containers back to the crew cabin and opened it. Inside were tubes with screw caps on one end. He opened one of the caps and found a string inside. Curious, he pulled the string on the ordnance. An illumination flare, intended to turn night into day on a battlefield, blasted out into the cabin. Fire spread quickly. Frantic, Haroon hauled the ammunition container out to the cargo deck, then rushed back to tackle the fire. He had to use his own jacket and hands to fight the flames because there was no fire extinguisher on board.

Severely burned now, Haroon realized the fire was spreading out to the cargo deck where the rest of the ammunition was stashed. And he was alone. He knew there were only a few soldiers working the Landing Craft Unit that night. Desperate, he ran to the next boat and dragged Lieutenant Raad out of the shower.

With the lieutenant's help, Haroon managed to control the fire and prevent a disaster that surely would have placed him before an execution squad. He was given a week off to tend to his injuries, and someone else was assigned to watch the L-93 until I returned from my leave. Surprisingly, Haroon was not punished at all. The officers probably decided that his burns and the scandal now associated with his name were punishment enough.

I had nothing against Haroon, but I was relieved the incident took place while I was hundreds of miles away. Otherwise, I was sure Lieutenant Ahmed would have found a way to pin it on me.

In mid-Octobér 1990, the L-93 became a day office where Haroon and Abu Wissam were assigned to process paperwork on the bridge. I was transferred to another landing craft, the L-88.

3. On Kuwaiti Soil

The other side was Candyland, a universe of toys and delicacies and fanciful inventions. At least that's how my crewmates described the spoils of Kuwait. As our new landing craft, the L-88, delivered shipments of barbed wire to Iraqi soldiers in Kuwait, many returned with exotic souvenirs and eyes aglow. They raved about the city with the euphoria of men who had been to heaven and back. Then again, these fellows were easily impressed. Many of them had barely left their native villages, much less traveled to a place as sophisticated as Kuwait City.

One comrade marveled as he described the abandoned home of a wealthy family. How lucky they had been to live in such splendor, he enthused. He was particularly impressed by their collection of cars—toy cars, that is. In fact, he brought one back for show-and-tell. It was a thin-walled plastic gadget, about twelve inches tall. The entire car was painted the same bright red, and all of its pieces were melded together in such a way that the wheels didn't even turn.

Another soldier flashed his loot, a clunky object he had snatched from an abandoned house, with a mix of pride and bewilderment.

"I don't know what's wrong with this iron," he confided. "I plugged it in, but it never got hot. Can you fix it?"

It was a handheld cake mixer, and its mixing rods were
missing.

Granted, I had not seen Kuwait City up to that point. I had
stayed close to port. I had no desire to roam its streets with Ali
Baba's Forty.

When I finally rode through the city on January 10, 1991, I
realized it was as lovely as everyone said, although to my eyes it
wasn't nearly as striking as Baghdad. My native city glistened
with grand streets, wide freeways, and impressive monuments.
An inviting energy charged through its population, which seemed
far more modern in its everyday style than that of Kuwait. For
one, Baghdad was not a city of men in solemn robes and women
in black gowns. We wore contemporary clothes. In the evenings
of my younger years, my friends and I would stroll up and down
Mansour Street, past upscale shops and cafés and familiar faces.
My high school was nearby, as were the headquarters of a couple
of popular soccer teams. That was life, *my* life. So I wasn't daz-
zled by Kuwait City's worldly charm. But I was forever changed
by what I would find in its hidden layers.

One day, as I ventured from the port of Kuwait into the city,
I wandered into a busy farmers' market. Amid the haggling and
the bustle of gowns, I heard a familiar sound, a language that
seemed spoken by angels. Armenian words. I looked up to find
an elderly couple poring over a basket of eggplant. Their conversation was mundane enough—did they want eggplant for dinner
that night? But it didn't matter what they were talking about.
They spoke in the language of my parents and my grandparents,
the language that always made me feel like I belonged. I drew
closer to them. Secretly I wanted to be part of their family, even
for just a few moments. I was tempted to ask them where the
Armenian church was, so I could attend Mass. But then I real-

ized that I was in uniform. I was the enemy of this unassuming old couple. I was an invader in their country. And I knew that, certainly, it would be best for them if they were not seen talking to me. As much as I wanted to vanish into their world that day, run away from Iraq for good, I knew I couldn't. Even though I was in a Kuwaiti farmers' market, outside conventional Iraqi borders, I knew I was still trapped. In Saddam's redrawn map of the world, I wasn't in Kuwait at all, but in territory newly conquered by Iraq.

The elderly couple decided against the eggplant and disappeared into the crowd without ever realizing that we had almost met. I left the marketplace without buying anything that day. I walked back toward the port, my hands in my pockets and my eyes cast downward, ashamed of my presence on Kuwaiti soil. Not only was I an invader of innocent people, that day I was also an enemy to my fellow Armenians. I tried to tell myself that if I was bothered, then how should Iraqi Arabs feel after invading their kinsmen in Kuwait? But rationalizations didn't work.

I took brisk steps, hoping to shake off the guilt that weighed upon me. Before I reached the boat, I passed a Kuwaiti child sitting on a curb. He waved hello. He didn't speak, but he didn't have to. His eyes, filled with fear, spoke volumes:

Why are you here? When will you go away? Please, don't hurt me.

I reached the boat, vowing that I would never leave port again.

I had reasons beyond the heartache I had felt that day. Just weeks earlier, on the night of December 9, 1990, we had delivered a routine shipment of barbed wire to the port of Kuwait. The following morning, we heard a ruckus not far from the dock. A noisy mob surrounded a group of Iraqi military police and army officers. We rushed to find out what the commotion was about. I craned my neck to see that the mob and the officers were crowding around six Iraqi soldiers. The soldiers were handcuffed and tied to a chain-link fence with their backs to the water. The men had been caught looting inside an abandoned hotel. When a Kuwaiti janitor surprised one of them, the soldier shot and killed him. Now, the six soldiers stood facing an Iraqi execution squad.

One of the condemned men was only a teenager who had been picked up off the street and forced to serve in Saddam Hussein's Popular Army. The Popular Army was intended for civilian volunteers who were supposed to serve for a specified time. But a few years into the Iran-Iraq War, it became a favorite dumping ground for Iraqi police operatives who'd grab random civilians off the streets and shove them into boot camps. Sometimes they'd even ship them directly to the front lines, where they were to serve indefinitely. I've heard stories of young men landing in boot camps still wearing their pajamas. We called it being "volunteered."

At the chain-link fence near the port that day, I watched five of the six soldiers stand in stone-faced silence as they awaited their fate. But the teenage boy screamed for mercy. I imagined it gave him something to do with his terror, although it did not sway his captors in the least.

The military officials assigned two executioners to each soldier, one to stand and aim at the head, the other to kneel and aim at the chest. In a thunderous voice, a captain read the execution order as signed by Saddam Hussein. I saw the guards blindfold the men and give them each one last cigarette. My heart pounded as I watched the soldiers puff furiously on their cigarettes, as if the smoke itself could save them. The cigarettes burned away all too quickly, leaving them with only a final prayer, the "Witnessing" of Islamic faith.

"I witness that there is no god but Allah and I witness that Muhammad is the messenger of Allah."

The next instant, the command was given. Almost in unison, twelve guns blazed and roared as each executioner emptied a thirty-bullet magazine into his target. The blindfolds ripped to pieces in the hail of bullets and fell to the ground in bloody shreds. Women wailed. A crew commander vomited. Streams of blood pooled and flowed on the ground.

When it was over, all six bodies slumped over each other, almost protectively. In a matter of seconds, all were motionless.

I watched the captain approach the men and shoot one bullet in each of their heads. A doctor came to verify the deaths, but he came across one detail that startled him: The boy's heart was still beating.

The captain sauntered back and fired another bullet into the young soldier's head. That seemed to do it.

The entire episode happened too quickly to absorb. Those of us who witnessed it walked away dumbfounded. I remained speechless for the remainder of the day, the same ten gruesome seconds playing over and over in my memory.

That's all it took, ten seconds for all 360 bullets to find their targets. And then there were the 7 coup de grâce bullets—367 bullets to kill five men and one boy. The boy had raised his knees at the last second to protect his chest, but that didn't stop bullets.

He was sixteen and had stolen a watch.

Two days after we witnessed the sextuple execution, on December 12, my ship commander and I were listening to the radio and heard the news that the United Nations had set a deadline for

Iraq to withdraw from Kuwait or face imminent war with the Allied forces. The deadline was January 15, 1991, barely one month
away.

My commander, Lieutenant Munther, was a pensive sort, a
man full of questions about theology and the meaning of life. We
often engaged in spirited discussions about our different back-
grounds. A devout Muslim, he wanted to understand the Christian concept of the Holy Trinity. Very delicately, I tried to explain
to him that Christians believe that the Father, the Son, and the
Holy Spirit are all God. And, no, Mary did not bear a child car-
nally fathered by God, a widespread misconception among Mus-
lims. The concept that God is one but somehow also three was
considered a blasphemy in Islam, not to mention, all too confusing, just as it sometimes proves to be for Christians themselves.
When I explained these concepts to Lieutenant Munther, I had to
be careful not to sound like I was trying to convert him. That
would have been punishable by death for the both of us.

The truth is, I welcomed his questions. Unlike some of the
know-it-alls I had encountered throughout my life, he was not
the kind of man who asked questions to ridicule me or to attempt to prove me wrong. He seemed truly interested.

"You know, I think I could be a good Christian," he confided
to me one day.

"I'm sure you could. You're probably a good Muslim, too," I
replied.

In turn, he explained to me some Islamic and Arab tribal traditions that a city boy, especially a Christian Armenian one,
would not be familiar with. That helped me better understand
the people I dealt with on a daily basis.

On the day that we heard the radio announcement about the
January 15 deadline, my commander and I were united by some-

thing more powerful than religious curiosity. When we were alone, I sensed he was as worried as I was about the grim news.

"What do you think about this deadline?" he asked me.

"I think they're probably allowing us one last New Year's Eve to celebrate before we die."

"But who can celebrate knowing that our days are numbered?" he asked.

He seemed lost in thought, prayerful, for a long time. Then he wondered aloud.

"Do you think those six soldiers were able to enjoy their last cigarette?"

I can't begin to describe the sense of loneliness and despair that engulfed me as the days passed and the deadline neared. What made things worse was that my closest friend back home, Father Vahan, was no longer there. He had flown to the United States just one day before I returned to Baghdad for what would be my last week off. I was distraught at the news: He had been accepted into a PhD program in divinity at Fordham University in New York, and he had obtained special permission through the Armenian Church to leave the country.

Father Vahan's departure made me realize how lonely I had become. I had lost all my immediate family, either to flight from Saddam or to death. Three of my childhood friends—two who had served in the Popular Army and one in the regular army—were now dead. While other young engineers around the world were growing in their professional experience and starting their own families, I was dodging bullets in a state of never-ending warfare and watching the years drift by. Alone.

I suffered from bouts of depression that always hit when I

was alone. I wasn't sure if self-pity was therapeutic or damaging to my already-scarred psyche, but I often found myself licking my wounds and counting my losses. Searching for some kind of consolation, I searched my memory for Father Vahan's words of wisdom. And in my darkest hour, I remembered something he told me during our last farewell.

"Whenever you think you are alone, remember that Christ said, 'I am with you always.'" (Mt: 28:20)

I let those words settle into my heart: Indeed, my best friend is Christ and with Him, I will never be alone.

Those words lifted my spirits to a high I had never experienced. I felt a new sense of strength and confidence about me. All things were possible, even the dim hope that I would see my family in America once again. Then, in my heightened Christian state, a devilish idea struck me.

If I wanted to get to America, I had to reach the Americans. I had to get closer to the Allied forces at the front lines.

The very idea that I might get lucky enough to be captured by the Americans blinded me to the risk of getting killed. As a POW, I reasoned, I would have some kind of a chance to reactivate my green card and return to the States for good.

So I volunteered for the January crew of the L-87, knowing that the war was expected to start that month. The L-87 was a landing-craft boat at the navy base in Ra's Al-Qulay'ah, in southern Kuwait. This Iraqi naval unit was closer than any other to the front lines, and the front lines were where American forces were preparing to pounce.

The crew of the L-87 changed every month. There was usually a long list of volunteers every month. Although I was assigned to the L-88, I had already been pulled away to serve on the L-87 during the month of November. But with the expected counterinvasion of the Allied forces, my name was the only one on the list for January. Completing the roster was a challenge as excuses flew among the enlisted. Some of the soldiers said that they had family matters to take care of. Others claimed that they were building a house and didn't want to die before it was finished. In the end, my fellow crewmen were handpicked by the fleet commander. To his credit, he tried to talk me out of volunteering, but he had no option other than to write in my name after I insisted upon the assignment.

For his part, Lieutenant Munther also tried to change my mind, but as an officer, he couldn't go so far as to forbid me to be so "heroic."

"Shant, you've already been in Ra's Al-Qulay'ah last month," he argued. "You don't have to go again, and they wouldn't make you."

"I want to go."

"The waves are high in January. You will get sea sick."

"I never get sea sick."

"Don't you know what I'm trying to say? The war will start in January."

"When the war starts, it will start everywhere, not just on the front lines."

"True, but everyone will be hiding in their shelters while your boat will go out on sailing missions."

"I will give Caesar what is Caesar's and God what is God's."

"What does that mean?"

"When Jesus was asked if the Jews should pay taxes to the Romans, the Pharisees were actually trying to trap Him. If He says, 'Yes,' then the Jews would reject Him as a national hero. If He says 'No,' then He is a rebel against the Roman Empire."

"What did He say?"

"He asked them to show Him a coin, and asked whose picture was on it. They said it was Caesar's."

"Right, and He said, 'Give Caesar what is Caesar's and God what is God's.'"

"Yes."

"How does that relate to you?"

"I am the coin. I will give my body, and maybe my life, to the army but my soul will always belong to God." That either confused him or made him angry. After that, he left me alone about it.

On December 13, we sailed through the night. I was unable to close my eyes or bring my body to rest in my bed. Out on the deck, I began a nightly habit of looking at the millions of stars in the pitch-black sky. I stayed up all night and watched the sunrise in the morning, while seagulls followed the boat in their flight and dolphins leaped playfully in and out of the water. The seagulls and dolphins both loved to come close to the boat and look at us; we watched them with the same curiosity.

Sometime during one of those first long nights, I decided that if I had to choose a place where I wanted to die, this would be it. That pleasant thought helped to stave off the dread that I'd probably die shredded by bullets, burned in an onboard fire, eaten by sharks, drowned in saltwater, or any combination of the four.

It was better to watch the stars.

4. Scarcity

The severity of the embargo imposed on Iraq by the United Nations following the invasion of Kuwait was becoming increasingly noticeable. With every passing day, food became more scarce, even in Baghdad. Longer and longer lines were forming before sunrise, waiting for bakeries to open their doors. Nonessential foods such as pastries and beverages were banned, to conserve sugar and flour. When the taste and color of bread changed, a rumor circulated that date pits, corncobs, and barley were ground and mixed with the flour. The flour was distributed by the government, of course. The rumor was widely accepted as truth, since one could easily see and taste foreign textures in the dough. The stuff tasted more like forage than bread.

In the military, food crises were even more severe than in the city. Aside from the fact that our daily rations were ruthlessly reduced, food was being stolen when it was passed from supply houses to delivery trucks, then to the cooks, and finally to the soldiers down at the bottom of the food chain. Still, deliveries were made and some modest amounts of food were served.

At the Landing Craft Unit, the engineering and technical staff was overwhelmed with maintenance tasks in an effort to make every boat ready for war. The remaining crew spent thirty minutes each day hosing the boat with water and the rest of the day hanging around in the crew cabin. After a twelve-hour workday, a weakly built workaholic mechanical engineer in his fifties named Qassim and I went to rest in the crew cabin just in time for dinner. We had had nothing to eat since breakfast and, because of our work schedule, we were the last to show up, as usual. Ahmed, the cook, reached out with his spatula from a little window that opened to the crew cabin and placed three thin rings of fried eggplant on my plate.

"Is this it? I've been working hard all day. I'm exhausted and hungry."

"I have no more."

"What happened? There are only fifteen soldiers on this boat. Couldn't you divide the food equally so that the people who come last get an equal share as the ones who came first?"

"This is your equal share, you and Qassim together. This is what I gave everyone else."

"Even you?" I asked.

"Yes, even me," he said.

I turned around and saw that the soldiers were paired up still sitting in front of an empty plate licked clean. Judging by the misery on their faces, I was convinced that the cook was being truthful. I knew that if I ate my portion, I would be as miserable as they were. Instead of teasing my appetite, I decided to let Qassim have all three eggplant rings. I filled my stomach with water and went to sleep.

Evidently, one of the cooks, Ali, had been stealing our food. Whenever soup was served during his shift, it consisted of some onions, a trace of meat, and a lot of bones and water. One night, after we had chicken bone soup, he stood packed and ready to go home. I was standing guard when he asked me to help him off the boat with his duffel bag. Bashir, the Kurdish cook, pointed out that Ali had stolen our chicken. I looked at his duffel bag and saw a wet spot where the chicken had started to thaw. "Do you want me to call the officers?" Bashir asked. Thinking how things could escalate in the Iraqi military, I said no. I didn't want the responsibility for Ali's execution. So instead, I handed him his duffel bag, certain that my missing towel and bed sheet were also inside.

As the days went by, there came a time when we considered it a luxury to see chicken bones in our soup at all—judging by the size of bones that were appearing now, we were convinced that the military was slaughtering old camels for food. Half the bone would stick outside the pot and the meat would cook for hours, but it remained tough as leather. To make matters worse, the propane tank and supply of rice eventually ran out.

We had all brought small supplies of food with us from home. I had a bag of almonds. During my last visit to Baghdad, I read that, among dry foods, almonds rank high in supplying the body with the nutrition it needs. The article went on to say that six almonds per day could deliver more complete nutrition to the body than one would imagine. I figured that if I were up eighteen hours on an average day, then every three hours I needed to eat an almond. According to this, my bag of almonds should have lasted me two months. But I was hungry. At first, I justified that my almonds were probably smaller than those used in the study, so I started with two almonds to mark the first three-hour period. But before the first hour was over, I had already finished my adjusted daily ration of twelve almonds. Before the second hour was over, I ate another daily ration to compensate my body for the nutrition it lacked the previous day. Within three days, the bag of almonds was empty.

Still, most Iraqi soldiers were entrenched in the desert, deprived of food and water, and practically starving. The few of us who were in the navy knew how fortunate we were to have fish to supplement our diet, plus plenty of drinking water stored in our boats. But because the sound of running engines scared away most of the fish, the largest fish we were able to catch was no more than five inches long. We had to catch several dozen every day so that each soldier would have three or four fish for dinner. In the beginning, I was given the largest share because by observing Islamic law, my crewmates refused to eat half the fish, which was without scale. But as starvation became unbearable, they started to see scales on everything that came out of the water.

With the onset of war, not only were we unable to throw our fishing lines in the water under the constant air raids and falling bombs, but also the trucks were not able to deliver bread or bones anymore. Very wisely, like Joseph in Egypt, the base had saved some bread back in the days when deliveries were still made. When the deliveries stopped, the base began to issue one bagel-size piece of old bread per soldier each day. We broke the bread into two pieces, ate one half in the morning and saved the other half for dinner so that we would not sleep on an empty stomach. Between the two halves of bread, we drank a lot of water to fill our stomachs. I was losing weight so rapidly under my new hydro-carbohydrate diet that I had to cut a piece of rope and tighten it around my waist to keep my work pants from falling.

Nevertheless, food crises were not nearly as critical as cigarette crises. Most Middle Eastern men are smokers. Some smoked as many as three or four packs each day. Luckily for me, half of the crew on my landing craft boat didn't smoke. This made us earn the nickname of "The Nonsmoking Boat." During the embargo, cigarettes were considered nonessential and were harder to find than food. When I passed two patrol boats that were docked at the pier in Failaka, one soldier was inside each boat and I overheard them talking.

"I need a screwdriver. Do you have one that I can borrow?" asked the first soldier.

"Yes," replied the second soldier and handed him a screwdriver.

"Thank you. Do you have another one?"

"Yes."

"Then let me have this one. What do you need two for?"

"I'll trade it for a cigarette."

"You want one whole cigarette for a screwdriver? I'm not going to take it home with me. I'm going to use it for the Iraqi Navy."

"I don't care what you do with it. I'll give you the whole boat for a pack of cigarettes, if you want."

5. Our Ticking Time Bomb

The second week of January began with the ill-fated January crew of the L-87 still in Umm Qasr in southern Iraq. The December crew was beginning to worry, wondering if they would ever be replaced before the war started. Most of the boats of the Landing Craft Unit were scattered and anchored at different locations in the Abdullah Canal. This was to make them less susceptible to American strikes, but to me, they were sitting ducks no matter where they docked.

With fewer boats on base, our duties were generally relaxed. Abdullah, a mechanic assigned to the January crew, was sitting with me in the crew cabin along with some other soldiers on a warm winter morning. We were making jokes about how unrealistic this war was for Iraq and managed to get a good laugh on more than one occasion. In an awkward moment when the sound of laughter stopped, someone looked at us and, with a frightful solemn expression on his face, said, "You are all going to die." The words hit deep because we knew they were not far from the truth.

On January 10, we anchored the last remaining boats in the Abdullah Canal. With the fleet commander, I ended up on one of the two large Iraqi landing craft boats. A speedboat came to collect the rest of the January crew of the L-87 and take them back to the base. Ahmed, the cook who served me three rings of egg-plant, was sitting on the antiaircraft gun atop the highest point of the Polish landing craft. He was shocked to see me descend to the speedboat along with the others, then remembered my hope of being captured by the Americans. He crossed his wrists to-gether, raised them above his head, and with a big smile he waved good-bye. I waved back as the speedboat sped away. He, too, wanted to get captured but was concerned that the Ameri-cans might mistreat him because he was black.

"There are a lot of blacks in America, you know," I explained.

"Oh yeah, maybe I'll be like Michael Jackson." He said it with a smile.

Secretly, I viewed Ahmed as the Robin Hood of the Second Naval Brigade. Although I loathed thieves profoundly, I did not seem to mind his little adventures. He was an unselfish thief with character.

My favorite story of Ahmed was his incident with Mo-hammed, who was a very arrogant young sergeant. One day, Mo-hammed picked up a busted-up swivel office chair from the Kuwaiti trash, brought it into the crew cabin, and forbade anyone from sitting on it. Days later, he was talking to us, the common-ers, in his usual condescending way. He said that sergeants in other units did not talk to their soldiers and that we should con-sider ourselves lucky that he did not mind talking to us. Qassim, who was old enough to be Mohammed's father, looked at me and shook his head. I could not bear the silence nor could I accept the crew's passive submission to Mohammed's insults. I replied, "Maybe it's better that you don't talk to us." Everyone remained silent after this comment. The crew was glowing with content-ment in contrast to Mohammed's fury.

Mohammed had a pink-and-white fragranced bar of soap of

the brand Fa. It was a rare brand, not easily found in Basra, that he had purchased in Kuwait. Like the swivel chair, no one was allowed to touch this foreign-made soap, but all had plenty of opportunity to look at and admire it. He would use the soap daily and put it back in its pretty pink-and-white paper box. On his way to the showers one day, he passed by the crew cabin and heard the soldiers talking about his favorite subject—prostitutes. He sat down on his chair, placed his towel and soap box on the counter next to the galley/cabin wall, and started to swivel. When he swiveled to the left, the towel and box were within his sight and when he swiveled to the right, they were not. Fifteen minutes later, when the stories ended, he stood up to go to the shower. His towel and pretty box were still there but the soap was gone. Ahmed, who was the cook on duty, suggested that we all get up and search the whole boat for the sergeant's soap. Mohammed agreed and made us all search every inch of the hundred-foot boat. But after thirty minutes of searching, it became clear that the soap was nowhere to be found.

"Are you sure that the soap was in the box when you came here?" asked Ahmed.

"I'm positive," replied the broken-spirited Mohammed.

"Too bad, it was a very nice soap."

A week later, we were all sitting in the crew cabin when Ahmed came to Mohammed.

"Look! I found your soap," he said and he handed him a paper-thin remnant of his pink and white Fa soap.

"Where did you find it?"

"In the bathroom, it was behind the door."

"But I repeatedly looked behind the door; it wasn't there. Everyone's been to the showers several times by now, how is it that no one saw it?"

"It was in the corner; you must have hidden it there and forgotten. What's wrong with you Mohammed? Don't you know that if you leave your soap in the bathroom, everyone's going to use it? Good thing I found it before it was finished."

After the speedboat took us to the base, I collected my belongings and joined the rest of the January L-87 crew. We were gathered in a minibus waiting to be dispatched to Ra's Al-Qulay'ah. But before the bus took off, a few more soldiers came to remind us that we were all going to die. This time, no one could save us from the abyss of depression.

Once on the road, we were all lost in our thoughts. I sat looking out the window, gazing at the desert and the sky. Every piece of land and shrub we passed, we would never see again. How soon our young lives would have to end. The desert that I once hated seemed very dear and sweet that day. I looked at the sun as it traveled slowly across the sky and thought that when I die, I wanted to be able to look at the sun one last time before I closed my eyes. I wanted to embrace the sun and set my spirit free from a world I tried so hard to belong to but where I was somehow always a stranger. This became a promise to me, as if from God, that I would be looking at the sun when I die.

I turned around and looked at the others behind me. They were all silent, their thoughts hundreds of miles away. These are the faces of heroes, I thought to myself, I should consider myself lucky to be in their company.

Aside from the bus driver, we were all sailors and did not know the way to Ra's Al-Qulay'ah by land, but we had heard that it was supposed to be a two-hour trip by car. The bus driver was also burdened with thoughts of family and the looming war. Driving absentmindedly, he got us lost in the Kuwaiti desert. He refused to admit that, but we all became convinced of it when we entered the fourth hour of our trip. All the while, there were no more troops or any signs of life in the surrounding areas. The driver continued to drive south, the general direction of our destination.

We knew something was suddenly very wrong when we came to a checkpoint and a military police officer wrote down our names on a piece of paper before allowing us to continue. Although we had run into hundreds of checkpoints in our military lives, never had our names been scribbled down on a piece of paper before. Beyond the checkpoint, we ran into an area of dense barbed wire and saw a wooden post with a strange sign reading THE FRONT EDGE. The jargon was unfamiliar but we knew its meaning wasn't good.

Still, we continued south, passing an intricate maze of trenches all filled with black petroleum. The trenches were dug on the western side of the road, extending to the horizon. Fifteen minutes later, there were no more trenches. Instead, ditches were dug across the road every hundred meters forcing vehicles to drive off the road. This would provide a perfect setup for a minefield, we all thought. But the driver and 1st Lieutenant Mahdi weren't sure if the bus had enough fuel to backtrack toward civilization. Although they finally admitted that we were lost, the two determined that it was safer to drive through what seemed like a minefield than run out of gas in the open desert.

When we had driven long enough to be near the Saudi border, I began to wonder if my plans of getting captured by the Americans might come easier than I thought. But my hopes of easy capture vanished when we were stopped at the next checkpoint. A small guardhouse with four or five Iraqis holding machine guns blocked the road with barbed wire and a few pieces of wood. The force did not seem formidable enough to stop an army, but the guards told us that they had orders to shoot anyone who went beyond that barricade. Our lieutenant asked them why.

"God has granted you all a second life," the military police said, "you've been driving through a minefield ever since you got off the main road." Then they told us that we were at the Kuwaiti-Saudi border. They said that an Iraqi colonel snuck through the barricade and across the border with a handful of soldiers early a few mornings ago to surrender to the Americans. A few miles into the Saudi desert, the colonel saw some Saudis and surrendered to them with his soldiers. To make his capture more attractive, he offered to divulge valuable information to the Americans and to the Saudi government only to find out that they were Iraqi intelligence officers disguised as Saudi bedouins.

Near the checkpoint were a few abandoned Kuwaiti cars. We tried to siphon some gasoline out of their fuel tanks, but they were all empty. One of the military police from the checkpoint needed a ride, so he offered to show us the safe way back: driving under the high-power electrical lines on the eastern side of the road. Then he directed us to the nearest gas station.

We were finally on the L-87 a few minutes before midnight. As soon as we arrived, the December crew rushed off the boat without looking back. Most of them didn't even waste a minute in saying a good-bye. They fled the doomed vessel like it was a ticking bomb.

Iraqi frogmen detonated bombs in the water all through the night, so that if U.S. Navy SEALs were present, the concussion from the explosion would kill them underwater. The concussions traveled through the water and shook our boat like a drum.

There was an explosion approximately every five minutes throughout the night, hour after hour.

"These bombs are going off too close to us. How am I supposed to know when the Americans are attacking?" I asked one night.

A disconnected voice replied from the darkness. "Theirs are the ones that kill you."

PART TWO

6. Under Attack

In the early hours of January 17, I was out on the deck of the L-87, pacing back and forth along the hundred-foot-long vessel. It was January 16 in the Western Hemisphere, one day past the deadline, and war was bound to start any minute. I sang prayers and ran the beautiful music of the Armenian Church in my mind. Good and bad memories from various stages of my strange life interrupted from time to time, but the music always prevailed.

A little before 4:00 A.M., I surrendered to fatigue and went back to bed knowing that sleep would come in an instant. I said the Lord's Prayer, a habit carried since I was a boy, then lay down and pulled up the covers. Before my eyes had the chance to close, a few isolated gunshots ripped away the heavy silence. In a matter of seconds, all the Iraqi artilleries were engaged, rattling loud and spitting up continuous fire into the blackened sky. This footage has been shown over and over in America since that day, and I understand that much of the world watched it unfold in real time on CNN's live broadcasts.

Down under the antiaircraft fire, I ran around making sure everyone was up and on their way off the boat, and reminded them to take their gas masks before we ran to the air raid shelter under the pier.

We found the shelter without a problem, but it was the first time we had entered the place. We discovered that the base's remaining soldiers were already down there, well situated, having arrived days in advance. The shelter itself was comprised of a very long reinforced concrete tunnel running under the pier alongside the water. One wall was on the waterside while the other wall led to many rooms inside. There was an intricate net of pipes running in and out of the inner rooms and along the walls to carry water, fuel, and compressed air out to the boats. Inside the tunnel, it was dark and humid. The smell of mold and decay was carried by water that seemed to drip everywhere.

I collected little empty glass bottles, filled them with diesel fuel, dropped one end of a rope inside the bottles and lit the other end to create a lamp. To cork the bottles and support the rope, I used my own share of precious bread and assembled eight pre-industrial-revolution-style lamps and distributed them among the crew.

Nobody slept on that first night, so the lamps came in handy right away. But by the second night, we resigned ourselves to the surroundings and brought down our mattresses and blankets from the boat, enough to settle down in some comfort. At first, we stayed inside most of the time but we always had to go back to the boat for food, which could only be prepared and eaten with any level of sanitation on the boat. Although we didn't care about that much, with the food being scarce and falling bombs being plentiful. We generally ate and returned to the shelter in less than five minutes. The cooks, who not only arrived on the boat early to prepare the meals but then stayed to clean up afterward, were considered the bravest of us all.

The L-87 was of Kuwaiti origin and had not been equipped for war. However, prior to the January 15 deadline, the Iraqis mounted an antiaircraft gun on its upper deck and supplied us with ammunition. There was enough of the ammo to fill the little storage room where we once had food, so it represented a significant trade-off for us. But at least it was a relief to have that much protection on board.

Once the war began, the officers decided to try out the new gun and see how it operated. So we all gathered around while First Lieutenant Mahdi removed the covers and folded them away very carefully, as if unwrapping a present. The soldiers marveled and praised the gun while the officers took turns handling the controls and rotating the weapon in different directions. On orders, a box of ammunition was brought out on deck and pried open—only to find out that the bullets were too big for the gun.

"Wrong caliber!" murmured words traveled across the deck. "How could they do this to us?"

"This is treason!" exclaimed Lieutenant Raad, the engineering officer.

All the others made it plain that they agreed. Personally, I didn't know what to make of this incident. On one hand, the mismatch between the gun and bullets represented the underlying truth of an army that was revered as "the fourth largest army in the world." According to Saddam Hussein, the might of this army would punish the Americans in a display of power he called "The Mother of All Battles."

On the other hand, I wondered whether, since we had no gun to shoot at an airplane, we might be lucky enough that an airplane might not feel compelled to shoot at us. No matter how I looked at it, though, it was disappointing to realize how insignificant our lives were in the eyes of our own Iraqi leaders. No one cared enough to confirm the caliber of the ammunition before the war started. It was Abdullah who had carried the box out from the storage room, and he didn't seem to care too much about the philosophy behind the incident. He closed the ammunition box and put it back in the little storage room where, for some reason, it still "belonged."

Having bullets of the wrong caliber wasn't the most shocking secret of the L-87. That honor was reserved for the fact that the L-87 was the most active boat on base, but among a crew of fifteen soldiers, only two were armed. I was not one of the privileged. Because of our proximity to the Allied forces, First Lieutenant Mahdi sent Lieutenant Ahmed back to headquarters to bring a supply of thirteen guns so that everyone on board would at least have a sidearm. Two days later, Lieutenant Ahmed came back with a supply of life jackets—but still no guns.

At least we will continue floating after we die, I thought. In matters of death, the Iraqi government always made sure to be considerate to its people.

7. Mounting Pressure

Inside the tunnel, we could hear the crash and rattle of Iraqi guns for extended periods, stopping briefly, then starting up again. What those of us below would only discover later, was that the planes of the Allied forces were flying comfortably above the range of the Iraqi artillery. They found their targets easily and their bombs made their presence known with deafening explosions and depressurization winds that ripped through the tunnel. On the first night, the artillery fired at every plane in the sky until an officer finally instructed them not to waste their bullets—the enemy targets were out of range.

Huddling in the darkness, we didn't know how close the Allied forces had come to conquering our base or how many dead bodies we should expect to see when we went outside. We all knew that the Americans weren't far away though, and we fully expected them to swiftly and efficiently kill us all as soon as they arrived.

When we made it through the first night and the Americans didn't show up, we were still certain that they would come on the following day. Or the next. Every extra day that we survived became a bonus.

We talked some of our fears over with each other. Others we

held private and kept inside our heads. Mine were specific. Would they kill me even though I am unarmed? Would they give me time to explain that I am a resident of the United States who has been trapped in Iraq for ten years, before they pull the trigger? Would they believe that they could find someone like me in uniform, unarmed, on the front lines of the Iraqi military? The answers were anyone's guess, at that moment, but our perspective brightened a little when we eventually emerged from the shelter and didn't discover any dead bodies on the ground—only thousands of spent bullet shells and a few bombed-out buildings.

At the time, the only means of contact that we had with the outside world was the radio. The Americans jammed all the radio stations to disable Iraqi communications but we managed to find an Iraqi, Kuwaiti, or Saudi station every now and then. None of these stations were realistic. The Iraqi station, traditionally cumbersome and heavy with news, was playing songs all day long, as if nothing had happened. Once or twice a day, the station announced Iraq's missile attacks on Tel Aviv and explained the tactic as "hitting the heart of the spoiled daughter of America."

I had no doubt that Saddam was trying to lure Israel to strike Iraq, which would most certainly anger all the Arabs and bring about a holy war. The Iraqi radio also claimed unreasonably high numbers of Allied forces' planes that were supposedly shot down. The number accumulated to two hundred before the war entered its second week.

The Kuwaiti and Saudi radio stations were no closer to the truth than their former sister Iraqi radio station. They both announced that Kuwait was completely liberated before the Iraqi radio reached its "one hundredth plane shot down." But the Kuwaiti and Saudi broadcasts allowed us to hope that the Americans might possibly liberate Kuwait and forget to knock on our door.

In the meantime, the constant sound of artillery, planes, and bombs deprived us of precious sleep. Even in the most peaceful moments, we never wanted to close our eyes, not knowing when the Americans might barge in. Gradually, we began to develop the talent of falling asleep instantly and waking up just as fast. On a good day, we would gather a total of four hours of fragmented catnaps no longer than ten to twenty minutes each. Mostly, we were running high on adrenaline and could easily spend forty-eight hours awake before our first nap. We had to be alert in our sleep so that we would be ready within ten seconds when called upon. We slept in our uniforms and kept the helmet, gas mask, and boots under our blankets where they could easily be found in the dark. Those who had a gun, a precious commodity in any war, placed it between their legs when they slept. Risks are all relative.

I had no gun, but was the only one among the L-87 crew who had a helmet. My boots were laced with a special zipper, which enabled me to slip them on very quickly when I woke up. As a result, both my helmet and boots were sought-after items, so I slept with them to protect them from theft. All of us had gas masks, supplied in a pouch we slung over our shoulders. Inside the pouch, we were provided with a medical kit, but the potency of the medicine was questionable. Inside each medical kit there were some bandages, cotton, ointment, and three needles. To each needle a transparent plastic bubble was attached that contained a small dose of antidote. We were to inject ourselves in the thigh with these needles in case of exposure to a chemical attack, then stick the needle in our collar so that the medics would know how many injections we'd had before we passed out. At least that was what we were told. The true effect was to comfort the dying with the thought that medical help was on the way.

My bubbles contained nothing but crystallized yellow dust. Presumably, the medicine they once contained had evaporated during the Iran-Iraq War. When a group of us opened our medical kits for the first time, we discovered that fewer than five needles in a hundred contained usable serum. The remaining had crystallized or condensed to thick molasses.

After combat began, a total blackout was imposed each night. Out on the pier, I was unable to see my hand inches away from my face. We often bumped into each other and asked who the other person was, not knowing if he was sent to slit our throat. It was customary in the Iraqi military for each soldier to stand a two-hour watch before being replaced, but with the base so dark and the Allied forces so near, it was a frightening experience to stand by the boat alone for two hours—especially since most of us didn't have so much as a slingshot. So we obtained special permission from First Lieutenant Mahdi to not post a watch during the day so that we would have enough soldiers to cover the night with only one hour of watch for each of us.

When it was my turn, I tried to borrow a gun.

"No one is going to lend you his gun at a time like this," said Waheed, our soft-spoken sergeant.

"At a time like this? What am I supposed to do if I'm attacked?"

"When you see the Americans, you're just supposed to yell 'Landing!' Over and over. Keep yelling."

"If I do that, they'll just kill me to shut me up."

He grinned. "But you'll die for your country."

8. Spare Parts

A boat similar to the L-87 was abandoned in the dry dock at the navy base in Ra's Al-Qulay'ah. The Kuwaitis were apparently working on the boat when their repair job was interrupted by the invasion. The Iraqis, of course, were not in the business of finishing the job, or doing anything constructive in Kuwait for that matter. The only access to the boat was through an extremely unbalanced, flimsy hundred-and-fifty-foot-long pipe-frame ladder. By then I had lost so much weight that I was one of only a few scavengers who dared to climb the ladder all the way to the top and board the abandoned vessel. Near the bottom and top, the ladder was a little shaky but tolerable. Midway up the ladder, I found myself riding on a swinging wave of squeaky metal and wondered if the little rope tying the top of the ladder to the boat would hold. Up there in the middle, most sane people opted to go back down and stand on firm ground, but I had to go all the way to the top.

The first time that I boarded it, I was just trying to find some tools so that we could perform our mechanical and electrical duties on the L-87. Although mechanics, Bassim and Abdullah refused to climb the ladder with me, so a sailor named Munther came along. Our expedition wasn't successful, since there were no tools or anything of value left on the boat. All Kuwaiti boats were originally equipped with complete sets of tools. However, like the dirty leftover piece of fitted carpet, tools also quickly disappeared. Our extensive tool set on the L-87 was reduced to a single screwdriver and a wrench. I kept those in my pocket at all times so that I would not be caught in the engine room without my tools. As a soldier, I didn't mind not having a gun, but as an engineer, I refused to go to war without my screwdriver.

I had to climb the ladder a second time when the hose that supplied cooling water to the generators on the L-87 ruptured. Despite the rain and ongoing air raid, Lieutenant Raad insisted that I scavenge the abandoned vessel for a similar hose to replace the one we had just lost. I tried to convince the young lieutenant to postpone his request until the air raid subsided, but he refused to change his mind. No one knew when we might be requested to set sail and the boat had to be in a state of readiness at all times. Slipperiness and falling bombs were now added to the list of challenges I had to face when climbing the ladder. I wanted someone to come along so that if I were injured they would be there to help, but my crewmates refused to leave the shelter during the raid.

It was not long before I found the hose, still attached to the generator. I disconnected the hose, folded it away and walked along the deck of the abandoned vessel. I stumbled upon a collection of naval flags scattered in the storage room, and realized that in order to surrender to the Americans, I would need a white piece of cloth. I examined all the flags and chose a blue and white one since it had the largest area of white.

No one was present on the vessel to see me commit the crime of possessing a white cloth. I tore the flag in half and hid the white portion in my gas mask pouch. I tore the blue portion into small pieces and smeared them with oil to make them look like rags so that nobody would come along and notice the missing white half.

I left that boat thanking God for the ruptured hose, Lieutenant Raad for his stubbornness, and my crewmates for the weakness that kept them in the shelter. Back at the L-87, I replaced the hose and reported the results to Lieutenant Raad.

By the time I had to return to the abandoned vessel for a third and last time, I was an experienced ladder cowboy; the shaky pipe structure complied like a tamed bull. This time I took Munther and Tahir with me and asked them to collect all the life jackets and fire extinguishers that we could find. Returning to my crime scene to search the storage room again, I found an emergency flare beneath the heap of scattered naval flags. I took the flare with me, then the three of us brought everything down to the L-87.

Back aboard, I checked all the fire extinguishers and gathered up the bad ones in one corner, then scattered the good ones throughout the boat. I also locked all of the compartment hatches so that water wouldn't flood the entire boat if its hull were ruptured. I instructed everyone, emphatically, to remember to lock the hatches whenever they went in and out of the compartments. Some crewmates doubted if these measures could increase our survival odds, especially since our boat had no means to fend off an attack if confronted by a warplane. But then Lieutenant Raad stepped forward to help me test the fire extinguishers, and he also reemphasized that the hatches must always stay locked. The crew's attitude quickly changed. They realized that keeping the boat afloat could mean the difference between life and death.

"What else can we do?" asked Lieutenant Raad.

I was fresh out of physical solutions. "The only thing left is to pray and wait," I said.

9. On Edge

Every night brought terror and fear. We recognized the events surrounding us from the sounds we heard in the darkness of the tunnel. The buzzing of a warplane was always accompanied by the rattling of Iraqi artillery, then inevitably followed by the deafening explosion of a falling bomb. When the American airplanes gave us a break, the Iraqi headquarters seemed to heighten our alert status and agitate the peaceful night. They circulated alarms of possible threats such as a landing on a moonless night, a destroyer approaching the base, Navy SEALs invading, or infantry advancing from the south. This caused a great deal of anxiety. It was no secret that the Allied forces were in close proximity. Any of these threats was more than likely to happen on any given night. However, when none of them came true, we began to theorize that headquarters fabricated these alarms just to keep us all on our toes. Sleep was optional at the front line, but being frightened was a must. Others said that these threats weren't real but were psychological tactics planted by the Americans.

One day, Bassim broke down under the pressure. He left the shelter and decided to take a suicidal stroll in open air while the airplanes attacked. Realizing what his intention was, I went after him to convince him to return to the shelter. Bombs were falling on the base and a few buildings were destroyed while we walked. I had to speak louder than the sound of war and try to rekindle his desire to live before we both got killed.

"What are you doing, Bassim?"

"I want to die."

"Why?"

"We're as good as dead anyway. I want to finish it today."

"You know, there's a possibility that we might get captured."

"Yes, a five-percent possibility that we might get captured and a ninety-five-percent possibility that we will get killed."

"Five percent is better than nothing."

Bassim didn't respond. He continued to walk. I walked with him a little more. A stray dog passed us by, frightened and scrambling for cover. "I'm not going to die out here like a dog," I said and went back to the shelter. I had done my duty and the rest was for him to figure out.

Within a couple of minutes, I felt a deep and genuine relief when I saw Bassim entering the shelter. I did not comment nor did I make eye contact, so as not to appear to want credit for his wise decision.

The most terrifying night came when someone finally yelled, "*Landing!*" Everyone charged outside and started shooting into the air. Officers and soldiers were yelling frantically, giving out orders and clashing with one another. Solo pistol shots joined a cacophony of machine guns and artillery. For the climax, the big cannon joined with its heavy-caliber projectiles. Looking out through the manhole opening, I saw the night sky lit with Iraqi fireworks. A young officer took out his pistol and started shooting from inside the shelter out through the manhole where we were gathered. A captain stopped him and sent him outside.

I went back to the shelter and waited inside with the other unarmed soldiers. Scared and frightened, we envisioned how the Americans would first kill everyone outside then chase the remaining soldiers inside the shelter. Gunfights might break out inside the shelter itself, where both Iraqi and American bullets would be equally fatal.

In what form was death coming to me? Would they slit my throat while my nose and mouth were muffled? Would it be a long-suffering death from a single bullet wound, or would I be baptized with my own blood like the boy who stole a watch? Perhaps the Americans would simply drop a bomb through the manhole and instantly kill everyone inside.

My eyes were fixed on the shelter entrance to see who would enter next, Iraqis or the Americans. Without diverting my attention from the manhole, I reached for my gas mask pouch and felt the white flag. I made sure to have easy access so that I might be able to wave it faster than an American could pull his trigger.

Fifteen minutes later, the sound of guns subsided and the Iraqis started to come back inside the shelter, one after the other. There was no landing or any indication that the Allied forces were attempting to attack by air, land, or sea. An Iraqi boat docked at the base was completing their annual training program and yelled "Landing" as part of a drill scheduled for that day.

Nobody had told them that their training schedules weren't in effect during wartime.

10. Midnight Assignment

Shortly after the landing drill was over, everything went back to normal. My guard shift began at 11:00 P.M., so I took my turn standing alone in the dark and guarding our defenseless boat from an enemy I could not see, with a weapon I did not have.

However, the empty bullet shells that covered the ground like peanut shells in a crowded bar served as a primitive warning system. I heard someone approach only minutes after I went on duty. He was a military policeman who had come to tell me that our commanding officer's presence was "requested" at headquarters. This usually meant that we had to set sail an hour or two before sunrise.

When First Lieutenant Mahdi came back from headquarters, he told me to get the engines ready immediately.

In half an hour, the engines were hot. We were out in the Persian Gulf by midnight, after leaving the cook behind so that he could collect our daily ration of fifteen pieces of bread while we were gone. During our departure he had bid farewell as if we would never see each other again.

We all wore our life jackets and wrote our names, addresses, and telephone numbers on them. We also wrote our contact information on all our limbs. This provided us with the comfort that our families might be notified if our bodies or body parts were found floating in the water.

Other than the unusual timing of our mission, we knew nothing about its purpose. When the other officers asked First Lieutenant Mahdi about the destination or purpose of our assignment, he became aggravated and started to yell, "I don't want anyone to interfere with my business." This secrecy bothered us because we felt that we had the right to know what we were going to die for. It was also disheartening to see First Lieutenant Mahdi loosing his calm under the pressure and burden of his secret. Minutes after leaving the base, Riyadh, the soldier behind the wheel, took a bathroom break so that he could come down to the crew cabin and tell us that the direction of our navigation was ninety degrees—which meant that we were going out to tiny Qaro Island. There, nothing rose above the yellow sand except a U-shaped chain of single-level rooms where soldiers worked and lived.

To reach the island, we had to sail through the oil-slick area, where the Iraqis had dumped thousands of barrels of oil into the Persian Gulf during the previous two days. We began to notice seagulls with tarred feathers flapping in the water. Saddam's strategy was probably to set everything ablaze, should he start to lose the battle. Or perhaps, it was nothing more than malicious destruction of Kuwaiti resources. Everything was possible for a leader who was not reluctant to use chemical weapons on hand-to-hand battlegrounds, killing both sides when the outcome of the battle was not secured in his favor.

Sailing through the night, we were unable to see the petroleum-covered waters in the dark, but there was no mistaking the odor. It reminded me of the January 10 minibus journey, when we drove through the Kuwaiti desert. Not only because the trenches we saw were filled with petroleum, but also because we were going through a minefield again. But this time, knowingly. During the previous two nights the Iraqis were tossing mines in these waters. Because the team that was assigned with the task was understaffed, they were recruiting two soldiers from our boat each night to help them with the mine-tossing business. In fact, if it were not for the midnight assignment, I was scheduled to toss mines myself at 2:00 A.M. that same night.

It would be incorrect to use the term "laying mines" instead of "tossing mines." On a little patrol boat, the crew carried four mines at a time, each on a wooden pallet. The patrol boat stopped at a randomly selected location, a mine was activated, and two soldiers pushed the four-hundred-pound mine and its wooden pallet off the boat with their legs. There was no effort to anchor the mines against random drifting, so the crew sped away as fast as they could before the mine might bounce back, hit the hull, and explode.

All we knew was that there were approximately two hundred mines drifting in the general area between our base and the little island of Qaro, and that they floated back and forth with the tides. Saddam hoped that they might hit American ships that were otherwise out of reach. The mines were supposed to float on the surface of the water and should have been visible during the day, but I never saw one.

As the L-87 proceeded through the night toward Qaro, two soldiers were assigned to sit on top of the landing craft ramp in the bow. They were given a pair of night-vision binoculars and told to take turns watching for the mines. There were no walkie-talkies, however, so they had to rely on basic oral communication. A third soldier stood ten yards behind them on a raised anchor chamber in the bow, to signal between the two soldiers on the

ramp and a fourth soldier ten yards behind him. The fourth signaled to First Lieutenant Mahdi on the bridge outside the wheelhouse. The officers remained up in the wheelhouse; everyone else
was demoralized, sitting around the crew cabin and speculating
on the level of danger during our unknown assignment.

The previous night, a boat from the Red Crescent (equivalent
in the Muslim world to the Red Cross) was sent out to an oil-rig
platform to retrieve dead bodies after a swift American Navy
SEAL attack. The Red Crescent boat was too small to carry all
thirty-five soldiers who were stationed on Qaro Island. We feared
it might be our job to retrieve the dead bodies instead. It seemed
unlikely, though, because we knew that our chances were slim of
surviving a round trip through mine-infested and petroleum-
covered waters while under fighter- jet attacks.

No one had spoken of his fears, yet, until Jassim finally said
out loud, "Tonight, some of us here will die." He said this and sat
on the floor and started to sing a beautiful but very sad melody. It
was as if he had predicted his own death and was mourning his
own soul. Grief began to fester in our already demoralized spirits.
It felt like a blanket of lead had settled down on my chest, like
mud settling down to the bottom of a murky pond. I became
aware of the additional effort that it took just to breathe.

Inside the crew cabin, everyone was silent but Jassim. They
were mesmerized by his song, and some trembled under the
shadow of the mournful lyrics. My eyes stumbled on Munther,
who at the moment was looking right back at me. The song
stopped, and I broke the silence. "There's nothing we can do now
anyway, except our jobs as usual." I looked at Tahir, who was the
youngest and never seemed bothered by holding the lowest rank
on the boat. A flicker of spirit started to glow in his eyes again.
He pursed his lips, nodded his head, and left the room to go do

his usual job outside. I followed Tahir's example and went to check on the engine room, just as I did every time the boat was sailing. Munther rallied the remaining soldiers and pretty soon everyone got back to business.

The boat was completely blacked out against detection by air. While I carefully felt my way to the engine room, I came across Lieutenant Raad, the engineering officer, and stopped to talk with him a little. But as it happened, we had paused at a perfect point to observe a freakish sight in the water immediately surrounding the boat. It wasn't the first time that we had seen this phenomenon, but on this night it was extreme. The glow was caused by a certain kind of bioluminescent marine microorganism, activated by the friction from contact with the boat. We must have been sailing through a giant cloud of them.

We couldn't tell if the green light was bright enough to be seen from the sky. But if it was, the boat would present a clear silhouette inside the glowing green blot. There was nothing to be done but to sail through. It was a perfect compliment to the mood of paranoia.

First Lieutenant Mahdi started yelling for me to stand on the cargo deck, where they needed someone in the third position: atop the raised anchor chamber near the bow, four steps above the deck. So I asked Abdullah to take my place and check on the engines while I stood watch.

While my eyes were gazing out into the darkness, Jassim's horrific words would not go away. It was true; some of us were going to die that night. My thoughts of being captured alive began to wither under the prospect of encountering either an airplane or a mine.

Strangely, I didn't care to know if I would be among the survivors. All my days on the L-87 were almost identical and equal

in misery. It did not matter to me if I lived one day more or one
day less. Since January 10, the day that we set foot on the L-87, I
considered myself a dead man. Each morning, I woke up with
the ritual of thanking God for the new life I was given. Although
unintended, by accepting death as reality and surrendering my
fate, I became almost fearless and was able to perform my duties.

There was a clatter of thoughts in my head. My brain buzzed
like a computer before it is about to crash, but it suddenly subsided when I remembered that I would be looking at the sun
when I die. But since we were sailing through the night, I comforted myself that I was not going to die, not at night, anyway. A
host of invisible angels must have been dancing to my prayers
and songs. I felt an enormous source of energy lingering in the
air and a great mysterious presence. I realized then, Tonight, God
is here with us on the deck of the L-87. I made the sign of the
cross on my face and stood in reverence. A lot of people must
have been praying for me. I wondered if my mother, in Los Angeles, had somehow summoned the angels for my protection. My
mother was a very persistent and tenacious little woman, capable
of doing that and more.

From afar, I noticed more green glowing lights. This time
they made the shape of three torpedo-like objects headed toward
our boat. The torpedoes were moving fast and in a straight line.
They were about to hit the boat at exactly the spot where I was
standing. I did not react in any way or run to tell anyone to
change the direction of the boat. The torpedoes would hit the
boat before I could announce their presence. My heart started to
beat very fast and strong; I felt it pound violently and bounce like
a rubber ball inside my ribs. I heard its echo drumming very
loudly in my ears. When the torpedoes were inches away, I took a
deep breath and prepared myself to be thrown into the water. My

heart almost stopped—or should I say, skipped a beat—so as not to interrupt the sound of the explosion. The torpedoes went under the boat and came out on the other side. They were only dolphins, friends of the sailors. I paused for a few seconds until my breathing and heart rate returned to normal and pondered the way that my body welcomed death. The extremely high confidence I had, only seconds ago, that I would survive the night was humbled to the lowest of the low. I thanked God for granting me another life, my guardian angel for watching over me, and my mother for her prayers. I turned around and looked at Tahir who was standing in his fourth position behind me. I could not see his face in the dark but I wanted to know if he saw what I saw.

"Did you see that?" I asked.

"Yes," he said. His voice was still quivering.

"I thought they were torpedoes."

"So did I," he said.

Shortly after, Bassim started calling from his position on the ramp. His voice was lost amidst the rumbling engines and splashing waves. Thinking that he might have spotted a mine, I climbed the ramp very quickly so that I could hear what he wanted to say. Bassim and Ahmed had been atop the ramp for about forty minutes and wanted to come down. Bassim asked me to get two other soldiers to relieve them from their positions on the ramp. I had no authority to assign people to their tasks. But mostly, I did not want to ask anyone to sit in a deadly position and bear the responsibility of his death on my conscious for the rest of my life. I told Bassim that I would take his place so that he could come down and ask the officers to assign others to fill in the remaining positions. Minutes later, Dhafir climbed up the ramp. He took the night-vision binoculars away from Ahmed the radio operator, and sat beside me. We stood our most careful watch, with plans no grander than to live through each passing minute. And so the reins of our fate were now in our hands, and some of its mysterious workings were about to be revealed to us.

Dhafir gave me the binoculars when his eyes were tired. The binoculars mounted on my head so that my hands were free. The principal concept of the binoculars was that they detected in-frared heat waves and converted the signal to a monochromatic green image. The image I saw was not very clear. We were able to make out the outline of large objects very well but whether we would be able to identify floating mines among the waves was very doubtful.

"Do we have only one pair of binoculars?" Dhafir asked.

"Yes."

"Where did we get them from?"

"Headquarters gave them to First Lieutenant Mahdi. They said they were very expensive and told him not to lose them."

"Can you see anything?"

"I see waves in light and dark shades of green but what's a mine supposed to look like anyway?"

"You'd see only the top part of the mine barely floating above water. They said it would be a dark spot through these binocu-lars. I was also told to look in the distance ahead of us and not worry about the sides. What we see in front of us is plenty of water for the boat to go through."

"But the waves are hitting the boat hard from the left. The mines could be moving with the current from left to right. I think we should concentrate on the left side and on the distance straight ahead."

"I agree; I was doing that anyway," said Dhafir.

Since the tactic of using floating mines was relatively new in the Iraqi Navy, I was certain that no one knew what a floating mine looked like through night-vision binoculars. I looked at the structure of our boat to see how a metallic surface would appear. It was bright because it was near. Other metallic surfaces were dark or bright depending on their distance and orientation with respect to the binoculars. When I stuck my hand, a warm object, in front of my face, I was almost blinded by the brightness of the image I saw. In the end, I convinced myself that, like any round object, a floating mine would appear bright at a certain location surrounded by gradually darkening hues of gray. Dark or bright, it was not going to be easy to distinguish a mine among the thousands of dark and bright spots that were reflecting from the waves in the water. These floating mines were not easy to see in broad daylight to begin with.

Through the binoculars, I looked at the horizon and saw flashing lights moving from side to side back and forth over a short distance in the sky. Dhafir could not see the lights with his eyes so I gave him the binoculars.

"Do you see them now?"

"Yes, what are they?"

"I think they are airplanes."

"No they're not. These are only stars."

"Do you see flashing lights moving horizontally back and forth in the sky?"

"Yes, but if they were airplanes, then why can't I see them without the binoculars?"

"The binoculars are more sensitive to light than our naked eyes."

"Airplanes don't go back and forth like that."

"They're flying in circles above the island."

"I still think they're twinkling stars."

I did not care to win this debate. The idea of sailing the boat into a swarm of warplanes was not particularly comforting. Dhafir refused to believe that we were about to add another element of danger to our suicidal mission. I, on the other hand, reminded myself that I was as good as dead since January 10. We each had our own survival technique.

After spending the first hour on the ramp, Dhafir suggested that we ask to be replaced. I wasn't tired and wanted to stay. At first he didn't argue, but five minutes later he asked again.

I felt stubborn and said, "If you're tired, you can go. I want to stay here and make it all the way to the island."

"But I want you to come down with me, so we can be together when it's our turn again."

At first I was determined to be hardheaded. In a place where I had no control over anything in my life, it somehow seemed important to have my way on this tiny matter. And for that reason, I can't explain why I soon gave in to his persistence. Only God knows why Dhafir was able to change my mind so easily. The cook Jassim came up along with Ali and the two took our positions. Abdullah stood in the third position, atop the anchor chamber.

On the bridge, the officers were not aware of the changes we had just made on the deck, nor could they see out through the dark. Lieutenant Raad did not know who else was out there with me but he noticed that I had been standing watch for more than two hours, by far longer than anyone else. He decided to bring me back in, not knowing that I had already been replaced. He sent Tahir to get me and bring me down to the engine room not realizing that he had just sent Tahir to his death on my behalf.

11. Der Voghormiah

Before checking the engine room, I wanted to rest a little in the crew cabin. Bassim, Ahmed, Munther, and Dhafir were already there, resting in their beds, alone in the darkness with their thoughts. Without removing my helmet or life jacket, I lay down on my bed and stared at the space above me. The silence lasted for about five minutes.

There was a powerful explosion on board—I jerked up and saw fire through the open door. It looked as if the power of the explosion had flung the wooden door open, but an instant later I realized that in fact the door had been shredded into confetti and was covering the floor.

We all ran outside and confronted a wall of fire that separated the cargo deck from the rest of the boat. We wanted to check on our four crewmates who had been standing watch for the mines, but there was no way to penetrate the fire.

Adrenaline can have strange effects on the body and mind; I saw thick white smoke rising from the engine room and rushed to the entrance, grabbing the ladder with my hands and sliding down like a fireman through the narrow hatch. It felt as if I made the acrobatic moves all in a single motion, and I was amazed that I didn't get a single scratch. In more peaceful days, we all fre-

quently banged our heads and shins, while climbing in or out of
that hatch at normal speed.

In the engine room, the first thing I tried was to start the
water pumps, but there was no electricity flowing to them.
Thinking that the generators had stopped, I stumbled through
the dense smoke to restart the generators and restore electricity
to the pumps before the fire destroyed the entire boat.

I reached the generators to find that they were still working,
but all the cables running from the generators were destroyed
and the hoses that supplied the generators with cooling water
were flat. Since the hoses ran through the burning cargo deck
outside, they were shredded by the explosion, so it was the over-
heated generators that created all the smoke in the engine room.
The fumes became very dense and the two generators started to
make a screeching sound. There was nothing else to do but
switch the generators off, knowing that I would never be able to
restart them again.

I went back on the deck and looked for the fire extinguishers
that I had already scattered around the boat. For some mysterious reason, the bad extinguishers were still all piled up in the
corner where I left them, but the good ones were nowhere to be
found. I ran toward the stairs to check on the four officers and
three soldiers who had been on the upper deck before the blast. I
nearly collided with Riyadh on the bottom step. The flames lit his
face, which was completely covered with blood. I was startled by
his appearance and helped him to the benches in the stern behind the crew cabin. He was followed by Lieutenant Raad with
wounds around his eyes; Lieutenant Ahmed with minor injuries
to his head; First Lieutenant Wafi with a wounded leg; Waheed
with injuries to his arm and chest; and Ahmed, the radio operator, sustained no injuries at all. I couldn't see First Lieutenant

Mahdi so I reported the engine room status to First Lieutenant Wafi, the second in command.

First Lieutenant Wafi, Munther, and I were the only ones in motion. The other soldiers were still in shock. Ahmed sat on the floor next to the wounded and started to cry.

"What about the others? Are they all gone? Are they gone?"

"What others?" I asked.

"The ones who were in the front!" he said with obvious disgust at my stupid question.

Suddenly, I realized that up until that moment, I had not allowed myself a chance to consider that those who took our positions were now dead. Ahmed's emotional outburst brought me a long way back to reality and made me realize that the four soldiers had no chance of surviving. It was only with faint and dimming hope that we considered the chances of the four being alive. I leaned over the side of the boat and started to shout their names, searching the fire-lit waters.

"What are you doing?" Lieutenant Ahmed asked.

"Maybe they fell in the water. Maybe they need help."

"Look at where they were standing! Do you think anybody could've survived that?"

"What if they fell in the water?"

"Either way, they're gone."

Lieutenant Ahmed simply walked away. I realized that I had been on the ramp only a few minutes prior to the explosion. If it were not for Dhafir, I would have been among the dead. Did my guardian angel speak to me through Dhafir, softening my otherwise stubborn head? I crossed myself and whispered, *"Der Voghormiah,"* the Armenian words for Lord have mercy. The only person who saw me do this was Riyadh. He was a Muslim, but I don't think he minded a Christian's prayer on a night like that.

The fire came closer to the little storage room where all the boxes of wrong-caliber ammunition were stashed. Not wanting more fireworks for the night, I started to throw the boxes in the water. Without a word, the others joined me. It was the first time that we saw an agile and swift Waheed. By nature, he usually moved and talked slower than the rest of us. Now he was throwing the ammunition boxes out faster than any of us. We all stopped for a second to catch a glimpse of this rare event. We were probably all high-strung; the ammunition was dumped ten times faster than it was loaded.

Meanwhile, the fire was growing fast; within ten minutes it engulfed the cargo deck, flames forty feet high burned on top of the thirty-six-ton fuel tank. Munther hung from the anchor in the stern, dipping pots and pans in the water and handing them over to us. Fortunately, the boat had already come out of the oil-slick area.

We ran toward the fire stumbling over debris and someone's dead body, bumping into one another, and spilling half the water before getting to the fire. When the water hit the fire, the flames swallowed it unchallenged. After a few attempts, we realized that our efforts were futile. Half the boat was burning and we were fighting it as if it were a kitchen fire. Munther climbed back up from the anchor and waited with us on the benches.

We were drained physically and mentally. Those who were healthy, such as myself, began to sustain injuries while running around on the wrecked boat in the dark. The blast had blown the lid off the anchor chamber, leaving an open hole in the stern. We fell in the hole repeatedly while we ran around. The scars I have on my shins today tell me that I fell in the anchor chamber at least four times. Both my shins bled to my ankles and my thighs were severely bruised from my hips to my knees.

It became clear that the only remaining option was to abandon the boat, but our lifeboat lay wrecked on the cargo deck. If First Lieutenant Wafi gave the order to abandon the boat, we would have jumped into the water, despite the prospect of hypothermia and wrestling with sharks.

Riyadh, calm and soft-spoken, tall and gentle with wavy blond hair, always reminded me of a camel. Now he was agonizing from his facial injuries and was apparently thinking of abandoning the boat.

"Whatever happened to the Red Crescent boat? When are they going to come and get us?"

"Where is the Red Crescent going to come from?" I replied.

"Headquarters knew that our assignment was dangerous. They dispatched the Red Crescent boat and it was behind us all along."

"Did you see it?"

"Yes, it was behind us the whole time. They probably thought we were hit by an airplane and decided to stay away."

"What hit us?"

"I don't know. An airplane, a mine."

"Did you see where the explosion came from?"

"The left side of the ramp in the bow."

"Then it was probably a mine—that's the direction the waves were coming from."

Everyone was talking about the Red Crescent boat now. Many confirmed that it had been sailing right behind us before the explosion, but now it was nowhere to be seen. I took out the handheld flare that I brought down from the abandoned vessel, pulled the string to light it, then waved it above my head. In case the Red Crescent boat didn't notice the forty-foot fire behind me, they would surely notice my flare, I thought. But I wasn't the only one losing his mind that night. Lieutenant Ahmed ordered me to throw the flare away, because it might "give away our position to American airplanes." I was in such a state that I threw the flare away immediately, then stood to watch it burn underwater for a few seconds before it disappeared.

So now we were safe from air attack.

12. Controlling the Fire

Bassim was standing next to me when First Lieutenant Wafi came imploring, "Please, put out the fire, just put it out and I'll do the rest." I began to tell him about the engines, generators, and pumps, but I heard myself say out loud, "The fresh-water pump!" Bassim and I ran down to the engine room. The fresh-water pump didn't need electricity; it was a crank-start diesel engine. I held the prime button down with one hand and a flashlight with the other while Bassim tried to spin the crank lever with both hands, but he had no stamina left in him and was not able to put a good spin on the lever. We switched positions. I worried that my strength might fail me or that the little pump might betray us like so much other equipment had that night. With my eyes shut, I spun the lever with both hands and the last breath of energy still in me. I channeled my anger into the pump handle and continued to spin as if I were stabbing a beast that refused to die. I didn't open my eyes or stop spinning until I felt Bassim's hand on my shoulder.

"That's enough. It's working. The pump is working now."

When we got back out to the deck, First Lieutenant Wafi was manning the hose. The fire was out in a matter of minutes, we were finally able to catch our breath and check out the damage.

Everyone was sitting on the benches and floor in the stern behind the crew cabin. The crew cabin was located in the rear right
corner of the boat, the farthest away from the front left corner
where the mine hit. Other than the shattered windows and missing door, the crew cabin was virtually intact compared to the rest
of the boat. I went up to the wheelhouse to see if I could find
First Lieutenant Mahdi. He was on the floor among the rubble
and shattered glass. When I called his name, he replied with a
faint voice. I helped him to his feet, took him downstairs, and
laid him near the benches next to the others, so that at least he
wouldn't be alone.

While everyone was sitting, I took a flashlight and went
down to check on the engine room. Of the five compartments on
the boat, the front two were completely flooded. The hatch between the second and third compartments was slightly bent from
the explosion—water was leaking into the third compartment
with high pressure from a very small gap in the upper right corner of the hatch. I estimated that the leak was not critical and left
it alone. It was clear that if I had not shut all the hatches the
night before, the whole boat would have been underwater within
minutes of the explosion.

The third compartment held the pumps and the water, fuel,
and sewage tanks. The fourth compartment had the two generators and two engines, of which only the right-side engine was
still running. And the fifth compartment had the rudder system,
which was inoperable due to damage that the hydraulic system
had sustained. I went outside and reported everything to our new
commander, First Lieutenant Wafi.

We tried to sail the ruins of our half-sunken boat to the island, less than ten miles away, but with only one engine and no
rudder support, the vessel only traveled in circles. I asked

Munther, Dhafir, Ahmed, and Bassim to come down to the engine room with me and help try to start the left engine so that the boat could at least travel in a straight line. We tried everything we knew, but the engine wouldn't start. The batteries seemed to be dead. Armed with the screwdriver and wrench that I had kept in my pocket, I disconnected the batteries from the two dead generators and also disconnected the batteries from the right engine, since it didn't need a battery while the engine was running. We tried the batteries on the left engine, separately and together, but all our attempts failed.

I reported our hopeless engine situation to First Lieutenant Wafi. He decided to try to make it to the island anyway. Instead of going in circles, he sailed the boat in half a circle and allowed the waves to push the boat back in the proper direction. Luckily, the waves were hitting from left to right while our boat veered left due to the incapacitated left engine. The boat limped very slowly during this very unusual maneuver. It was obviously the last journey of its operational life. Our compass was another item that was damaged. To make sure that we were going in the correct direction, First Lieutenant Wafi decided to take the risk of using the radar. We were forbidden from using radar because American airplanes had the ability to detect the signals and immediately find our position.

I found myself praying for God's mercy yet another time. I did not know what to pray for without being greedy. Would it be too much if I asked that we find the soldiers who were missing, injured but not dead? Perhaps I should be content if the boat did not sink or hit another mine or get hit by an airplane. Should I settle for the island or is a warm bed in a hospital too much to ask for? Instead of burdening God with my demands, I thought that He would know best what was good for me. In the end, the

most powerful and satisfying prayer came from a few and simple
words. They were spoken by Christ with His last breath on the
cross. "Father, into Your hands I commit my spirit." (Lk 23:46).

First Lieutenant Wafi found a flare gun and lit the dark sky
with a red flare so that the Red Crescent boat could come to our
rescue. Bassim and I stood on the deck near where the firewall
had been. We searched the bow to see if we could distinguish any
shapes while the sky was briefly lit, still hoping to find our missing friends. But it was still too dark to see anything.

"Who was on watch there?" Bassim asked.

"Ali and Jassim were on the ramp, Abdullah and Tahir on the
deck. One of them was on the floor near the galley. I tripped over
him when we were throwing water on the fire."

"That's Tahir. Munther found him hanging on the side of the
boat and took him down when you were in the engine room."

"I don't want the sun to rise today. I don't want to see any
body parts."

"I don't want to see that either."

A red flare and a green flare went off together and lit up the
sky for about two seconds. This time the flares provided enough
light for us to quickly examine the damage in the bow. Bassim
and I didn't see any bodies on the deck but the ramp was completely gone; the lifeboat was shredded to pieces, a big hole
marked the spot where the mine hit the boat. The three-eighths-
inch-thick metal plate of the hull had a ten-foot horizontal tear
through it, as if it were made out of paper. The bow was submerged underwater. When the boat surged forward in its half-
circular navigation plan, the waterline reached the firewall line
and entirely covered the cargo deck. We realized that even if
there were any dead or unconscious bodies on the deck, they
would have already been washed away.

I smelled a strange odor that made me feel extremely uncomfortable. "Do you smell that?" I asked Bassim.

"It's the mixture of wet ashes and diesel fuel," he replied.

"No, I've never smelled this before. It's something else."

"What is it then?"

"I think it's the smell of death."

"What are you talking about?"

"I don't know. I don't want to stay here anymore. Let's go."

We still had hopes that the Red Crescent boat might come to our rescue. First Lieutenant Wafi fired red and green flares sporadically. After firing the last flare, he shot bullets in the air. The rest of us used flashlights and lit up cigarette lighters and waved them in the dark. But it soon became clear to all of us that the Red Crescent boat had abandoned us.

The anguish of knowing that we were abandoned by our own when we were facing most certain death exceeded any disappointment or anger that I had ever experienced. Two months after this incident, I was told that the commanding officer of the Red Crescent boat was publicly executed upon his return to the base in Ra's Al-Qulay'ah. I was quite indifferent when I received the news. Knowing how the Iraqi military operated, everyone should have expected execution for this cowardly act, including the officer himself.

As I sat on the L-87, I was baffled by the strange series of events and circumstances. Most of us had no guns, we were given ammunition of the wrong caliber, we had to go through a minefield that we planted ourselves, all the good fire extinguishers had disappeared even though they were scattered around the boat, the batteries of the engines all died together, the rudders and compass were destroyed, and—the Mother of All Puzzles— our own Red Crescent boat abandoned us. Nothing made sense to me and I was convinced that I would never live long enough to receive any explanations.

I wanted to sit down and rest on the benches with the others but I was restless and could not relax. When all of this was over, there would be plenty of time to rest, safe and sound in our beds or for eternity in our graves. Instead of sitting, I made a round and checked on the injured. The explosion took out First Lieutenant Mahdi's left eye and smashed his ribcage. His sweater was soaked with blood like a wet towel. I held his smashed ribs together to provide him some support and make it easier for him to breathe. He had lost a lot of blood and his body was getting very cold. He did not have energy to move or talk, but when I held his hands with mine to keep them warm, he whispered, "Yes."

Lieutenant Raad called me and said "Shant, I'm blind." I tried to calm him down and reassure him that everything was going to be OK. Small shrapnel was embedded under the skin on his cheeks and forehead around his eyes. Seeing that his eyes were not injured, I told him that he should be able to see soon. Of course I didn't really know if he would be able to see, but I wanted to offer any strength that I could. He took out his locker keys and his pistol and gave them to me, telling me to hand them over to the Second Naval Brigade in Umm Qasr, if he didn't survive. I took the keys and pistol and said, "You'll be fine, sir. You'll be fine."

Dhafir was still hoping for the Red Crescent boat to come to our rescue, so he took Lieutenant Raad's pistol away from me and shot our last bullets in the air. The empty pistol remained in Dhafir's possession after that.

Among those who were able to walk and talk, Riyadh had the most severe injuries. His nose was broken and he had a lot of deep cuts all over his face. Not surprisingly, we had no first aid kit, no alcohol, no bandages or even aspirin on the boat. But among other things that I had collected from the abandoned vessel was a roll of bandages that I had kept hidden under my mattress. Now I brought the roll out and started to help bandage his face and stop the bleeding. I had also hidden a small container of multivitamin pills. I took the container out and gave each person two pills, including myself. Clearly, vitamins were not going to revive a dying person but they were the closest thing we had to medicine. Even a placebo was better than nothing.

As we approached the early hours before sunrise, the temperature started to drop. I collected all the blankets from the boat and gave them to the injured. At first, I didn't put any on Tahir, thinking he was dead. Later, when we found out that he was still alive, I also placed two on him and on First Lieutenant Mahdi. When we ran out of blankets, I gave away my coat.

It wasn't anywhere close to being enough.

13. Sunrise

Beam by beam, the rising sun pierced the dark sky. Once there was enough light, we realized that Tahir had no visible injuries. He did move his fingers once, very slightly, giving us hope that he might regain consciousness. We kept vigilance and talked to him sporadically, hoping that he might give off another sign of life, but his fingers would never move again. He was already in a no man's land, lingering somewhere between this world and the afterlife. As for the rest, nothing of Ali, Jassim, or Abdullah was ever found.

The cargo deck was charred and submerged with the bow at least four feet underwater. Everyone was still gathered in the stern behind the crew cabin. Some started to shiver with the early morning's near-freezing temperatures. I climbed the ladder to see if I could find any blankets left behind in the wheelhouse, and saw an airplane approaching from the southern horizon. There was only one plane in the sky and we were the only target in sight. "A plane!" I yelled to the others, then threw myself to the deck. Everyone hid away. First Lieutenant Wafi shifted the engine to neutral, then ducked in the wheelhouse to help make the boat look lifeless. He and I were the only ones on the upper deck, which was the most susceptible to airplane attacks. I pressed myself against the metal floor, fixed my eyes on the sun, and listened carefully to see if I could hear the sound of the explosion that would kill me.

The plane flew very fast and low passing directly above the boat. I felt the metal floor vibrate under the roaring jet engines, then turned and ran down to the lowest point in the boat and hid by the sewage tank. There, I was shielded by the largest number of metal walls between me and the pilot—but I knew that the tank was nearly full. The tank would burst from the depressurization caused by an explosion and cover me with fermented sewage. Even so, I hesitated less than a second, then decided that even if the tank burst, I might still be among the fortunate living.

After three or four passes, the pilot apparently decided that the boat was not worth bombing and went away. Or maybe he had already dumped his bombs elsewhere, before finding us. The reason remained hidden, but our lives were spared and the sewage tank was left undisturbed.

With daybreak, we realized that we were not far from the island. Qaro was within sight, a little more than a mile away. But our half-sunken boat was now so heavy that it wouldn't budge an inch. We hoped that the Iraqi soldiers on the island would realize that we were in trouble and come to our rescue, but it seemed as if something was preventing them from doing so.

"What is wrong with these people?" Lieutenant Raad exclaimed. "The Red Crescent boat abandoned us and now the island is watching us slowly die. What do they know that we don't?"

At 9:00 A.M. we were all relieved to see a little speedboat from the island headed in our direction. When they were within a few feet of the L-87, Lieutenant Raad was the first to greet them.

"What were you waiting for?" he shouted.

"Our fuel tank is almost empty. We were waiting to see if you could come any closer."

The little speedboat was going to have to make several trips, so we decided that First Lieutenant Mahdi and those who needed the most immediate medical attention should make the first trip.

I went to First Lieutenant Mahdi to prepare him.

"They are here for our rescue, sir."

"Who came?" he whispered.

"The soldiers from Qaro are here."

"What about the Red Crescent boat?"

"They never showed up. We will have to carry you down to the speedboat, sir."

We had a stretcher on the boat but it was stored in the first compartment, which was near the explosion and was now completely submerged.

We picked up First Lieutenant Mahdi and placed him on a blanket. Six of us held the cloth and carried him down to the speedboat. Needless to say, suspended on a blanket with a smashed ribcage, he was in a lot of pain.

"No, no," he groaned, gnashing his teeth.

"Hang on, sir, we are almost there."

But he surrendered to eternal sleep just before his body was lowered to the speedboat.

It turned out that the speedboat had enough fuel to make three trips and take us all to the island. Tahir, Dhafir, Munther, and I were among those on the second trip. First Lieutenant Wafi, Lieutenant Ahmed, and the remaining soldiers were on the third and last trip.

The soldiers on the island helped us off the speedboat and carried our belongings. As soon as we set foot on the island, several of us were overcome by an uncontrollable urge to cry. We felt intensely guilty that we had come to safety without our friends. Dhafir sat down on the sand and started to weep; Munther shed silent tears and walked away while I felt pain like thorns in my throat.

An officer from the island came and started to give orders and instructions to his soldiers.

"Take good care of these heroes. Help them with their stuff. I don't want to hear from them that they're missing anything."

Two soldiers found a wet wallet at the bottom of the speedboat. They opened the wallet and took out a black-and-white photograph of a man in his youth looking pleasantly back at the camera. They asked. "Is he one of the dead?"

"No. That's me," I said—and took my wallet back.

The communications soldier on Qaro picked up my duffel bag and walked me to the communications room where my crewmates were gathered.

"We have to walk faster," he said. "The planes are coming."

"I can't walk faster than this."

"Are you wounded?"

"No, it's just—my legs are bruised and bleeding. I can't walk faster than this."

"Don't worry, you're doing OK."

"Do you know why we are here? First Lieutenant Mahdi was the only one who did, but now he is dead."

"You came to evacuate us. We were all packed and ready to go."

"In that case, I'm sorry about the explosion."

"We've been watching your boat all night long through our

binoculars. We saw everything and relayed your status in thirty
different messages to Ra's Al-Qulay'ah. They dispatched a patrol
boat two hours ago, so it should be here any minute. Then you
guys can go back to the base."

As we walked toward the communications room, we saw another officer with his soldiers. They were beginning to show concern over the increasing number of airplanes circling the island.
The officer emphatically stressed that no one should shoot.

"If I even see anyone starting to fire, I will shoot him myself."

In the communications room, the island soldiers showed
heart by serving us from their precious supplies of tea and crackers. Some of them wanted to eat the crackers, too, but the officers stopped them because they were only meant for an
emergency—a definition under which we qualified but they did
not.

While we warmed up with a cup of tea, one more message
was transmitted to the navy base, giving the latest update. We
heard First Lieutenant Wafi report the damage to the boat and
the status of the L-87 personnel. Upon hearing the names of the
dead and missing in action, another wave of crying broke out.

First Lieutenant Muhsin, who was the commanding officer of
the patrol boat that came to our rescue, stepped into the communications room while First Lieutenant Wafi was still transmitting
the last words of his grieving message. Seeing that some of us
were crying, he decided to help with some sort of twisted reverse
psychology. First Lieutenant Muhsin yelled, "Why are you crying? You are warriors and warriors don't cry." Everyone stopped
crying except for Bassim who was still overcome by his emotions.
"I want your name soldier!" yelled First Lieutenant Muhsin, who
was now pretending to threaten Bassim. Finally, Bassim sup-

pressed his tears, not for fear of the lieutenant but rather as a courtesy for us, his comrades. After going through what we had just experienced, nothing was more annoying than being lectured on how to be a warrior from someone who had not yet seen any action.

Apparently, we were not the only ones annoyed by this. To give us a break, the officers on the island took First Lieutenant Muhsin away to show him the body of his friend, First Lieutenant Mahdi, in the other room. Upon seeing the lifeless body, First Lieutenant Muhsin held the door posts with his two hands and, while swinging his head from shoulder to shoulder, he let out a loud howl and a shriek. He started to beat his chest with his fists like a gorilla and wail. Then he grabbed his own jersey and tried to rip it down the middle. Two officers rushed to his side, supported him from both arms and walked him back to the communications room. Handling him as if he were fragile, they seated him down very carefully on the floor next to us and gave him a cup of tea and some crackers. While he held the cup of tea with two hands, sipping and whimpering, everyone looked at him in shock. The words, "warriors don't cry" were still resonating inside the room's walls. Bassim looked at me from the corner of his still-wet eyes and smirked while shaking his head. I nodded.

Airplanes and helicopters were flying over the island like flies over honey. They were probably attracted to the deserted L-87, standing off not too far from the island like a hulking ghost. On shore, we took positions in foxholes and waited until the airplanes and helicopters were completely gone. We boarded First Lieutenant Muhsin's patrol boat, quickly left the island, and broke out for our navy base in Ra's Al-Qulay'ah.

14. Breaking Saddam's Grip

The patrol boat was capable of completing the trip from the island to the base in a little more than two hours. In our fantasy, we would sail west at full speed, neither detected by airplanes nor tripped by mines. We would sneak into our home base while the Americans were not looking and glide over the waters without anything in the sky but the brilliant sun.

Still, we all knew that a confrontation with American warplanes at some point was inevitable. My original fantasy of getting captured by the Americans involved a land siege and a peaceful surrender, not exploding boats, invisible drifting mines, and random airplane attacks. Again, I considered my plans naive and stupid and chastised myself for not considering Lieutenant Munther's advice to stay in Umm Qasr.

As we sped recklessly through the waters, Munther pointed out two mines that came pretty close to hitting our patrol boat. I was not able to see the mines even as he pointed to them. My angel was still at work, protecting me. Munther turned to First Lieutenant Muhsin and asked him if anyone was looking out for mines. The commander of the patrol boat did not seem to think that that was necessary. Knowing firsthand the magnitude of destruction that could result from these mines, Munther and First

Lieutenant Wafi took the initiative to keep out a watchful eye for them and help us navigate safely to the promised land.

It had been only thirty minutes when I looked at my watch for the tenth time, hoping that we wouldn't arrive too late to save Tahir's life. Riyadh and the others had received some medical attention on the island and were beginning to feel better. But Tahir was still unconscious, with an IV bag resting on his chest and a needle stuck in his arm. At precisely 11:30 A.M., I saw an airplane. It was flying low at the horizon, ominous like a black eagle who would bring with him our judgment day.

We wanted to lower the lifeboat into the water but our efforts were extremely uncoordinated. We pushed the lifeboat overboard headfirst and it plunged to the bottom of the sea like an anvil. As the airplane drew nearer, First Lieutenant Muhsin ordered one of his soldiers to sit at the antiaircraft guns and try to shoot the airplane down. When the soldier approached the guns, everyone—soldiers and officers—yelled *"No!"* We knew that if the pilot saw someone at the guns, then there would be no mercy. The soldier stepped back and First Lieutenant Muhsin didn't order him to take his position. In a way, First Lieutenant Muhsin didn't really want to duel with the plane but, for the record, he gave the command that was expected of him.

Nevertheless, the fighter jet rose up to a higher altitude and went into a dive toward our boat. We scrambled around and panicked like rats in an overcrowded shoebox. From the stern, I ran to the galley while one of First Lieutenant Muhsin's soldiers jumped overboard. The plane dropped a bomb, missing the speed boat by mere inches. The bomb exploded in the water, but it fell so close to the rudders that they were affected. Before the plane came back, First Lieutenant Muhsin struggled to turn the boat and go back to pick up his soldier from the water.

"Why did he jump?" he asked.

"He did not jump! He tripped and fell," his friends replied.

Abandoning the boat was one of many crimes punishable by death in Iraq. First Lieutenant Muhsin was no fool, but he played along.

I never saw the plane coming the second time, but I took cover when everyone else did. The plane strafed the fiberglass boat. Its ceiling and walls were no match for the bullets. They drew a dotted line within inches of my hiding spot in a corner. They split the wooden floor and kicked dust up in the air. Learning a lesson from the sixteen-year old kid who was executed not too long ago, I held my knees up against my chest to sacrifice my legs for my vital organs and to make myself a smaller target for the airplane. I covered my face with my helmet and heard the bullets rip the wooden platform again.

After strafing the boat three times, the plane was gone for a short while. Dust floated in the air all around us. We got up and checked each other for wounds. Miraculously, no one was killed. Although I was on top of Riyadh, somehow a bullet managed to hit him in the leg. I was feeling no pain and there were no bullet holes in my uniform. One of the patrol boat officers threw his body over Tahir to protect him from the bullets. When someone pointed out that his butt was bleeding, he was upset. "What am I going to do when my family wants to see my scar?" Luckily, we found three more bullet holes, in the back of his thigh. This would give him plenty to display without getting too intimate with his family and friends. None of the four bullets had exited his body. In the beginning, he was high on adrenaline and was not aware of his wounds until we pointed them out. An hour later, he was unable to walk unassisted.

First Lieutenant Muhsin was still hoping that he could escape the airplane attack and push all the way to Ra's Al-Qulay'ah. But he finally realized that his rudders were damaged. A small fire started in the engine room. The patrol boat crew put it out very quickly and I went down to see if they needed my assistance there. On the lower deck, I found that most of the soldiers were hiding under a very thick wooden table in the crew cabin, below the galley. Realizing that this was a safer place than the galley, I decided to join them but a faint and very distinguished scent began to intrude.

"It's that smell again," I whispered to myself.

Riyadh overheard me and asked, "What smell?"

It was the smell of death, but that was the last thing that Riyadh needed to hear from me. I spared him and just said, "I smelled the same thing on the L-87 last night." Then I went back up to the galley, choosing the risk of bullets over that awful smell.

The plane came back for a fifth time and made one final pass over us. This time it dropped a small bomb in the wheelhouse that completely disabled the boat. Luckily, no one was in the wheelhouse at the moment other than the dead body of First Lieutenant Mahdi. To my joy and disbelief, First Lieutenant Muhsin finally uttered the words, "We have to surrender." He ordered one of his soldiers to wave to the pilot with an orange life jacket. I took the white piece of cloth out of my gas mask pouch and handed it over to the soldier. "Here, this might work better." He took the impermissible piece of cloth from me and waved it at the pilot. At the sight of the white flag, the plane was gone and everything was calm again in the Persian Gulf. For fifteen minutes we strained our ears for airplanes, but all we heard was the sound of splashing waves. The boat was disabled and we couldn't go anywhere.

We didn't have to speculate for long about what the Americans might do next—our attention was drawn to the southern horizon, where three helicopters emerged and immediately took command of our theater of operations.

When the helicopters came closer, we all went out to see what was going to happen. The gunner from the helicopter signaled with his hand that we should abandon the boat and jump in the water. We had three life rafts on the boat, each contained in a small white fiberglass barrel. A rope was attached to a hook on the barrel at one end and to the boat at the other, so that when we tossed one barrel overboard, the hook was released and the raft inflated. Each raft was made to accommodate six people, with a three-day supply of food, water, and other necessities.

Before getting off the patrol boat, I went away for about ten seconds to bring some of my belongings with me. When I returned with my backpack, I found ten soldiers and a warrant officer crammed together in the little life raft. They were waiting for me. I told them to go without me since there were two more life rafts. My crewmates from the L-87 pushed together to clear some space for me and insisted that I complete their dozen.

Once on the life raft, the twelve of us started to push away and paddle using our hands and the two oars that the raft was equipped with. We wanted to be as far as possible from the boat, not knowing what was to come next. Although we were proceeding toward our captivity, I felt more like I was paddling toward my freedom. After ten years of oppression, I was finally managing to break free of Saddam's grip and cross the Iraqi border.

My naive plan had actually worked.

I was transitioning from captivity as a "free man" besieged by the Iraqi government, to freedom under American custody. The war was over for me now. All I had to do was face the uncertainty of being a POW.

I remained taciturn and reserved on the outside, afraid to express my feelings in the presence of my future POW companions. Anxiety could spread among the others, and relief might portray me as a traitor.

The warrant officer threw his rank insignia and identification cards in the water, then instructed us that while in captivity, we were not to address the officers using the usual "Sir." "Our first names will suffice," he said. The title "Sir" is highly formal and not used in common speech as in the West. Warrant officers were notorious for being resentful about the fact that they do not receive the same honors as the officers—the salute and the title "Sir." Some soldiers agreed with the warrant officers, while I joined the silent minority on this issue; this was a cheap shot and malicious. It revealed a lack of character and integrity and I wanted no part of it. I was even willing to give Lieutenant Ahmed, who gave me a hard time about the leftover piece of fitted carpet, the respect due to his rank.

We were now at a considerable distance from the boat. One of the helicopters was flying in a big loop encircling both the boat and raft within its circumference. The other two helicopters flew back south and disappeared beyond the horizon, about two miles away.

We were anxious and restless because we did not know what was going to happen to us next. I found out in the months that followed that waiting indefinitely for the unknown was one of the most difficult parts of being a POW, but I got my first practical lesson in it on that day. While the helicopter orbited around the life raft and boat, it passed by the raft once every few minutes. Ahmed, the radio operator, was excited like a little puppy. He followed the helicopter with his eyes and whole body making it very uncomfortable in the overly crowded raft. When the helicopter made a sudden turn, Ahmed, too, swung around and elbowed Riyadh in the face. Riyadh's nose started to bleed again. We all yelled at Ahmed, gave him an oar, and told him to row.

Whenever the helicopter came close to the raft, we cheered and waved at the pilot in an overly friendly gesture. After doing this a dozen times, I explained to my Iraqi friends that the pilot understood the message. We didn't need to cheer anymore. Minutes later the two helicopters came back, this time followed by a large missile frigate.

"They're going to kill us," cried Ahmed.

"Don't be ridiculous, we surrendered!" I told him. "They're here to pick us up."

While the first helicopter was still flying in circles, the gunner wanted to ease our tension and gave us the thumbs-up. I found out later that the pilots were told not to use the OK sign because in the Middle East it might be misinterpreted for profanity. Actually, most Iraqis were familiar with the OK sign but had no idea what the thumbs-up gesture meant.

"They're going to kill us! Their pilot did this," the warrant officer made a tight fist with his hand and stabbed the air with an invisible dagger.

"No, he did like this." I showed them the thumb-up sign. "It means that everything will be OK." But looking at the expression in their faces, I wasn't sure if my raftmates believed me. They must have thought that I was being awfully optimistic.

The two helicopters that led the way for the frigate found the two mines that Munther had pointed out earlier that day. They threw a smoke signal next to each mine so the frigate would not come near them. The frigate decided to stay behind and not maneuver its way around the mines. This meant that we had to paddle our way to the frigate. The wind blew the smoke away from the raft and the waves moved with the wind creating an illusion that, instead of stationary smoke signals, they were moving objects like torpedoes aimed at the raft.

"What are these? They're coming toward us. You see? They're going to kill us!" Ahmed started another panic wave.

"They're not torpedoes. You survived mine explosions, fire and airplane attacks, and now you are afraid of smoke." I continued to attempt to calm them down. Their panic and scrambling were threatening to tip the overcrowded raft.

"What are they, then?"

"I don't know, a cigarette butt, maybe. You know, American cigarettes are big." But seeing that they were not receptive to my humor, I continued. "They are probably smoke signals." Then I turned to Munther, "Aren't those the approximate locations where you saw the two mines?"

Munther nodded his head in agreement. "That makes sense," he said.

"Why do you keep defending them?" asked the warrant officer while we took turns paddling.

"Look, if they wanted to kill us, then we would've been dead by now. Why should they drop a torpedo far away and see if they aimed right? Why not drop it straight on top of our heads? Forget the torpedo, bullets are cheaper."

At this time I thought I was beginning to lose my mind but to them, I started to make more sense. Munther's support began to build some confidence in the remaining ten—they started to listen.

"We won't be POWs for long, right?" Waheed asked softly.

"Believe me, this will be a short war." In my mind I was thinking that the superior American arsenal and technology were capable of winning the war in days, but out loud I said, "The Americans can't fight long wars like the Iraqis and Iranians."

"Yeah, it will be a short war," the others confirmed.

"Do you speak English?" Ahmed asked.

"Yes, I do."

"Then talk to them when they take us."

"Of course, I will. All I need is a chance to talk to them and I will tell them." I pondered for a moment and then asked, "What do people usually say when they are captured?" With this, I was finally able to crack a smile on their faces.

"Do you think they will beat us up or torture us?" Munther asked this time.

"I don't think so."

"But weren't they the ones who dropped nuclear bombs on Japan? And what about the war they fought in Vietnam? I read that many Americans married Vietnamese women and, when the war was over, they left them behind with their children."

Apparently, Munther had been reading some Iraqi propaganda, which usually depicted Americans as evil people without a fear of God.

"They didn't do this to torture the Vietnamese women. Unfortunately, what they did to the women in Vietnam they do everyday to the women in America too. But things have changed now. I really don't think that anyone is going to marry you and leave you behind." A wave of laughter shook the raft.

The remaining two life rafts on the boat did not inflate. The soldiers and officers who were still on the patrol boat refused to jump in the water, although they all had life jackets. The helicopter gunner started to shoot in the water near the boat, which immediately drove them all in like a herd. The gunner then dropped a couple of self-inflating rafts and everyone was snagged out of the water safely. No one was left on the boat other than the body of First Lieutenant Mahdi and the nineteen-year-old unconscious Tahir. The helicopter hovered over the boat and showered it with bullets completely and thoroughly. My raftmates urged me to tell the Americans to stop because Tahir was still alive inside the boat. But we were far away and my voice was overwhelmed by the sound of guns and helicopter blades. Tahir was one of our own, but he was left to complete his journey through this world alone.

I saw the serial number on the missile frigate, M-38, and was happy to see the American flag. The remaining eleven did not recognize it.

"Is this the British flag?"

"No, it's the American flag."

"But the British flag is red, white, and blue."

"So is the American and French, but when you see a lot of stars and stripes, you should know that it is the American flag you are looking at."

There were approximately one hundred Americans out on the deck of the missile frigate. We saw smiling faces, cameras flashing, and video cameras. For each Iraqi on the life raft there were at least two or three guns and one camera ready to go off. Most noticeable was a soldier crouched atop the highest point on the frigate. His face was hidden behind his helmet, goggles, and bandanna. His body was low, his legs spread apart, and he moved very cautiously from side to side like a crab. He never diverted his attention away from us. It felt like his gun was fixed at the center of my chest. My attention was fixed to the barrel of his gun while my Iraqi friends were still arguing about whether the frigate was indeed American.

"It's not an American boat," said one of them, "it's the United Nations."

"Why do you say that?" I asked.

"They have white people, black people, brown people, Chinese, Indians, and people from everywhere."

"When you see a flag with lots of stars and stripes and people of different colors, you are looking at Americans." With that, I modified my earlier simplified definition of the Americans.

The Americans had a special gun they used to shoot a tow line toward the life raft. On the second attempt it fell within paddling distance and we pulled ourselves closer to the frigate. When the raft touched the frigate, a ladder was rolled down, and we started to climb very eagerly to our captivity, one after the other. In the meanwhile, a speedboat of SEALs had arrived at our patrol boat. They searched the boat and carried off the two dead bodies and the radio so that they could decipher the code. The first ten Iraqis were up on the frigate but Munther and I were still on the life raft. He held the ladder with courtesy and invited me to go first.

"May I bring my backpack with me?" I asked the Americans but no one answered.

"Why don't you go?" Munther asked.

"I don't want them to shoot me thinking that my backpack is a bomb."

Finally, I heard someone say, "*Yes!*" very distinctively, and I began to climb the ladder of dreams. When I was at the top, a Hawaiian American assisted me. Keeping his elbow bent, he flexed to show off his big biceps and extended his hand to help me climb aboard. They took my backpack away and said, "You'll get this back" to assure me, but I never saw it again. Before lining up with the others against the wall, I managed to say, "These soldiers were all against this war, please go easy on them."

I was the eleventh prisoner aboard the USS *Curts*. Three days earlier, the Americans had captured twelve Iraqis from an oil-rig platform, where the Red Crescent boat had gone to retrieve the dead bodies left behind. We were the second group of prisoners, and I was the twenty-third POW of Desert Storm. It was noon on January 24, 1991.

PART THREE

15. POW 007

The Americans were noticeably in better shape than we were. Their bodies were graceful and strong like swimmers and gymnasts, chiseled like boxers and body builders, and big and tall like football and basketball players. And then, there was us. We stood with our wasted bodies, malnourished and plagued, inundated with feelings of shame and disgrace not only because we were defeated, but because we felt like an inferior species.

The Americans first took the injured away for medical attention and then asked me if there were any other injuries among those who were still in the water. I told them that they should expect three or four more with light injuries and an officer with four bullets in his leg. The Americans frisked us, one at a time, emptied our pockets and took away our jackets, boots, and belts.

Although it was a cold winter, I did not bring my jacket along. It was on the stern of the patrol boat drenched with seawater, so I left it behind. I was the only POW who had a helmet. I brought it with me—or should I say, it stayed on my head. Surprisingly, although we all had gas masks, I was the only POW who brought his along. My frisker allowed me to keep my helmet but took away the gas mask. He placed all my possessions in a plastic trash bag, tagged my back and the bag with a piece of masking tape and wrote the number 007 on both pieces. He dismissed me to the other guard who took me inside, just as he had taken POWs number 001 through 006 before me.

"I'd like to have my boots, please," I asked the frisker before they took me away.

"But they're wet. Are you sure you want to wear them?"

"Yes, please."

I never knew why they took my boots away or gave them back. The remaining POWs were barefoot. During the days that followed, I was thankful for the warmth that my wet boots provided in the freezing-cold nights of the desert.

Inside the frigate, the Americans gathered us at the closed end of a corridor and assigned two guards to watch over us from the open end. When the remaining POWs were all picked up from the water, the Americans again took the injured for medical treatment and brought the others to the corridor where we were all gathered. The Americans then handcuffed us, using flex cuffs, and blindfolded us. While blindfolded, I heard the heavy cannons from the frigate. They were sinking our patrol boat and trying to hit the two mines that the helicopters spotted in the area.

My fluency in English and unverified American status were enough to convince the Americans to remove my handcuffs and blindfold and use me to communicate with the Iraqi POWs. The Iraqis were weak, wet, and cold. The first thing I asked on their behalf was for the Americans to provide them with blankets. They brought a large roll of fuchsia-colored fabric and started to cut it up into appropriate lengths for each POW to use as a blanket.

While everyone else was blindfolded, I saw the soldiers from Qaro being brought in. They were already blindfolded, handcuffed, and barefoot. First Lieutenant Wafi was sitting near me. I told him that the island had been captured but he didn't react to the news. The communications soldier from the island, who helped me with my duffel bag three hours earlier, was seated next to me. We were not allowed to talk, but while the Americans celebrated capturing fifty-one Iraqi POWs and liberating the first Kuwaiti real estate, I turned toward the communications soldier and whispered.

"Did anyone get killed on the island?"

"No," he said, "but who are you?"

"I'm from the landing craft. They destroyed the patrol boat and captured us."

"Did you guys survive that? We were watching you with the binoculars and thought for sure you were all dead. We sent a message to the navy base telling them that you were all killed."

"Thank you. It's better if the base thinks we're dead."

"Shut up!" yelled one of the American guards, and we were all quiet.

The contrast between the American and Iraqi soldiers and the way they were equipped was astounding. The fifteen soldiers on the L-87 had—collectively—two guns, one helmet, and fifteen old gas masks with ineffective medical kits.

The American soldiers each had a gun, helmet, gas mask, bulletproof vest, eye-protection goggles, earplugs, flashlight, and other supplementary items. They had regular meals, plenty of water, and supplies of sun-block lotion, skin-care lotion, foot powder, and so on. I must have stared too long because the guard became uncomfortable and told me to look away. The way the two countries equipped their soldiers reflected very clearly the manner in which the two governments respected life, took pride in their soldiers, and cared about their people.

Waheed came back from the medical room and sat next to me. The doctors treated his fractured arm and wounded knuckles. In the process, they tore the only shirt he had. It was very cold. He saw that I was wearing two shirts and asked if I could give him one of them. I gave him the one on top, which was a thick woven wool shirt, leaving only one thin shirt on my body. In the days that followed, I suffered from the severe cold weather but never had remorse for giving away my shirt to Waheed. I was only thankful that my injuries were light and that my plans to cross over to the American side were materializing.

Although we did not know it, it became evident from the reaction of those passing through the hallway that we stank. At the time, there was nothing to be done about it. The end of the corridor was clogged with POWs and brimming with body odor. I was placed in the beginning of the POW line between the Iraqis and American guards to help distribute food and communicate between the two sides. Todd, Matt, and Corey were three American SEALs who sat on the ground and started to talk to me. They asked how I was. I answered, "Considering everything that happened today, I'm great." They asked where I learned English. I told them about living as a legal resident of the United States and that I had lived in Chicago.

"My first cousin, Haig, joined the U.S. military in Los Angeles and was being sent to Kuwait. I'm not sure what branch of the military he is in, but wouldn't it be something if I found him on this ship?"

"We don't know anyone by that name on this ship."

They nicknamed me "Chicago," since it was easier to remember than Shant. Personally, I would have preferred 007 but I was proud to be named after a city I loved.

I admired Matt's tattoo of a black panther crawling down his forearm. "Do you have family in Chicago?" he asked.

"I still have an uncle in Chicago but my family moved to Los Angeles a long time ago. This is where I would like to go after all this is over."

"We're from California, too. Have you been there?"

"Unfortunately, not."

"California is beautiful. You should come and see the girls and the beaches in California. Do you like American or Iraqi girls better?"

"I like them all."

"Good answer!" said Corey, who was part Native American.

Todd asked if I was the commanding officer.

"No, I'm not an officer at all."

"Did anyone get killed during the attack?"

Again I said no, but then I told him about First Lieutenant Mahdi and young Tahir being left on the boat.

"We brought their bodies down. They will be handed over to the Red Cross who will make sure to deliver them to their families." Then he continued, "I could tell that you guys didn't want to fight. That's why I wanted to spare your lives. Our orders were 'free weapons.' That means I could have blown up the whole boat with everybody in it." From the remarks he made and his blond hair and blue eyes, I realized that he was the gunner on the helicopter who gave us the thumbs-up.

"I could tell that you wanted to spare lives. We would have been dead otherwise."

I wanted to ask Todd if Tahir's body was bleeding from the bullet holes that Tahir received when Todd strafed the abandoned boat. I wanted to know if Tahir was still alive when we abandoned him, but I was not prepared to know the truth and could not bring the words out of my mouth. First Lieutenant Wafi had told me that he checked Tahir's breathing and concluded that he was dead before he left him behind.

One year later, however, I would learn that Tahir's body bled from six bullet holes, which meant that his heart was still beating when he was shot.

16. On the Frigate

I was the first to be summoned for interrogation. In a little corner not far away but out of sight from where the rest of us were
gathered, a blue-eyed and relatively young interrogator with pre-
maturely gray hair stood waiting with a broad smile on his face.
He was accompanied by a man I presumed to be a Kuwaiti interpreter. Both men were very polite. They told me that I had been
chosen first because I spoke English, but I had a feeling that they
already knew that I came with a strange story. They began the
session with the usual questions about my name, rank, unit, education, and military experience. They wanted to know what my
job on the patrol boat was. I told them about the patrol boat,
about Qaro Island, and about the L-87.

"You mean you were on both boats?"

"Yes."

"This has been a bad day for you."

"It's been a bad decade."

"What do you mean?"

I told him about Chicago and Los Angeles, and explained
that I was a permanent resident of the United States but had
been stuck in Iraq for a little more than ten years.

"Did you fight in the Iran-Iraq War?"

"I served."

"You served but did you fight?"

"I served in both wars but never had a gun. You can't fight when you don't have a gun."

The Kuwaiti interpreter interrupted and asked me in Arabic. "What is your name again?"

"Shant."

"Again please."

"Shant."

"How do you spell that in Arabic?"

"*Sheen-Aleph-Noon-Taa.*"

"You don't have an Arabic name?"

"No."

In Kuwait and Saudi Arabia, people cannot earn citizenship by birth alone. They had to be direct descendants of citizens of the country. An Armenian, such as myself, would never be a Kuwaiti or a Saudi citizen. This was not the case in Iraq, however. The interpreter turned to the American interrogator and said in astonishment, "This is not an Arabic name!"

"No. I'm Armenian," I said.

"If you are Armenian, then what are you doing in the Iraqi Army?" the American asked.

"I was born in Iraq. I am Armenian, a citizen of Iraq, and a permanent resident of the United States. In Iraq, I became a citizen by birth, but my citizenship documents show that my nationality is Armenian." In 1915, on the verge of collapse, Ottoman Turkey carried out a brutal plan of genocide to annihilate the Armenians. The Armenians were the rightful owners of the eastern provinces of Turkey, going back four thousand years. Their kingdoms prospered on this land for thousands of years until the Turkic race advanced from central Asia. The Ottomans feared that Armenia might be annexed. They had recently lost the Balkan countries and were losing control over North Africa and the Arab peninsula. In the end, one and a half million people—more than half the Armenian population—were brutally massacred. Among those who perished were my mother's grandparents and some of her uncles. The survivors scattered across the four corners of the world, so I was born in Baghdad. For this reason, even today, there are more Armenians living outside Armenia than inside its borders.

"Tomorrow we will send you all to another place," said the American interrogator. "You specifically will attract a lot of attention and will be interrogated over and over again. They will ask you a lot of questions. If you want to go back to the U.S., you need to tell them the truth. Whatever you do, don't lie to them."

"I understand."

"Before I let you go, is there anything you need?"

"Yes, we need to write letters and inform our families of our safety."

"Once you are in a POW camp, you will see the Red Cross. They will help you."

"We also need some food."

"We will bring some food soon."

I nodded and thanked him. He called the guard and dismissed me. When the guard came to take me back to our corridor of body odor, I stood up but the interrogator started to talk again.

"By the way, we have your backpack." Then he asked in disbelief, "You brought your books with you?"

"They're my bedtime reading."

"You read *Quantum Theory* and *Nuclear Physics* before you go to bed?"

"Wouldn't you?"

The two polite men laughed while the guard took me away.

Being the only English-speaking POW, I often found myself to be the spokesperson of the group. Mostly, my job was to get permission from the guards whenever one of the POWs needed to go to the bathroom. With fifty-one POWs in the corridor, this happened every other minute. Like a guest in a stranger's house, I was a little bashful to ask the host for the bathroom too many times in the same visit. I held back and went only once a day myself, which made me resentful toward those who went twice.

The Americans came up with a better solution after this. They placed a bucket in the corner near the place where we were interrogated and told us to relieve ourselves in the bucket whenever we had to go. Because of my English-speaking ability, I also ended up with the responsibility of dumping the contents of the bucket overboard at the end of the day.

In addition to being the bathroom messenger, I was also the food distributor. When it was feeding time, the Americans removed our handcuffs and blindfolds. They gave me food bags and apologized because they thought that the food was mediocre in quantity and quality. "We weren't prepared to receive this many prisoners today," they explained. The Iraqis were happy to receive more food in one meal as POWs than a whole day as soldiers in the Iraqi Army. They also ate fruit, which they had not done since the UN had imposed an embargo in the aftermath of Iraq's invasion of Kuwait. After we finished eating our meals, the guards handcuffed and blindfolded us again so that we could go to sleep like parrots.

On a normal day, it would have been impossible for me to sleep on a hard metal floor, blindfolded, handcuffed, and wet on a cold winter night. The corridor was not wide enough for one person to stretch his body across, let alone for two people to sleep opposite from each other while being crowded by others from both sides. No matter, I was exhausted and had not slept in two days. I was lost in a dreamless sleep as soon as I lay down.

The next morning, on January 25, I heard the Americans talk about our transfer to a POW camp. A Lebanese interpreter came to explain in Arabic what was going to happen to us. He was very friendly, but we could tell from his accent and poor choice of words that he had been living abroad a long time and needed to brush up on his Arabic. He told us that we would be treated well by the Saudis and that their jails were constructed buildings with good facilities. I knew he meant to say "POW camps," but hearing him use the word "jail" instead reminded me that the *P* in POW stood for "prisoner."

Helicopters were transferring prisoners in groups of ten. The Americans kept me on the frigate until the last group. Matt and Corey visited me one last time and introduced me to Mike. "In a little while, Mike will be escorting you to the helicopter and hand you over to the Marines at the Saudi POW camp. You will be staying there for a few days." Then they turned to Mike and said, "This is Chicago, the guy we told you about. He's one of us, take good care of him."

When it was my time to go, only Matt was nearby.

"Where are Todd and Corey?"

"They have to be somewhere else right now."

"I want you to have this." I gave him my dog tags.

"Cool! Thank you, Chicago. AB-positive—that's my blood type too. Surely, I won't forget you."

Mike came to take me away. The soldier who had to blindfold and handcuff me apologized first and then applied my bonds very loosely. I gave him my helmet for a souvenir. As I walked with Mike, I heard voices of my American captors and felt their hands on my shoulders.

"Take care, Chicago."

"Hang on, guy."

"Good luck."

I heard the helicopter engines approaching and felt the sharp bite of the cold wind as soon as I stepped out on the deck.

17. The Marine Corps Camp

The blindfold took a lot out of my first experience in a helicopter. Mike sat next to me throughout the forty-minute flight and helped me out of the helicopter when we arrived somewhere in Saudi Arabia. Eventually, he handed me over to a Marine and told him that I was Chicago—and that he should take good care of me. The new guard was curious and started to ask me a lot of questions while we walked away. I told him a brief version of my strange story but my mind was preoccupied with the words of the Lebanese interpreter. He told us that the Saudi jails were constructed buildings, with bricks and cement, but all I could feel was the sand beneath my feet and the wind blowing in an open desert as if nothing rose to slow it down.

As we continued to walk, voices of more Americans became louder and clearer. Suddenly, I felt a sharp pain when my injured shin hit the edge of a wooden bar. I hopped and grimaced when the jolt of pain electrified every nerve in my body.

"God damn it, Pete, watch out for the guy's leg, will you?"

"Right. Sorry," Pete muttered.

Two guards pulled me up into what seemed like a large army truck. I found myself with the other Iraqi POWs who were also on the helicopter. The truck drove for a short while and delivered us to another vehicle. We were blindfolded and handcuffed all day and went through cycles of being frisked, waiting, being loaded onto a vehicle, waiting, being transported, waiting, and then being frisked again. When we arrived at our final destination for the day, the guards lined us up on the sand. We stood there while one of the guards started to call out numbers. I smelled the alcohol and felt the chill of a permanent marker on my hand.

"Number 99," the voice said.

Another voice said, "You made a mistake, 97 . . . 98 . . . 99 . . . 100 . . . 101. He's 101."

I felt the marker on my hand again. He crossed out 99 and wrote 101 on the other hand. Seconds later I heard, "Now we have two 101s, we're missing 96."

"Are you positive?"

"Yes, he's 96."

He crossed out 101 and wrote 96 on the back of my shirt and on both my pants legs. I felt like I was an article in a badly managed warehouse. Even when I was being shot at, I felt more human than when under the mercy of the permanent marker.

When the guards were ready to take us away again, I asked them to take me to the bathroom. One of them took me for a ten-to-twenty-pace walk. He then stopped and said, "OK." I felt the desert sand still beneath my feet and cold wind in my face.

"You mean out here?"

"Do you need to shit*?"

"No."

"Then, do it here."

---

* As a Christian, I do not approve of vulgar language or profanity. However, I thought it was important to adhere to the actual dialogue for accuracy throughout this part of my captivity.

I was still handcuffed and blindfolded, a guard with a gun stood behind my back and a cold wind blew in different directions. I tried to urinate but could not do it. I discovered a human body mechanism that I had not yet known. My mind was preoccupied more with the guard and his gun behind me than with my own bladder. I started to think of some unrealistic excuses. *What if there was an audience in front of me?* I was thinking that this could be a practical joke and that others were ready with cameras and video cameras so that they could bring some humor to the monotony of the desert. I buttoned up my pants and asked the guard to take me back.

"It just doesn't work like that," I said.

"You'll get used to it."

The guard took me back, frisked me for the tenth time that day, then seated me in a bus where the other POWs were gathered. The Marines removed our blindfolds and gave us our dinner. They were young men in their late teens and early twenties, most of them from Pittsburgh, Pennsylvania. They liked to talk tough and use profanity in lieu of punctuation in their speech. Apparently, they learned that from Marine life and not necessarily from Pittsburgh. After we were done eating, they gathered the trash and blindfolded us again.

18. The Person I Am

A reputation of some sort had preceded me to the Marine camp. Again, I was the first in my batch to be summoned for interrogation. After dinner, a guard came and asked for me. I walked with him and followed his directions, but my injured legs were too weak to carry my stumbling weight. I was tripping over the little bumps in the sand, and because my hands were bound, I couldn't retain my balance and fell a few times.

After walking a short distance, the guard told me to stop. I stopped and waited for a few seconds, then heard a jeep passing us by. We resumed our walk and descended a slope where I was told to stop again. The guard said, "Duck!" I did not respond, thinking that this time instead of a jeep, we had stopped to allow a duck to pass by. When he pushed my head down, I understood that he wanted me to duck down and so I complied. I followed his orders of ducking, stepping in, then standing straight.

The guard removed my blindfold but kept my handcuffs on. I found myself in a small tent, dimly lit with a tungsten light bulb hanging from its wire in the center of the tent. There were four officers, mostly in their fifties, waiting for me with signs of fatigue and determination on their faces. Dense cigarette smoke was trapped inside the tent hovering above their heads. Clearly, they had been there for quite some time. They had probably been interrogating the POW groups that arrived before me all day long. One of the four officers was undoubtedly an Arab, either a Kuwaiti or a Saudi. The officer in the center of the tent was giving the guard abrupt orders, while the others remained silent. The guard placed me in front of the officer and waited outside. Everybody's hostile attention turned toward me.

The officer in the center had short stubby blond hair, rough bronze skin that was weathered by the desert sun and wind, a two-day unshaven chin, and a commanding voice. For some reason, he reminded me of John Wayne.

"Sit down!" He growled, snubbing his cigarette out in an ashtray.

I knelt.

"All the way down!" he yelled.

I rested my butt on my heels.

"All the way down, I said," he started to yell.

My butt finally made contact with the cold sand.

"What's your name?"

I told him and he wrote it down. I also answered the question of my rank and unit.

"How many languages do you speak?"

"I speak fluent Arabic and Armenian. I know some German and a little bit of Russian."

"And English, of course."

"Yes."

"Where did you learn all these languages?"

"I am Armenian, so I speak Armenian; I was born and raised in Iraq and therefore I speak Arabic; I studied English all my life and lived in Chicago for a while, which explains my American English; I studied German and sometimes practiced it with my

Swiss relatives; and Russian I learned from a friend because I think it is a beautiful language."

"Do you realize, Shant, that you are a prisoner of war now and your fate depends on the American military? We can starve you, strip you naked, and throw you out in the cold. We can make your life miserable and make you wish you were never born. We can even kill you if we want. It all depends on how you will answer our questions. Do I make myself clear?"

I swallowed hard and replied, "I know that I'm a POW now, and that you can kill me whenever you wish. But I also know that yesterday, I survived two sinking boats, a mine explosion, and repeated airplane attacks. My friends died in front of me and bombs and bullets were all around me. Yesterday, I was in the front lines and today I still am. I am a soldier and this is my job. It doesn't scare me that you threaten to kill me. But if you have questions, then fire away because I have nothing to hide."

"We will be asking you a lot of questions and we expect you to tell the truth. Everything you say will be documented and kept on record. We will check, double-check, and recheck. If we find out that you are lying, and we have ways of finding out, then you are in deep shit. I realize that you speak good English. Do you understand what I just said?"

"Yes, sir."

He was still holding his pen although he had not written anything beyond my name, rank, and unit. He proceeded with the interrogation.

"What was your job on the boat?"

"I am an engineer but I functioned as a mechanic on the boat."

"Are you an officer?"

"No."

"You mean you have all this education and you are not an officer?"

"They wouldn't make me an officer."

"Why is that?"

"I am a permanent resident of the U.S., my mother is a U.S. citizen, and my stepfather is a retired navy man."

"In the Iraqi Navy?"

"No, the U.S. Navy."

He dropped the pen from his hand, rubbed his stubby hair, and said, "You know what I think, Shant?"

I had a feeling that he was going to say that I was full of shit.

"What?"

"I think you are full of shit."

"Why?"

"Because you're lying."

"Why do you think that I'm lying?"

He got angry and yelled, "Don't interrupt when I'm talking!"

"I'm sorry, sir."

"I don't believe a word you said. I do believe, though, that you've been in the U.S."

"Everything I told you is true."

"Don't interrupt me, I said!" He yelled again, then continued in a calm voice.

"Now, we're going to give you another chance. We will consider that nothing has been said and start all over again tomorrow."

There was a long pause, so I figured it was my turn to talk.

"I want to say something, sir."

"Go ahead."

"I have always been a lousy liar. That's why I don't lie. You may give me a second chance but I won't be able to change my story."

"Why can't you?"

"Everything I told you is true. There is only one truth and if you want me to repeat my story to you tomorrow, it will sound exactly the same as it did today. I realize that my story is very strange and hard to believe but, if I wanted to lie to you, don't you think I could've fabricated a more believable story than this?" I said this with a very specific Iraqi saying in mind, "An organized lie is better than a messy truth."

He leaned back and said, "We're going to let you go. I want you to think very hard about what I said tonight. We will call you again tomorrow and start from the beginning. Don't underestimate me when I say that we can make your life miserable."

John Wayne called the guard and told him to take me away. The Arab officer volunteered to blindfold me. He tied the blindfold as hard as he could as if he were trying to crack my skull. From that, I concluded that he was Kuwaiti and not Saudi. As the guard escorted me out of the tent, someone said, *"Zdrastvuitye"* (Salute in Russian). At first, I did not respond because I could not visually recognize that the greeting was addressed to me. When I heard *"Zdrastvuitye"* again, I realized that the Kuwaiti and I were probably the only two who knew Russian. As a Kuwaiti officer, it was likely that he received some training in Russia like many of the officers in Iraq.

I turned my face toward John Wayne and said, "I told you that my Russian was not that good."

"What is your name?" asked the voice in Russian.

"My name is Shant. I do not speak Russian very well. I do not want to speak Russian now." I responded to the voice in Russian.

John Wayne didn't understand, but said, "Let him go."

The guard took me outside and told me to wait. He went inside the tent, received his instructions from John Wayne, then proceeded to escort me back to the bus.

"Why don't they believe me?" I said to him. "I didn't lie to them. If you have any influence, please tell them."

"Hey, I'm just a soldier. I don't have any influence around here. But if you were lying to them, they will find out. If you didn't lie, then you have nothing to worry about."

When we came to the bus, he handed me over to the two guards on the bus and said, "This is Chicago, he is special. He's not allowed to talk to anyone. Watch him very closely. He speaks perfect fuckin' English." Under normal circumstances, I would have considered his statement repulsive and offensive. But this time, it came as a strange compliment.

The two guards on the bus removed my blindfold and seated me in the front row, where no other Iraqi was allowed. One of the guards was thin and tall, with red hair. The other was shorter, but well built, and with brownish blond hair. He seemed to like hearing himself pronounce the word "Pittsburgh" by stressing both the *P* and *B* sounds in the name. Of the two, "Pittsburgh" did most of the talking. It was not too long before the two guards asked me my story. I was exhausted and tired of repeating the abstract to my biography over and over again. I gave them a very brief version, but it was enough for an icebreaker. They were mostly nice although they liked to play tough and intimidating, which made them seem hostile at times. The same was true with the remaining guards in general.

"Look at what you Iraqis did! For fifty years my family got together for Christmas. Now I broke the tradition because I have to babysit you guys."

"You will be home soon but some never will. I've been away from my family for more than ten years. A lot of people suffer and die in Iraq everyday. I count my blessings for being alive and celebrate Christmas in my heart."

But at the mention of the suffering Iraqis and celebrating Christmas in the heart, Pittsburgh said, "Hey, Chicago, I want to go and kill all the Iraqis. Do you see this M16? I'm pretty good at it."

"Do you enjoy killing people?"

"No, but how come the Iraqis raped the women and killed the babies in Kuwait?"

"Some people were killed in opposition, and empty houses were looted, but I didn't hear about women raped or babies killed, directly or indirectly. In any case, rape and murder happens everyday in the U.S. more than anywhere else in the world. You really didn't have to come this far to make your point."

"It's different when it's sponsored by the state."

"Yes, but I think the Kuwaiti propaganda may have twisted the truth and exaggerated a little to motivate some countries to fight for them."

"Did the Iraqis think that they could invade a country and no one would do anything about it?"

"Look, I'm not saying that what Saddam did was right. Most of the Iraqi soldiers are planning to surrender and not fight. Not only because they know they stand no chance against the U.S., but also because they know that Iraq shouldn't be in Kuwait. Three-quarters of the draftees never reported for duty. They chose desertion at the risk of being executed if they were caught on the street. But to answer your question, the Middle East has been at war for a few thousand years and no one seemed to care. So, why now?"

"The way I see it is like this: The world is like a schoolyard. A little bully beats on a little kid and a big bully beats on the little bully. We're the big bully and you're the little bully."

"You can't simplify it more than this. But let's talk about something else."

"OK! Are all the Iraqis homosexual?"

"Why do you ask?"

"We caught two guys in the act a few days ago."

In the Middle East, people of same sex hold hands, put their arms around each other, and kiss on the cheeks with no sexual implications whatsoever. These are only gestures of friendship and greeting. I was not sure what Pittsburgh meant when he said, "We caught two guys in the act. . . ." I couldn't imagine how that might have been possible. We were handcuffed, blindfolded, freezing, exhausted, dirty, worried, nervous, and under the watchful eyes of our guards every minute of the day. I could not even urinate when I needed to.

"Maybe it's in your imagination," I said.

"That's disgusting Chicago. How can you say that?"

The guards blindfolded us again so we knew it was time to sleep.

"Do we have to sleep like this?"

"Like what?"

"Blindfolded and handcuffed in our seats on the bus?"

"Yes."

"But it's dark out there and we can't see anything anyway. Even if we could, we know what the desert looks like. Why blindfold us?"

"These are the regulations."

I said my prayers while the guards started to wonder among themselves why they had to blindfold us.

There were no roosters or work sirens to declare the beginning of a new day but everyone was awake with the rising sun. The guards took us outside to a hundred-by-thirty-foot pit that the Marines had dug twelve feet deep to protect us from falling bombs. The pit was only a few feet away from the bus, but we had not noticed it in the dark of the night. We entered the pit from a downhill slope, much like the one I descended prior to entering the interrogation tent. The entrance was gated with sandbags and barbed wire. They seated me closest to the barbed-wire gate and farthest away from everyone else. Four guards stood on top, one on each side of the rectangular pit, to watch every movement we made. No talking was allowed at any time and the words "Shut up!" were very frequently heard. In the corner diagonally opposite from where I sat was our bathroom: the bottom half of a barrel, surrounded by bamboo sticks and a piece of cloth for pseudoprivacy.

We spent most of our days in the pit and ate all our meals there. We were served beans and rice for lunch and packages of Meals, Ready-to-Eat (MRE) for breakfast and dinner. The Americans must have been under the impression that the food in the Iraqi Army was better than theirs. Every time they brought us a meal, they felt the need to justify that they ate the same thing. The food, which was not bad at all, was a most welcome change from the dry forage bread that we got in the Iraqi Army, when we were given any food at all. But the Marines had probably been eating the same food for months. Even if they were served filet mignon every day, they would have felt that their Geneva Convention human rights were being violated. No matter how good the food, monotony ruins everybody's appetite.

As usual, I was both the food distributor and trash collector, a benefit package that came with my linguistic skills.

19. The Second Round

Inside the pit, the guards didn't blindfold us, but our handcuffs remained unless it was feeding time. When one of us was blindfolded, it usually meant that he had been summoned for interrogation.

When a guard came and blindfolded me, I knew that John Wayne had kept his word and invited me for another session. He had already grilled me for more than an hour and didn't believe a word I said. This time, I was prepared to be on the receiving end of his anger, but even so, an interrogation was the only thing that broke up the monotony of the pit. There, neither talking nor walking was allowed, unless we had to go to the half barrel over in the corner. Most important, however, was that the interrogation was the only means for me to tell my story and seek help from the Americans.

While we walked, I asked the guard to tell me where we were. He said that he was not allowed to disclose any information. I could hear the sound of exploding bombs, which told me that we were close to the front lines. The weather was mostly damp in this part of the desert, which told me that we were close to the water. When I told the guard that I had a hunch that we were near the northern Kuwaiti-Saudi border and the Persian

Gulf on the east, he did not respond verbally but seemed a little agitated, which told me that I might have been correct.

We descended a slope leading to the entrance of the interrogators' pit. The guard ordered me to wait while he went inside the tent. In less than a minute, he came out and ordered me to duck, step in, and stand straight. When he removed my blindfold I found John Wayne and the rest of the gang, still in the same clothes. They even seemed to be sitting in the same positions.

"Sit down!"

I did it right this time, and sat all the way down.

"On your knees," he yelled.

I realized that there was no correct way of sitting down; he just wanted to show me who the boss was in this tent.

"Did you think about what I told you?"

"Yes."

"Do you want to change anything you said last night?"

"No."

"What was your mission the day you hit the mine?"

"We were sent to evacuate Qaro Island."

"What kind of a boat were you on?"

"It was a one-hundred-foot landing craft boat."

"Tell me about the boat."

"It has two 368 horsepower Rolls Royce engines and two Mercedes generators. The hull was made in Taiwan."

"I don't care about that. I want to know all the other details."

"The boat was brought from Kuwait after the invasion. When I was assigned to the boat, a lot of things were missing, including the blueprints and manuals. The Kuwaitis might still have those; they can probably answer all your questions."

The Kuwaiti officer could not sit still in his chair. He interrupted the interrogation and asked, "You mean you sank a Kuwaiti boat that day?"

"No, that day we sank two. The patrol boat, which came to our rescue, was also Kuwaiti."

The Kuwaiti officer showed signs of frustration, but John Wayne, who did not like to be interrupted, gave him a look and continued with his interrogation.

"I don't need the blueprints. I need you to tell me what kind of guns and weapons the boat had."

"Originally, none at all. A few days before the war started, they installed a gun and gave us boxes of ammunition. A few days later, we discovered that the bullets didn't fit."

"What, it was the wrong caliber?"

"Yes."

"What kind of artillery did they have at the navy base in Ra's Al-Qulay'ah?"

"I was never interested in learning about weapons. I'm afraid I can't give you specific details but I can say that they had a lot of small-caliber antiaircraft guns on almost every boat and one big cannon that shook the whole base when it fired."

"What kind of a weapon did you have?"

"I never had one."

"You were in the front lines and didn't have a gun?"

"A lot of people were drafted in a short time after the invasion. There was chaos and a shortage of supplies. Only two of the fifteen soldiers on our boat had guns."

"How did that make you feel?" he said, almost ridiculing me.

"Safe."

"Safe!"

"Yes, if I had a gun, I would have to shoot and be shot. Without a gun, I stood a better chance of getting captured, which was what I wanted."

"That's smart," he said. I finally felt that he was beginning to understand my strange circumstances.

"I know that you were in the navy, but can you tell me about the planes, tanks, missiles, and other weapons that Iraq has?"

Throughout the session, the interrogators didn't seem to believe anything I said. Everything I said was interpreted in a different way so that it confirmed their mind-set of whomever I was supposed to be, rather than inform them of who I actually was. The interrogators seemed to think that I was Saddam's right-hand man, or at least some sort of spy. When I realized that there was nothing I could say to change their minds, I became less delicate with my choice of words. "I don't know the answer to these questions," I said, "Like I told you, I'm just a soldier. But if you want, you can ask the U.S. government. They sold weapons to Iraq. All these countries that came together to free Kuwait have sold weapons to Iraq. Ask them. They can provide you with more accurate information, and I am sure you would consider them more trustworthy than me."

I knew that other countries sold weapons to Iraq. Among them were Russia, England, France, Italy, Yugoslavia, Jordan, and many others. But, at the time, I was not sure if the U.S. did as well. I said that it did, however, when I decided to switch my defense to offense. I was a POW who was suspected of being a spy. I was at the lowest point in my life, and things could not get much worse for me. Having said what I said, I was prepared to take a punch in the face and walk out of the John Wayne tent with a black eye and a bloody nose. To my greatest surprise, not one word was said to me nor did I have to face another burst of anger.

After a few moments of awkward silence, he resumed his questioning and started to ask about the mines.

"Do you know where these mines are?"

"They are not anchored to the bottom of the sea like they should be. They drift back and forth with the waves. Nobody knows their exact location but they're out there."

"How many mines are we talking about?"

"I don't know for sure."

"A hundred, two hundred?"

"There were two nights when some of us helped the mine-laying crew. Each night they tossed sixty mines in the water. They've been doing this for a few days. I would say that there are at least two hundred mines in the water."

"Did your boat sink after it hit the mine?"

"Yes, I mean, no. It was still partially floating the last time I saw it. I don't think it is still floating though."

"Why do you say that?"

"I heard the Iraqi frogmen on Qaro Island talk about sinking it so it would not attract attention to the island. I also heard the Americans on the frigate talk about wanting to sink it. It didn't have the strength to stay afloat for long anyway."

John Wayne nodded and said, "It is sunk now."

He said it in a courteous way, as if he were delivering news of a death in my family. To me, it felt that way too. I bowed my head and looked at the ground. With the sinking of the L-87, a small but important part of my life will forever lie underwater. It was the symbolic burial of the bodies we never found. Jassim, Abdullah, and Ali were finally laid to rest.

"You have a very strange story, Shant. I still don't believe that you're telling me the truth, but I'll take it for now. Do you need anything before we let you go?"

"Yes, it is very cold outside. Everyone has warm clothing on him but what I am wearing is very thin. I have a sweatshirt in my bag that I would like to have."

"Where are your belongings?"

"They were put in a plastic bag when I was captured."

"We can't find your bag."

"My number was 007 but now I am 96. I'm not sure which number the bag is tagged with now."

"OK, we'll see."

The Kuwaiti officer volunteered to blindfold me again. He tied the blindfolds twice as hard because of the sinking of two Kuwaiti boats. The guard took me back to the pit and then to the bus where I spent the night with the remaining POWs. I could not fall asleep very easily. I was bothered by the thought that the Americans were not willing to believe my story, and not only that the Americans did not believe me but they thought that I was a Saddam loyalist, more than any other POW. This concept revolted every fiber of my being and insulted me to the bone. I had nothing else to offer other than the truth. But the truth was being completely rejected.

After running these torturous thoughts in my mind to the point of exhaustion, I finally managed to fall asleep. But shortly after, an Iraqi POW started to call, "twalette . . . twalette." The guards woke me up.

"What is he saying, Chicago?"

"He's saying 'toilet,' he wants to go to the bathroom."

"Why is he saying it in French?"

"The word is sometimes used in everyday language in Iraq. To him, it's just a word of foreign origin and, since you are also of foreign origin, he figured that he was speaking your language."

20. Survival Mode

In the morning, we were escorted from the bus to the pit and assembled in our usual positions. While the guards stood in plain
view, I heard voices and fragments of speech not far from the pit.
The voices were talking about "blood tests" and "two test-tubes"
before they faded away in the distance. Shortly after, an American
interpreter, who had a few Arabic lessons on his résumé, came to
tell us what was going to happen. He stood behind the barbed-
wire gate and spoke very slowly with a heavy alien Arabic accent,
pronouncing each word separately. He uttered the following
words: "We . . . want . . . your . . . blood." Then he stuck two fingers in the air and said, "Two bottles."

There was no doubt in my mind that the Iraqi POWs thought
that we were going to be executed. During the Iran-Iraq War, we
were told that the Iranians replenished their hospitals' blood
bank by drawing all the blood from the Iraqi POWs before exe-
cuting them. No blood came out of the bullet holes of the dead
bodies.

I wanted to tell the others that the Americans wanted only
two test tubes instead of two bottles, but I was isolated from the
remaining POWs and was specifically not permitted to talk to
anyone. It was funny how fate chose Ahmed, the radio operator,

who was the most weak-spirited among us, to be the first to go. All eyes were fixed on him as he walked like a martyr, exiting the pit with his escort guard. His cheeks were sunk and his face turned pale as if his blood had already stopped flowing through his veins and his soul was halfway out of his body. On his way out of the pit, he was dragging his feet, his back was hunched and his shoulders were slumped. On the way back in, he was trotting like a hero rolling his sleeve down with a big smile on his face as if to say, "Nothing to it."

Before noon, buses were lined up outside. The Americans told us that we were going to be transferred to another camp. We were hoping that the new place might have better facilities, that it would provide better protection from the weather and have real bathrooms and showers. But in any case, anything was better than the pit and angry interrogators. The Americans started to call out our numbers one by one, and told us to fold our blankets and leave them on the ground in front of us as we left. They frisked, handcuffed, and blindfolded each POW, then took him to the bus before calling out the next number. The numbers were called in ascending order. At first, we were all curious why number 57, Lieutenant Ahmed, was skipped. Then we realized that all the officers and warrant officers had been omitted from the transfer.

One of the American officers from John Wayne's tent came to supervise the operation. He wore wire-framed round medical glasses and had peculiarly pinkish skin, which seemed more extreme with his bald head sticking out of his uniform. The pink officer had been present at all my interrogation sessions. "Make sure they're not officers," he told the guards as they loaded the bus. When the guards called number 94, I began to fold my blankets. When they took number 95 away and came back, I stood up expecting to hear my number, but I heard number 97 instead. I pretended to stretch and sat back down but could not fake why I folded my blankets away. I was disappointed not only because I was doomed to stay in the pit but also because I realized that the Americans did not believe the most fundamental and easily verifiable fact about me; that I was only a soldier.

The last POW to go was number 103. Before the buses drove away, the pink officer pointed to the pit and asked the guard, "Are you sure they're all officers?"

"Yes, sir," the guard answered.

"I'm not an officer," I called out from the bottom of the pit.

The supervising officer looked at me very briefly but did not respond.

"He says he's not an officer, sir," the guard repeated my plea.

"He's staying."

I was told to fold all the blankets that our friends left behind and pile them in the center of the pit. After the blankets were all folded and piled, First Lieutenant Wafi was chosen to help me carry the bathroom barrel to the barbed-wire gate. Two guards took the barrel away. Two other guards then took us to a new pit and brought us our dinner. The new pit looked exactly like the first one only that it was equipped with a light bulb, hung in the center. Instead of taking us to the bus to spend the night when darkness fell, the guards turned on the light. It was a very cold desert night with strong winds and near-freezing temperatures. The two blankets that we each had were not nearly enough to keep us warm during the day, when the temperatures were much higher, let alone at night.

"Are we going to spend the night here?" I asked the guard.

"I think so, yes."

"This is going to be tough."

"Yes," said the guard considerately.

At that moment, it struck me that during my college years and throughout my military service, I had been training myself for days like this. Not that I had the foresight that I would become a POW, but simply to condition myself for any harsh environments that my military service might subject me to. From that time on, I never used a heater in my room in Baghdad, and kept my windows open throughout the winter, year after year. You could see your breath inside my room during the winter. I slept with very thin clothing or none at all and covered myself with only one blanket. After the initial sting of my cold sheets, I would stay still for ten minutes until the sheets and blanket were warm from the heat of my body. When the space around me was warm, my muscles would relax and only then would I be able to sleep. Once or twice each winter, I took a cold shower and broke it down to a science. First, I would wet my hands and rub them against my body to cool it down and then I would walk under the shower.

My self-training was not exclusive to winter days. During the hot summer, I never used the air conditioner in my room and rarely turned my ceiling fan on, although in hot and humid Basra, the AC was a must. One afternoon, I blindfolded myself. Again, not that I had the foresight that I would be a POW one day, but I wanted to see how much I needed my sight in an environment that I knew well, such as my room. Sightless, I managed to find a certain cassette among a collection of two hundred, set the music to play, tidy up the room, and then go to bed with my blindfold still on. I also trained myself to eat all sorts of food, cooked or raw, edible or nonedible. Though, from a very young age, I had a tendency to do that. But during my college years, I began to build and develop this skill.

Despite my ardent self-trained endurance program, it was

still very difficult to sleep in the pit that night. The initial sting of a cold bed, which in my room only lasted ten minutes or so, lasted forever in the pit. The sand under my body and the two blankets that covered me never retained my body heat. A strong cold wind blew constantly after dark and penetrated my blankets and uniform as well. I knew that I had to optimize the use of my two blankets and retain my body heat before I could sleep. In the end, after more than half an hour of trial and error, I folded one blanket and placed it on top, then rolled myself with the second blanket like a burrito. I thought it impressive that I was able to do that with my hands cuffed together. Now, with the burrito-style blanket wrap, I had three layers on top, one underneath and both sides covered from the wind.

My muscles began to relax, and I knew that if I were able to stay still and not disturb the geometry of my blankets, I would soon be able to sleep.

It started to rain.

The guards were well equipped with rain coats, warm jackets, gloves, and hats. The rain did not seem to bother them as much as it bothered us. One of the guards went to their supervisors to ask them if we should continue to be punished under the weather or should be allowed to take refuge on the bus, which was available all night. The good-news bearer came back running and told the guards to take all POWs to the bus. By the time the guards blindfolded us and took us out of the rain, our blankets were already wet. They stayed wet throughout the remainder of our stay at the Marine Corps camp.

It was not John Wayne this time. The new interrogator had
Latino features, with light brown skin and a wide black mus-
tache. His speech indicated that he was born in the U.S. or had
been there since childhood. The pink officer and the others were
all sitting in their usual positions.

"Sit down," said the new interrogator.

I knelt but that did not seem to bother him. He proceeded to
ask me all the questions that John Wayne asked me before, and I
gave him all the same answers. The pink officer wrote everything
down again.

There was a big map of Kuwait hanging on the wall behind the
new interrogator. Wishing that I was free again, I retraced the path
that brought me from Umm Qasr to the pit in the Marine Corps
camp. Every city along the way brought memories, good and bad.

"Ah . . . ah . . ." said the interrogator interrupting my drifting
thoughts.

"Look right here," he said and pointed to the area between
his eyes, almost touching the bridge of his nose. He fixed his
angry eyes on me to make sure that I did not lose my focus again.

"A beautiful map, isn't it?"

"Yes, it is."

"It bothers me when you look at it."

"I'm sorry. I didn't mean to bother you."

"What countries have you been to?"

"Iraq, Lebanon, England, and the U.S."

"What else?"

"Kuwait, after the invasion, and now I guess I'm in Saudi
Arabia, if you want to count that."

"Are you sure that these are all the countries you've visited?"

"Yes, I am."

He took out my key chain and held it in front of my eyes.

21. Not as Planned

After breakfast, an American soldier gave me back my gas mask. From this I knew that my belongings were finally found. I was the only POW who brought his gas mask with him. I had no use for it while on the Iraqi side. I knew that the Americans would not use chemical weapons but that Saddam might. The Americans apparently appreciated my strategy and rewarded me by granting me possession of my gas mask. They were actually making a statement to the other POWs, or were confirming the statement that I made when I brought the gas mask into captivity with me.

Later in the morning, I was blindfolded and escorted out of the pit in the usual manner when I was taken for interrogation. After descending the sloping entrance, the guard told me to wait while he went inside the interrogator's tent. The cold wind blew ruthlessly through my uniform. My muscles were tense. They were shrinking away from the cold fabric that covered my naked skin. The uniform, which was now too large for my starving body, flapped like a raggedy flag on a flimsy post. I was too weak to stand in the face of the wind. With no one near me to give me permission, I lowered my body to a crouching position and waited for the guard who was delayed for some reason. Ten minutes later, the guard came out and took me inside.

"We found this in your bag."

"Yes, that's mine."

"Do you know what this is?"

"It's a little bear. His name is Misha. He was the mascot for the Moscow Olympics in 1980."

"Where did you get it from?"

"A friend of mine lived in Russia while I lived in the U.S. We met in college and became very good friends in Iraq. He gave it to me."

"Who is he?"

"You don't know him. He's not here."

"What is his name?" he asked in anger.

"Ghassan."

"What kind of training have you had in the Iraqi military?"

"I've had three months of basic training in 1985 and two months of naval training in 1986."

"When in 1986."

Trying to juggle my memory, I looked away but avoided laying eyes on the map.

"Ah . . . ah . . . look right here," he pointed at the bridge of his nose again.

This was beginning to be annoying so I said, "I can't remember when I'm looking at you."

He opened his angry eyes wider and said in a threatening voice, "Why?"

"Because you don't let me think . . . June of '86."

"Did you fight in the Iranian war?"

"I served for three and a half years during the Iranian war and six months in this war. I did not really fight in either war because I never had a gun. I thank God for that because I did not want to be responsible for taking a human's life."

"If you did not fight during the Iranian war, then what did you do?"

"I worked in the Engineering Department of the Navy headquarters."

"Did you see any important documents?"

"The important documents were classified and kept by the officers."

I became tired of kneeling, so I sat all the way down the way John Wayne liked it.

"Ah . . . ah . . . you have to ask first."

I knelt back up and said, "I'm sorry."

There was a moment of suspense. He expected me to ask permission, but I did not want to take a chance to be humiliated if I asked and he denied.

"Do you have a girlfriend in Iraq?"

Although I did not have a girlfriend in Iraq, my eyes glazed at the thought of the life that I was leaving behind. I had a large circle of friends from the Armenian clubs, the different schools that I had attended since childhood, my grandfather's and my aunts' neighborhoods, the University of Technology, the Academy of Fine Arts, and the military. Despite the fact that most people considered me a popular guy, I felt as if I were living a lonely life in a barren land. I often retreated to my room, which was the only space on Earth where I felt I belonged.

Part of my spirit was still in my room enjoying the large collection of carefully selected books while listening to my favorite music: poetry with Armenian music, philosophy with Bach, classic novels with Beethoven, short stories with Mozart, art books with pop music. My walls were adorned with icons of my tormented soul. There was something strange and attractive about the silent and sad figures that I painted. They hung on the walls adorning my room, inside and out, and flowed down the staircase. I had received many offers, but the paintings were too precious for me to sell.

"I don't want to answer that," was my only response to the question about the girlfriend. I looked away for a moment to hide my eyes then composed myself and looked back at the interrogator.

"What's her name?" He asked.

"What's that got to do with the war?"

"Do you want to see her again?"

I realized that the new interrogator was not aware of my previous declaration that I had no desire of going back to Iraq and that I became a POW because I wanted to return to the United States.

"I don't know," I answered.

"It all depends on what you tell us."

"What difference does it make if you don't believe a word I say anyway?"

"I never said that I didn't believe you."

"The first interrogator said it openly several times."

"I'm a different person."

"You're asking me all the same questions again."

This was one of very few chances that the new interrogator allowed me to deviate from his line of questioning, and certainly the only time that I led the conversation. The session lasted between one and two hours, as usual. At the end, he asked if I needed anything.

"I see that now you have found my bag. I need my sweatshirt, please."

"We'll see what we can do."

Back in the pit, I had plenty of time to reevaluate the circumstance that I was in. Indeed, I was a POW like I had hoped to be. But that was only the first half of my master plan. The second half envisioned the Americans receiving me with open arms and rescuing me from my unfortunate past. Sure, they would verify my status. Meanwhile, I was being interrogated every day, for nearly two hours a session.

I could withstand the intimidation, the humiliation, and the anger in the interrogation tent, but being accused of lying was very unsettling to me. The truth of my strange story was the only thing I had on my side. I had to convince the Americans to save me from my predicament, but my words were being rejected. Although I played hard at times and didn't yield to the psychological games of the interrogators, my wounded body was exhausted and was on the verge of breaking down.

I have always been honest and true to myself and others. I had strived to be a model citizen but, of which country, I was no longer sure. It seemed like I was only half a citizen in Iraq because of my American status, but also only half a citizen in the U.S. because of my family's Iraqi background. Although my family, my features, my name, and my primary language were all Armenian, the land of Armenia was one I had never seen. It was only from photographs that I knew the streets, monuments, and churches of Armenia.

Deep in the pit, I came to feel that I didn't amount to a full citizen of any country. I was a permanent resident of the U.S. but not a citizen, an Iraqi citizen but with Armenian nationality, and an Armenian who had never been to Armenia. I was a man without a country, living in a pit with hostile eyes watching over me, among friends who were suspicious toward the special attention that the Americans were giving me. The Americans thought that I was an Iraqi spy because I spoke English and Arabic—and the

Iraqis were beginning to think that I was an American spy for the same reason. It was quiet in the pit. I wiped a tear off my face and set my mind on an optimistic future when I would be reunited with my family once again.

Moments later, the pink officer came to remind the guards to watch me very closely and keep me as far as possible from the remaining POWs. At first it started out to be another miserable night; the weather was cold and blankets still wet from the previous night's rain.

But my guardian angel was still at work; it started to rain again and the guards decided to take us inside the POW bus.

22. A Friend

We woke up in the morning to a new and friendly group of guards. They started to ask me questions; I gave them the usual two-minute version of my story, then we started to talk.

"You guys all look alike," said Mike, one of the friendly guards.

"That's because we're all blindfolded."

"No, I mean you guys have the same features and skin color and you're all hairy but you look different. Are you Italian?"

"No, I'm Armenian."

"Chicago, I want to see what you look like when we remove your blindfold for breakfast. I'll show you a picture of my girlfriend and my family."

When they removed my blindfold, Mike was standing in front of me. His smile and blue eyes were the first things I laid eyes on.

"Here is a photo of my girlfriend and this is my family."

"Your girlfriend is beautiful. Are you thinking of marrying her?"

"The first thing I'll do when I go home is propose to her."

"Your father looks Italian."

"He is, but my mother is Polish."

When the next shift came, Mike had to go.

"I hope to see you in better circumstances, Chicago."

"Any circumstance is better than this."

After we had breakfast in the bus, the guards took us out to the pit. While watching us, the guards were talking among themselves, surprised at how cold the weather was in the desert. Washington, one of very few black soldiers in the unit, said, "I thought it's supposed to be blazing hot in the desert. When will it be warm around here, Chicago?"

"In March it will be nice, in April warm, and in May it will be hot. By July and August, you will pray for a day like this."

"How hot will it be in July and August?"

"From mid-July to mid-August, the temperature in the shade can peak to one hundred and ten or one hundred and twenty. On the same day, the temperature usually drops to the seventies in the evening and as low as the fifties in the early morning hours."

"Oh my God, I hope we'll be gone by then."

"So do I."

"What about sandstorms? When will those come?"

"In March you will see a lot of dust flying around, but in April you will see a red cloud approaching quickly from the horizon. Before you figure out what it is, you will find yourself blasted by sand and running for shelter."

"How do people deal with these sandstorms in the city?" asked Washington.

"Trees are planted around the cities to reduce the severity of these storms. It's called the Green Belt."

"You know, Chicago, most people think I'm too nice to be a Marine. What do you think?"

What was I going to tell him? "You're a very nice person and a good Marine."

After the friendly conversation was over, we were back to business as usual. I was told to carry the barrel again, only this time one of the American soldiers was helping me. We carried the barrel to the barbed-wire gate, the way First Lieutenant Wafi and I did a few days earlier. The guard then asked his friends to take over for me because I was not allowed outside the pit without handcuffs and blindfolds. None of them wanted to volunteer. They decided that there was nothing to be seen on the outside and allowed me to go with the bathroom barrel, my hands and eyes unbound, to the surface of the Earth.

It was the only time that I got a chance to see what was on the outside. But other than a few soldiers and an army truck and desert sand, there was nothing within sight whatsoever. I realized that POWs and interrogators weren't the only ones living in a pit; the entire unit with all its machinery was hidden in pits.

Outside the pit, the cold wind blew freely in the open desert. I wore my blanket like a cape to keep warm from the wind. A second guard joined us and brought a five-gallon container full of gasoline with him. They poured the five gallons of fuel in the barrel then lit a match and threw it in. There was a lot of water in the barrel because of Muslim cleansing rituals. The fuel floated on the water and burned alone. "The shit is not burning," said the American guard, who helped me carry the barrel, "I'm going to bring a stick so that I can stir the barrel."

My blanket and uniform were still damp from the rain. While the first guard was gone, I drew closer to the fire and opened my arms holding my blanket so that it would dry. By doing this, I became a barrier and caused local turbulences in the wind. Suddenly, the fire, which was blowing away from me, reversed directions with the wind. The fire blew backwards, embraced my body, and scorched my face. I dropped myself quickly to the ground and was happy to feel the cold, wet sand on my uniform again. I smelled my burned hair and heard American soldiers running toward me. The guard who brought the fuel was still standing next to me.

"Are you OK?" He asked.

I stood up, shook the sand off my uniform, and said, "I'm fine, but is my hair all gone?"

"No, you're OK."

The first guard came back running with a stick in his hand. Seeing that I was OK, he said, "I thought I was going to witness someone burn with burning shit." He started to stir the barrel and curse.

"Is this the first time you see someone cook shit?" He said.

"It looks like the stuff witches brew in cartoons," I replied.

"It's a good thing you still have your sense of humor."

"Yeah. It's about all I've got left."

23. We Found This in Your Bag . . .

Despite its hazards, carrying "the shit barrel" and burning its contents was the most enjoyable experience I had at the Marine Corps camp, except that the sludge never burned, so eventually the American doctors instructed the soldiers to bury it like a corpse, six feet under. That brought my comparatively pleasant duty to an end.

Meanwhile, the soldiers took me back to the pit. I was soon summoned to what turned out to be the toughest interrogation session of my POW career. I found myself kneeling in front of the new interrogator again. He held up a small address book.

"We found this in your bag."

"It's mine," I acknowledged.

"I find it very interesting. Who gave it to you?"

"A friend. It's just a normal address book—what's so special about it?"

"Everything, the telephone numbers of all the girls, all the people you know."

The names that were written in Arabic were college or army friends; they were all guys. Those written in English were foreign friends or embassy connections, only one may have been a female. The other part of my social life took place within the tight Armenian community in Iraq. I wrote the names of my Armenian male and female friends in Armenian, which was not legible to the Arab interpreters or American interrogators.

The new interrogator had a specific style in which he liked to carry out his interrogation. Like a dancer, he choreographed his moves. He would start by asking a series of trivial questions then gradually steer the interrogation toward the main issue before firing away the big question. Although the plot was somewhat transparent, I had to do the dance. He rarely allowed me to veer from his line of questioning. I knew that it wasn't about girls that I was being interrogated. But since it wasn't a question, I didn't respond to his last remark.

"What about these telephone numbers?" He continued.

"What about them?"

"You have numbers of high-ranking officers in your book, colonels and brigadiers. How do you want me to believe that you are just a soldier?"

"During the Iran-Iraq War, I served in the Engineering Department of the Navy headquarters. We had six brigadiers and five colonels in the department. Baghdad, the capital city, was my hometown. From time to time, the officers sent me to Baghdad and asked me to hand deliver official documents to the main military offices there. They gave me their personal telephone numbers so that I could report to them the progress of my task. I also have a lot of phone numbers of low-level soldiers in my address book."

"Whose business card is this?"

I had collected a few business cards, which I kept in my wallet.

"This is Hans, a friend from Switzerland who visited Iraq with my Swiss relatives."

"And this?"

"This is written in Armenian. It's Father Oshagan from church."

He opened his eyes very widely, held another card a few inches away from my face, and said in a threatening tone, "And this!" The way he choreographed his presentation of the card and asked the question made me feel like a child; I knew that I was in deep trouble without knowing what wrong I had done.

"This is the first secretary of the German embassy in Baghdad."

But he must have known that already, since it was written in Arabic on the card. His eyes were still wide open and the card was still in my face. I figured that he was expecting me to say more.

"I'm an artist. I had exhibitions in the British Council and American Cultural Center in Baghdad. The staff from the American embassy should recognize my name."

"You mean the *former* American embassy in Iraq," he asserted.

"Yes, I'm sure the U.S. closed down their embassy in Baghdad while their troops were taking positions in Saudi. Anyway, the Germans had opened their Goethe Cultural Institute in Baghdad recently. I met Mr. Achim in my exhibition at the British Council. He gave me his card because he wanted me to do an exhibition in the Goethe Institute for publicity and exposure."

He reclined without making a comment. His mind started to work while his eyes wandered one foot above my head. Being an artist was a new twist to my strange story. I was sure he did not believe it.

"You can find my Iraqi Artists Association as well as my Iraqi Engineers Association membership cards in my wallet."

Moments later, the interrogator resumed with a sly look in his eyes.

"What kind of weapons do officers carry?"

"They carry pistols."

"What did you have?"

"I told you, I never had a weapon."

"What's this?"

"This is a magazine of a pistol."

He opened his eyes wide and gave me that choreographed scary look again. He brought his face closer to mine so as to tell me that what he was about to say was very important.

"We found this in your bag."

This came by total surprise to me. I did not know how the pistol magazine ended up in my bag. I was wondering why the interrogator was able to find all these things in my bag but never found my sweatshirt. The deeper he dug in my bag, the deeper in trouble I seemed to sink. It was not a matter of whether I was an officer or not. The Iraqi officers were waiting peacefully in the pit, undisturbed and rarely interrogated more than twice. I was suspected of being something much more than that, the nature of which I didn't care to speculate on. I took a deep breath and started to explain another story that he would most likely not believe.

"After we hit the mine, Lieutenant Raad thought that he was going to die. He gave me his locker key and his pistol. He told me to empty his locker and take its contents to his family in Baghdad and to return the pistol to the base. Minutes later, Dhafir took the pistol away from me and started to shoot in the air. He was signaling for the Red Crescent boat to come and rescue us, but the boat never came. When Lieutenant Raad came out of his shock, I gave him back his key but the pistol remained with Dhafir until we were captured. I have no clue how it ended up in my bag."

"Was your friend shooting at airplanes?"

"No, we were shooting to signal for help. There were no airplanes at that time."

The interrogator started yelling, "I thought you said you never had a gun!"

"That was not my gun. I only held it for a short time."

"So, you lied to us. You did have a gun." He yelled again.

"OK! If this is how you want it, then yes, I did have a gun. This is war and I'm a soldier in the front lines. If I had a gun, I'm not going to be shy about it."

Our tango turned to a boxing match. We both calmed down after our mutual outbursts and were ready for another dance. He held a roll of cash and proceeded with the interrogation.

"Why do you have a lot of money on you? How much is this?"

"I don't know. I never count my money."

"This is a lot of money for a soldier. Only officers make this much money."

"This is a lot of money for an officer, too. I receive a monthly salary of 138 dinars in cash. A soldier returned 50 dinars he had borrowed from me a month ago. In addition to that, I collected a 450 dinar rent from a property I own. All of this cash came to my hands shortly before my one-way trip to my boat. I also had some cash that was still in my wallet from last month."

"I understand that your family is rich."

"They are fairly wealthy people."

"Why did you join the army, then?"

I thought that he should have at least known, as an interrogator, that military service was compulsory during wartime for all males in Iraq.

"In the U.S., people enlist in the military by choice. I hear that it's mostly young people with financial difficulties who seize the opportunity. But in Iraq, every male between eighteen and fifty-five who has at least one arm and a finger to pull the trigger is drafted. Those outside the draft age are still made to volunteer in the Popular Army."

He dug deeper into my bag and took out a yellow "Survival in the Sea" booklet and put it in my face.

"What's this?"

"I picked it up from the life raft thinking it was a note book that I would use to write letters to my family from captivity."

"Didn't you read the title and see inside?" He opened the booklet, which contained all kinds of signals.

"No, I saw only the back cover and tossed it in my backpack."

He asked me why the L-87 was sent to Qaro and wanted to know every little detail of the mission and the events that transpired.

"When your commanding officer sent a message from Qaro and reported the damage and casualties to the base, did you hear the codes that they used?"

"I wasn't paying attention."

His eyes opened wide again. "You mean you didn't hear anything?"

"We spent the night on a half-sunken boat, we survived explosion and fire, we were abandoned by the Red Crescent boat, we lost three bodies and carried two with us to the island. The new commanding officer was reading names of friends who were missing in action or dead. We were very emotional, some of us were crying. Surely you can understand when I say that I had no desire to decipher the code."

With that, the interrogation session came to an end. Before calling the guard to blindfold and take me away, the officer with pink skin acknowledged my presence for the first time and started to talk to me.

"Whenever you see the people who laid the mines that hit your boat, I want you to thank them for us."

I had already explained to them how the mine-laying crew was shorthanded and was recruiting soldiers from different units each night, including us. But I did not want to go through that again. It did not seem important at this point since he was not really inquiring about it. So, I said whatever I could say that would satisfy him.

"There are a lot of things that I would like to say to those responsible for the mines, but I'm not sure I want to see them again."

The guard took me back to the bus and seated me in my usual first-class front-row seat. I started to think about what was happening to me. The way the Americans watched me very closely, isolated me from the others, and focused their interrogation energy on me had nothing to do with my rank or the way that I was captured. From a biography that I had read recently, my lifestyle and background were strikingly similar to those of a spy. Every piece of evidence that was found in my bag, whether it belonged there or not, supported that theory.

The Iraqi government would have executed me in reaction to those items, rather than have gone through the headache of verifying my weird story.

24. Validation

We spent one more night in the bus and had breakfast in the pit, then the pink officer approached the guards and started to talk to them about our transfer. Shortly after, a guard called out my number, blindfolded me, and escorted me away. Before descending a slope or entering a tent, the guard stopped. He told me to kneel and then he removed my blindfold. To my surprise and pleasure, I found myself in the presence of my old friend, John Wayne. I preferred him to his counterpart, not because he was softer than the new interrogator, but because he was more genuine, more direct in his interrogation. He was as straightforward with his questions as I was with my answers, and when he didn't believe me, he simply said so.

John Wayne was alone this time. He was sitting on a bench outside a tent under the partial shade of the canvas while I was on my knees in the sun. He did not specify the manner in which I should sit. I knew that this was not a formal interrogation session, but the casual setting was not the most unusual thing about this visit, it was his apology.

"I'm sorry I didn't believe you in the beginning. Most of what you said turned out to be accurate. But if you have anything that you want to add or change you can still tell me. It's not too late."

"No, everything I said is true. I can't think of anything to add right now."

"You'll be going to another camp today. I know that you can't wait to get out of here. But because of your situation, you'll be interrogated by a lot of people wherever you go. Always say the truth. You might be more intelligent than anyone else in this camp but, remember, you can't fool all of the people all of the time."

I wanted to say something intelligent and appropriate for the moment but my mind was still dwelling on the unexpected apology. There were many gestures that defined a gentleman but none exceeded that of an officer apologizing to an enemy POW soldier for not believing the answers that he gave during an interrogation.

"Abraham Lincoln was a great man," I said, "I, too, like his words of wisdom."

The guard took me back to the pit where I waited to board the bus, and a soldier came and quietly asked me for my mother's address so that he could write a letter and assure her of my safety. I have no reason to doubt his sincerity, but my mother never received his letter. One by one, we were frisked, blindfolded, handcuffed, and then escorted to the bus. The guard intentionally strapped the flex cuffs around my wrists very loosely, as if to voice his objection toward handcuffing me. The handcuffs were so loose that they could almost slip off my wrists under their own weight alone. I appreciated his gesture but wished that he had not done so. I didn't want to attract any more attention.

The guards escorted me out of the pit and stood me by the bus where I heard a man with a robotic-sounding voice say, "Num—ber—Nin—ty—Six," to verify my number before I boarded the bus. Another soldier frisked me again and took out my gas mask to search it. The guard then noticed that my handcuffs were loose. He pulled them hard, making the handcuffs tighter than they had ever been before.

25. The 401st

Minutes after the last POW was brought in, the bus drove away. I must have been sitting next to an open door or a large window; a very strong and cold draft blew against my body during the entire trip. We weren't allowed to take the compound's blankets with us, and my shirt was very thin and damp. It seemed that so far, the interrogators had succeeded in finding everything that was in my bag except the sweatshirt.

We weren't able to utter a single word before the nearest guard would yell, "Shut up!" The guards always performed their jobs with exuberance when an officer was present, so I assumed that one was with us on the bus. I had to struggle with the wind until the bus would come to a final stop. I brought my feet up and crouched in my seat. My knees were against my chest so that my legs could block the wind from my body. I knew that we were driving south—the sun was on the left side when we started in the morning and on the right side of the bus in the afternoon.

The bus finally stopped at the 401st MPPW Company in Sarrar, a little more than a hundred miles north of Dhahran. The man with the robotic voice announced his presence by calling out our numbers. The guards helped us get off the bus and seated us on the sand. The soldier who frisked me noticed the icy feeling of my shivering body and rushed to call a doctor. He came minutes later, felt my hands, checked my pulse, and dropped his jacket on my shoulders. The jacket was very warm. I realized that if the warmth of the jacket came from his body, rather than being electrically heated, then my body was colder than a fish.

"How long have you been like this?" The doctor asked.

"About four hours."

"I'll be right back."

The doctor went away for about fifteen minutes. When he came back, he took back his jacket and wrapped me with a blanket.

Two hours later, when they removed our blindfolds, I realized that I was the only POW who had his own blanket. It was Italian-made with a tan base color and red plaid design. The guards then took us to the two tents where we would temporarily spend the night. Zimmerman, who was a young lieutenant, showed us the tents and gave us each a sleeping bag. Only we, early-bird POWs, received this luxury of owning a sleeping bag. Clearly, the Americans did not expect to be hosting more than one hundred thousand POWs in a matter of a few weeks. We were told to drop our sleeping bags and follow the guards to the processing tent.

Zimmerman accompanied me and brought me to a young soldier who was sitting behind a laptop computer and a folding table. His job was to fill out some basic biographical information, but apparently the program that he was using was not designed to accommodate an unusual profile such as mine. The pull-down menus were not able to reflect my Armenian-Iraqi-American status. For languages, he entered Arabic and English. The menu didn't allow an entry for Armenian and, strangely, neither for German nor Russian.

"Do you have French?"

"Yes," he said and entered it quickly.

"I don't speak French, I was just checking."

For religion, I had to specify which Christian denomination I belonged to. The program failed to recognize the Armenian Orthodox Church, which is different from the Greek or any other Orthodox church.

"I'm sorry it's taking a long time. It's the first time I'm doing this."

"That's OK. It's the first time for me, too."

His eyes were fixed on the computer. His face was illuminated with a green glare, which shone from the computer screen. It took a few seconds before he realized my sarcastic remark. He stopped typing, looked up, and smiled.

After filling out the biographical information, they wrote my new POW number on a yellow wristband similar to those used in hospitals. The wristband stayed with me until the end of my captivity. They opened my bag, which still had the masking tape with the number 007 on it. They took out my possessions and itemized them. I was surprised to see Dhafir's possessions mixed with mine as well as the ranks of a first lieutenant. This explained why the pistol magazine was found in my bag and why the Marines refused to believe that I was not an officer.

I was taken to the photographer next. She handed me a little sign with my new POW number on it: 125039. Then she told me to hold it under my chin for the photograph.

After the photograph, a physical exam followed. Zimmerman wasn't with me at the time, but a different soldier tried to warn me about the prostate exam. I knew about the prostate gland but, at the age of twenty-seven, I never felt the need to know exactly how they examined it. I thought that it probably meant undergoing a dose of X-ray radiation, which I'm not particularly sensitive

to, so I told the soldier that it was OK. I'm sure that my body gesture said, "I don't understand why you feel you have to warn me."

The nurses measured my height and weight and checked my
pulse. The doctor took a look at my wounded shins and bruised
legs and asked me how I felt in general. After we were done with
our social patient-to-doctor chat, he said, "Now we will do the
prostate exam." The nurses scattered away. They were shuffling
papers and acting busy in the farthest corner of the tent, pur-
posely not looking in our direction. My escort guard disappeared
behind one of the flaps. I found myself alone on a little wooden
platform with the doctor who was trying to ease the tension with
a smile. He started to put on a rubber glove—just one.

I noticed that there was no X-ray machine.

"I want you to turn around, drop your pants, bend over, and
spread your cheeks," he said while putting gel on his finger.

"Do I have to do this?"

"Yes, it's important."

I obeyed his orders, thinking that this kind of torture was
much less glamorous than what I'd seen in the movies. Although
the poking lasted only a second or two, the impression it left will
stay with me for a lifetime. When people ask me what the worst
part of being a POW was, although rarely mentioned, the
prostate exam is among the first things that comes to mind. In
my college years I trained myself for cold and hot weather, being
blindfolded, and eating just about anything, but it never crossed
my mind to train for something like this.

The last stage of processing was fingerprinting. By that time, I
had become a popular friend among the Americans. My escort
guard took me back to the computer-photograph area where I

began to tell my American friends how I was captured. They had prior knowledge that Mr. Chicago was among the POWs who they were going to receive that night. They also knew about the Iraqi boat that hit an Iraqi mine and the first liberated Kuwaiti real estate, Qaro Island.

My socks were still wet from the day that I was captured, and the photographer was surprised at how I didn't get sick in this cold winter weather. The photographer's compassion reminded me of my mother; she was old enough but twice as tall. She brought me a pair of new socks and asked me if I wanted a cup of hot tea. While wearing my new pair of socks, I told her that I had not had anything warm to drink for weeks and thanked her for her kindness. She brought me a cup of tea, then a cup of coffee and a cup of hot chocolate followed by a meal with a bottle of water and a can of Pepsi.

To keep me there a little longer, the Americans used me as an interpreter while they processed the remaining POWs, even though there was already a sufficient number of interpreters on hand considering the relatively small number of POWs waiting in line. My services were not really needed but I took pleasure in telling Lieutenant Ahmed to turn around, drop his pants, bend over, and spread his cheeks. I was not one who sought revenge, but I could never forget how miserable I was when he accused me of stealing that dirty piece of leftover carpet.

"Do I have to?" Lieutenant Ahmed asked.

"Yes, they say it's important," I answered.

"Why do they do this? Tell him I refuse to do it."

I turned to the doctor and said, "He says he needs more privacy." The nurses and I exited the tent leaving Lieutenant Ahmed alone on the platform with the smiling doctor.

It was time to go back to my sleeping bag.

Inside the tent, there were no guards to watch over us. For the first time since we were captured, we could have talked freely without being told to shut up. For the first time in two decades, we could have criticized Saddam Hussein openly without fearing for our lives and the lives of the ones we loved. But no one said a single word; we were all exhausted and almost instantly, we were all lost in a deep sleep.

In the morning, I joined the Iraqi officers for a few moments. Lieutenant Ahmed started to explain to me that he did not steal the rug. I walked away and came upon First Lieutenant Wafi, who was explaining to the remaining officers what happened to us the night that we hit the mine. He was taking credit for all of my efforts that saved the boat. With the corner of his eye, he looked at me while explaining to the others that he told us to close the compartment doors and use the fresh-water pump to fight the fire. He said that everyone screamed and panicked, but regarding himself, he said, "Only I, only I remained calm." I had no intention to go back to Iraq or compete with him for glory. I continued to walk away until one of the American soldiers (who reminded me of a brigadier general named Sabah from the Iran-Iraq War) called out, "Come here, Chicago. There's a lady who wants to talk to you before you go."

"When are we going?"

"They're coming to take you away to another place very shortly."

We went into an empty tent, where a female officer was waiting for me. Brigadier Sabah and I sat opposite her. "Tell her your story," said Brigadier Sabah. I began to tell my story from beginning to end. Her eyes drifted away but her ears were listening to every word I said. She pulled out a little burgundy cigarette purse and lit up a smoke. Brigadier Sabah was studying her face with a twinkle in his blue eyes and a big smile on his face. Obviously, he had told her about me and she wanted proof. She seemed very concerned with what was going to happen to me, but she also had her doubts.

"You better not be lying to me."

"I'm not lying. I'll give you all the addresses of my relatives in the U.S. If you want, you can check with them to verify my story."

She turned to Brigadier Sabah and said, "What can we do to help him?"

"We already wrote a letter to his mother."

"I'll see what I can do," she said and started to put her pack of cigarettes in the little purse. But before she put it away, she turned to me and asked, "Do you smoke?"

"No."

"Good for you."

When I came back from my meeting with Brigadier Sabah and the female officer, the Iraqi POW officers were eating breakfast. Across the barbed wire, at a distance, we saw Dhafir, Ahmed, Riyadh, and the others who were captured with us but were separated a few days earlier. They were waving with excitement and calling my name. I waved back and expected to be reunited with them soon. Little did I know that this would be the last time I saw them. I was still eating when a truck came to take us away. They called out our new numbers, handcuffed and blindfolded us, and off we went to a new destination.

The unit was called JIF, which stood for Joint Interrogation Facility. That night, I was interrogated briefly on two separate occasions. My inquisitor was approximately my age, with definitive Scandinavian features, and who went by the name Dave. Interrogators don't wear their names or ranks on their uniforms, but that was of no significance to me. Overall, I was interrogated by many at JIF, but Dave was present almost every time. All of my interrogators were polite and friendly. However, regulations were strict at JIF and many precautionary measures had to be taken. My bootlaces were cut up and removed, my belt and gas mask were taken away, and I was kept alone in a tent under solitary confinement conditions. There was a cot in the middle of the tent, where I laid Zimmerman's sleeping bag and the doctor's blanket, but other than that, I was not allowed to have anything.

26. Under Surveillance

On the following night, Dave introduced me to a soldier named Heinz, then left us alone. Heinz didn't ask me about the war or any military information. His focus was on my American status, my relatives in the United States and in other countries. I made a long list of direct family members and close relatives in the U.S., Switzerland, and the United Arab Emirates. I wrote down where they lived, how they were related to me, and their occupations.

"I see that you have a very large family. Most of them are doctors, engineers, and professors. Do you think that they will support you if we send you to the U.S.?"

"I am confident that if you ask any one of them, they would not hesitate to say that they would."

"I don't know how much I can do but I will try to help you. Do you need anything for now?"

"Yes, my mother worries even when there's nothing to worry about. Not knowing anything about me is going to kill her. I need to write a letter and send it to her. Will you help me?"

Heinz helped me write a short note to the Red Cross asking them to contact my mother on my behalf and inform her of my safety. I signed the letter and was about to date it.

"Is it February yet?"

Heinz looked at his watch and laughed. "No, we're two hours short," he said with a smile still frozen on his placid face. Deep wrinkles radiated from the corners of his eyes revealing his friendly nature, which stood in obvious contrast to the hostile backdrop of war. I dated the letter and gave it to him.

Later, I learned that early in February, a Red Cross agent contacted my mother and informed her that I was safe and was a POW under American custody. Up until that moment, my mother was bedridden, nearing her death. Suffering a nervous breakdown and high blood pressure, she had neither the will nor energy to continue living. Nothing could have revived her other than that phone call by the Red Cross agent who refused to leave his name. My mother regained her health and started to do everything she could in order to bring me back to the U.S. She contacted her congressman, the State Department, the Department of Defense, the U.S. embassy in Saudi Arabia, the minster of defense of Saudi Arabia, and became a volunteer with the American Red Cross.

In the meantime, Father Vahan, who had started with his PhD program in divinity at Fordham University, was invited from New York to give a talk to the Armenian community in Connecticut about Armenians in Iraq. At the end of his talk, he was asked about a certain American-Iraqi-Armenian who had family in California and who had been drafted into the Iraqi military and captured by the American forces.

"Can you tell us anything about this person?" they asked.

"A good friend of mine fits this description," replied Father Vahan, "but to the best of my knowledge, he's not a POW."

My aunts were in the audience and approached him after the talk. They informed him that the American forces had captured me, and this astounding coincidence completed the linkup of my personal contacts.

• • •

Heinz interrogated me a few times. Dave spent more time at it than anyone else, but he never accused me of being a liar or threatened to torture me. He asked his questions with courtesy, and I answered with reciprocating respect. In addition to the usual questions, he wanted me to tell him something about the morale of the Iraqi soldiers.

"The Iraqis have a very low morale. They don't believe in this war. Most of them are waiting for an opportunity to surrender. They know that Saddam had no right to invade Kuwait, even if it belonged to Iraq decades ago."

"What do you think will happen to him?"

"A lot of Iraqis will die—but I don't think anything will happen to him."

"Why don't the Iraqis kill him?"

"He is too well protected. Half the country is spying on the other half. People are afraid to talk against him even in their own homes. In every gathering, however small, there are likely to be several informants that don't know each other. Each year there are attempts on his life. But somehow the perpetrators always get caught, tortured, and then executed with their whole families. He's wiped out entire villages just for being *rumored* to harbor people who attempted to kill him."

"We will kill him."

"Dictators die but tyrants flee."

"Where do you get that from?"

"From *The Social Contract* by Jean Jacques Rousseau."

"Mm-hm. Well, we will kill him. Believe me; the CIA is working on it."

"I hope so. God bless them if they do."

• • •

With the start of each shift, the guards were instructed to frisk me and search the tent for any questionable items. During the day, this wasn't much of a nuisance but at night it was a different story. Very often, the graveyard shift would wake me up to perform their duty. Although some looked around the tent without interrupting my sleep, the wrestler preferred to start his shift by kicking my cot to wake me up and blind my eyes with his flashlight. He would then frisk me and search the tent, cot, and sleeping bag and take away everything that he might find.

I wasn't able to save a napkin in my pocket or under my mattress in case I needed to blow my nose. Nor was I able to hide a cracker to eat if they forgot to bring me a meal. The wrestler would take away my water bottle and tell me that I had to ask the guards for it whenever I was thirsty. Because of him, I could not hold on to a toothbrush for more than two shifts. Every time he took my toothbrush away, it took several days before I was able to have another one.

One day, the wrestler escalated his security procedures and started to collect rocks from the sand inside my tent. But as he cleared one layer of earth of its rock contents, he uncovered more rocks in the layers beneath. After making a few rock-loaded trips between my tent and the outside world, he realized that he would never be able to make my tent completely safe and went away for the day. Another time, he stepped inside the latrine with me, as usual, and watched me while I crouched above the wooden bench aiming for the half barrel.

"We have to do this, you know. Do you think I like to stand here and watch you wipe your ass?"

"Yes, I actually do."

"Why?"

"Because, you're the only one who does it."

Truth be told, he was not the only one who stepped inside the latrine with me. But, something told me that he was not going to ask his friends to see whether they watched me like he did. He immediately stepped outside the latrine and waited for me until I finished, then he escorted me back to my tent. On the way between the latrine and my tent, he asked, "Am I the meanest guard you have ever met?" At first, I said "No," thinking that by saying "Yes" I might upset him. But before I finished uttering the word, I realized that he was going out of his way to be cruel and that he would not stop until he reached the nirvana state of cruelty. Quickly, I corrected myself.

"I mean, yes. There are some other mean guards but you are the meanest."

My words worked like magic. Never again did he step inside the latrine, kick my cot, shine his flashlight in my face, or take away my food and water. Even so, I still could not retain a toothbrush.

A few days later, while I was inside my tent and the wrestler stood outside on his guarding duty, I heard a loud explosion. It sounded like a missile falling one or two miles away from the camp. This was not the first time that I heard an explosion, but they were scarce and came from far away. The sound was consistent with the city-to-city missile warfare that occurred during the last year of the Iran-Iraq War.

Immediately after the explosion, the telephones at the guard tower and compound gate were ringing off the hook. I could sense chaos outside my tent. Guards were running from one point to another and yelling out instructions. I knew that it was not a chemical attack because chemical bombs are not loud. Ten minutes later, everything calmed down and went back to normal. The wrestler decided to take me out for my daily exercise a little ear-

lier than usual. I walked up and down the little compound counting the number of paces between my tent and the latrine and between the remaining tents in the compound. The wrestler waited
a little, expecting me to ask, but when I didn't, he spoke up.

"Do you know what that was?"

"You mean the explosion?"

"It wasn't an explosion. It was an airplane breaking the
sound barrier."

"No it wasn't."

"Yes it was."

"I didn't hear any airplanes in the sky. You usually hear the
sound of the airplane getting louder and higher in pitch before
the sonic boom arrives. We heard three explosions, my tent inflated and deflated under the depressurization that is usually
caused by large bombs and missiles. We used to wake up every
morning to one of those during the Iran-Iraq War."

The wrestler didn't argue. He let me walk around the compound until my fifteen minutes were over then took me back to
my tent.

Later I learned that some missiles did indeed fall close by,
but I have no means to verify this incident. All I was certain of
was that the wrestler wouldn't trust me alone in the latrine. He
wouldn't let me keep a napkin, cracker, toothbrush, or bottle of
water. And so, I wasn't about to be gullible enough to take every
word that came out of his mouth as absolute truth.

27. Reconciliation

Generally speaking, I was not the type who demanded company every minute of the day. In fact, I usually preferred being left alone. The lack of having immediate family members nearby gave me ample opportunity to maintain good relations with my extended family and a large circle of friends, but my solitude was also important to me. Before my capture, I spent at least two or three hours a day reading and painting. Two or three times a month, I reevaluated and wrote down my future objectives. At JIF, I had nothing to read or paint and no control over my future, but I had plenty of time to reevaluate my life and think about the past. This left me vulnerable to flashbacks of the events that transpired during the last journey of the L-87.

When the flashback episodes ended, I found myself alone in my tent again with a fast pounding heart, heavy breathing, and the smell of death lingering like a black cloud above my cot. During the night, my dreams were more intense and surreal than my daytime flashbacks. I feared closing my eyes and seeing the nineteen-year-old Tahir, appearing somber and somehow forgiving, while he looked at me with his sad eyes, saying, "I wasn't dead when you left me on the patrol boat."

• • •

I knew that I had to keep myself occupied so that I would not lose my mind. I read and memorized the nutritional facts on the food packages that came with my meals. That was only good for a few minutes each day—then the packages started to repeat. I told Dave and Heinz about my troubles and asked them if I could have the books that I brought with me, or a pen and paper so that I could occupy myself with some drawings. They told me that I couldn't have the books because my backpack had been lost, and that a POW was not allowed to have a pen and paper at JIF.

Still, even though the circumstances of my stay at JIF weren't ideal, they were better than what the Marine camp offered. JIF also appeared to be my last stop with the Americans. I was apprehensive of being handed over to the Saudis and made certain that Dave and Heinz knew how I felt.

"I want to make sure that you know I don't want to be transferred to the Saudis. I don't know how they might treat me, as a non-Arab, a non-Muslim, and an enemy POW."

"I don't think that the Saudis will discriminate against you," said Dave.

"I am a permanent resident of the United States and I want your protection. No matter how you do it, I want to remain in American custody. I'd rather be a POW indefinitely with the Americans than a free man tomorrow with the Saudis."

"We will do our best. The truth is we like you." Dave said this nodding his head and looking toward Heinz for support.

"That's right," said Heinz with a smile.

"Do you need anything else?"

"I need to wash, brush my teeth, and shave."

And so, on the morning of February 3, Dave entered my tent with a bag of toiletries for me. He sat down on my cot while I washed my dirty hair and brushed my teeth using only half a bottle of water. The remaining half, I saved for shaving a twelve-day beard using only two cups of water and a disposable razor. The clumsy process inspired Dave to tell me about the time he decided to grow a beard.

"My beard was reddish blond, but my mom didn't like it." I looked at Dave for a second, and visualized him with a reddish-blond beard, then resumed my struggle to shave. Dave could not stay long. He told the guards to let me use the razor for five more minutes and went back to his work.

When the five minutes were up, the guards retrieved all the toiletry items from me. By that time, I had managed to shave a small patch on the right side of my face. I tried to negotiate with the guards, but they refused to let me have the razor any longer. Having surrendered to my fate, I was burning with curiosity to see what I looked like in the mirror. We had no mirrors, so I asked the guards to take me to the latrine. I looked at my reflection in the stagnant urine and water in the barrel, and saw that my beard was noticeably thinner on the right side of my face, and that there was a bald spot in the middle of my cheek. Other than that, it was not as bad as I thought. I consoled myself thinking, Who's going to see me anyway?

That same evening, I heard Dave's voice outside my tent again. "Hi buddy, someone's here to see you." The visitor carried a Bible with a camouflage cover and wore a little cross on the front of his hat. He recited a beautiful little prayer and gave me a few small cards with prayers and psalms printed on them. He pretended not to notice my half-shaved beard. Two mornings later, I heard Dave's voice outside my tent again.

"Hi, buddy. The chaplain says hi and wants you to have this." Dave handed me a paper bag containing a Bible with my name written on it, and a double-blade razor.

I shaved the other half of my face and decided not to worry about shaving any more as long as I was in captivity. Then I took the Bible out of the bag and started to read.

I used one of the little prayer cards as a bookmark and the other to keep track of the date. The card would always fall between an even and an odd page number. To avoid confusion as to which marked the date, I multiplied the day of the month by two, so that the result was always an even number, then added the month multiplied by one hundred. I had to ask the guards for the date before I could start my calendar. The one who gave me the answer realized that it was actually his birthday. I started on February 13 and placed the card between pages 226 and 227.

I read the Bible daily, and somehow I was filled with the belief that on the day I finished reading through it—all the way from Genesis to Revelations—the war would be over. I was only one day short of finishing when the war actually ended. During those days, the Bible was my most prized possession. Reading helped to keep my mind off of my torturous thoughts and flashbacks, but it was the stories themselves that worked like therapeutic magic on me. It was as if every time I opened the Holy Book, the Holy Spirit would flow out and fill my tent, such that I was constantly conscious of its presence while I read along the pages of the Bible. I understood more deeply why Jesus called the Holy Spirit the Counselor when He promised to send it to the disciples after His death.

This was not the first time that I read the Bible straight though. Prior to Desert Storm, I completed it twice, once in Armenian and once in Arabic. But the combination of my strange circumstances and going through it in such a short time, gave me a new perspective. Instead of reading scattered stories, spanning a period of a few thousand years, I saw the Bible as a single, consolidated story. Every episode had a perfect place in God's plan, historically connected with the events that preceded it, and prophetically linked with the coming of Christ.

I read vigorously from sunrise to sunset. I stopped each day only after the white pages became too gray for me to distinguish the black print. But to keep my mind occupied, even when it was too dark to read, I memorized a new psalm every other night. After dark, I stowed my Bible under the mattress and recited psalms from memory until I fell asleep.

I started with Psalm 91, which was printed on one of the cards that the chaplain gave me. It was nicknamed "Desert Shield," a very fitting name, and a source of comfort to any soldier at war.

> He will cover you with His feathers, and under His
> wings you will find refuge . . . A thousand may fall
> at your side, ten thousand at your right hand, but it
> will not come near you. (Ps. 91:4-7)

As I read through the psalms, I recognized Psalm 24 from the Armenian liturgy. The psalm was short and beautiful, glorifying a majestic Lord. I knew the words in Armenian, so I memorized it with minimal effort. Then, when I read Psalm 40, I felt as if it were a prayer that I had written many years ago but had now forgotten. I memorized it easily, since it was almost mine.

> I waited patiently for the LORD; He turned to me
> and heard my cry. He lifted me out of the slimy pit,
> out of the mud and mire . . . He put a new song in my
> mouth, a hymn of praise to our God. (Ps. 40:1-3)

I also memorized Psalms 42, 46, 59, 62, 70, and 73. Each one addressed some aspect of hardship that I endured during different stages of my life. From age thirteen, I felt rejected and abandoned in the aftermath of my parents' bitter divorce. At age fifteen, I had to decide whether to immigrate to the U.S. with my mother and brother and never see my father in Iraq again, or stay with my father and never see my mother and brother again. When I came back to Iraq to visit my father, I was trapped for more than ten years with the outbreak of the Iran-Iraq War and I witnessed the death of many family members, one after the other. Those who didn't die fled the country. Three of my childhood friends were killed in the war, and the remaining ones were soldiers awaiting their turn to die.

These feelings of rejection and abandonment persisted throughout my life. However, I had always disguised my disappointments behind a friendly smile and carried on living in a very optimistic way, to the point that many of my college friends thought that I was a spoiled child who had never seen a bad day in my life. They assumed that my rich parents made sure to provide me with every luxury and remove every obstacle that might stand in my way. But when they knew my true story, they wondered where I got my love of life. I did excel in my studies, art, and extracurricular readings. I had a wide circle of friends and a variety of social activities, but I was still convinced that there was no place for me on this Earth so long as I remained in Iraq. This was perhaps one of the key elements that helped me decide to join the January crew of the L-87 with little hesitation.

With the Counselor in my tent, all the grief that I had buried in a graveyard of painful memories began to resurface. But the Bible brought me a serene sense of peace and helped me reconcile with my pain.

Fully dressed in my Navy uniform before leaving for the bus station to report to my unit in Basra City Christmas 1986.
(CREDIT: ESSAM BUNNY)

February 1988, again in my Navy uniform before leaving to report.
(CREDIT: MAHA KHOURI)

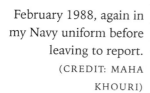

Me, sitting on the sand near the processing tent in the Admin
Compound at the 403rd. (CREDIT: CHRIS WHITTED)

From left to right: Chris Whitted, Douglas Ringer, Abe Wooster
(CREDIT: CHRIS WHITTED)

```
                        SHANT KENDERIAN
        7k4
ISN: US 718 125039EPW

Biographical information provided by the prisoner is attached.

Additional information:
    Mother: Janet Harris;  tele no. ████████████
    Uncle:  Sami Kanderian  resides in the United Arab Emirates
            ████████████
            tele no. work: ████████
            tele no. house: ██████

Captured on 24 Jan 91

    Has been issued a green card and a social security number.
    Does not know either number.  Discarded both cards rather
    than risk having the cards discovered on him by other Iraqi
    soldiers.
```

Most likely written by Heintz. The bottom paragraph reads,
"Has been issued a green card and a social security number. Does
not know either number. Discarded both cards rather than risk
having the cards discovered on him by other Iraqi soldiers."

```
PWIS-2                    EPW/CI PROPERTY INFORMATION          91.03.09

US7IZ-125039EPW  KENDERIAN, SHANT H              E3

   Enclosure: JF              Compound: A

Seq Property                        Inventory  ┌──Disposition──┐
 No. — Tag ──Description──────     ─Qty─ Date ─Type──────────Date─
  1 1042001  25 DINAR NOTES        .    10 91.01.29 SA(SAFE)     91.02.11
  2 1029002  10 DINAR NOTES             3 91.01.29 SA(SAFE)      91.01.29
  3 1029003  01 DINAR NOTES            11 91.01.29 SA(SAFE)      91.01.29
  4 1029004  1/2 DINAR NOTES           1 91.01.29 SA(SAFE)      91.01.29
  5 1029005  MEDICATION SEPTRIN, OPEN  1 91.01.29 SR(STORE ROOM) 91.01.29
  6 1029006  BOOK SURVIVAL AT SEA ORAN 1 91.01.29 SR(STORE ROOM) 91.01.29
  7 1029007  KEYS,METAL TYPE MATERIAL7 5 91.01.29 SR(STORE ROOM) 91.01.29
  8 1029008  KEY CHAIN, BEAR PLASTIC T 1 91.01.29 SR(STORE ROOM) 91.01.29
  9 1029009  WEB BELT NAVY IN COLOR    1 91.01.29 SR(STORE ROOM) 91.01.29
                            ── EDIT LIST ──

                   Edit an item in the data base
              Add      Edit      Delete     Previous    Menu
Move - - -                                        Select - <Enter>
                  ═══< Screen 2 of 2 >══
```

This is an itemized list of my belongings. The list was made when
I was processed at the 401st. You can see my POW number on the
top left, 125039. This was the day I received my prostate exam.
Item 6 is the booklet I picked up thinking it was a notebook but
it was actually a Survival at Sea manual.

This photo was taken at the 403rd POW camp in Saudi and sent by Monica to my mother. The note was written by Monica.

In my tent with Chris Whitted toward the end of my stay at the 403rd. (CREDIT: CHRIS WHITTED)

With Michael Rahilly at the 301st POW camp.
(CREDIT: MICHAEL RAHILLY)

You can see me here on the extreme left of the photo. I am sitting
in the kitchen tent eating dinner with the American and Iraqi cooks
at Enclosure 2 of the 403rd. Lieutenant Magee is to my left and
Grossman is the third person to my left. My beard had grown
because I had stopped shaving ever since my shaving incident at
JIF. You see me wearing my POW wristband and a dark blue
jump suit. (CREDIT: HUGH GROSSMAN)

View of Enclosure One, at the 403rd, as seen from the northeast
watch guard tower. To the left you can see some of the five hundred
prisoners held at Compound 7. (CREDIT: MICHAEL RAHILLY)

White tents seen in the horizon are part of the POW camp in the
desert of Hafr Al-Batin. The photos were taken from the American
compound. Latrine stalls are located in front of the truck.
(CREDIT: MICHAEL RAHILLY)

Michael Rahilly and I in the processing tent of the 301st in Hafr Al-Batin. I am wearing my pair of Reebocks and only one wristband. Although I was treated as a Trustee, I was not yet wearing the "Trustee" wristband. (CREDIT: MICHAEL RAHILLY)

Also in the processing tent of the 301st in Hafr Al-Batin, I'm seated with a soldier from Virginia. (CREDIT: MICHAEL RAHILLY)

These were taken at the 301st by Michael Rahilly. The two sweatsuits that Grossman gave me are shown in these pictures. I came back home wearing the black one (the one pictured in the two photos below).

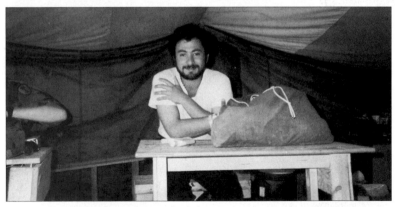

I am at the processing tent of the 301st. Based on the clothes I was wearing and the duffle bag on the table, which contained all my belongings, this might have been my last day as a POW. I was awaiting the truck that would carry me to freedom.

(CREDIT: MICHAEL RAHILLY)

28. Basic Needs

Besides Dave and Heinz, I was interrogated by many "guest inter-rogators" throughout my extended stay at JIF. During these ses-sions, Dave was always present in the tent. He would introduce me to the guest interrogator of the day, then recline in his seat to oversee the overall progress of the session, as if claiming owner-ship in an unspoken way.

One of the first of these visitors was sent under the direct or-ders of General Schwarzkopf to investigate the circumstances that led to Tahir's death. The U.S. forces wanted to make sure that there was no wrongdoing on behalf of the Americans. After we abandoned the boat, helicopters strafed it before the Ameri-can SEALs went on board to search it. As part of standard proce-dure, Corey "capped" Tahir by shooting him in the head. He hadn't noticed the IV bag to realize that Tahir was perhaps in-jured or unconscious. I told the interrogator that when we left Tahir on the boat, he was unconscious. He had no bullet holes nor was there any blood showing on him. Any bullet holes that he might have sustained were probably the result of the helicop-ters strafing the boat while Tahir was still inside.

A few days later, I was introduced to Jim who came back to in-terrogate me two more times. Since we both loved soccer, we talked about the sport on and off, before and after our sessions. From him, I learned that Karl-Heinz Granitza, who was a player with the Chicago Sting during the time that I lived in the Windy City, was now the head coach of the team. Of the many topics that he covered, Jim's interrogations always involved questions about the effects of the leaflets that the Americans dropped on Iraqi troops.

"I was captured very early from a boat. I have not seen these leaflets."

"What kind of propaganda do the Iraqis use against us?"

"They use the religious factor; the Crusaders are defiling the holy land of Islam: eating pork, drinking alcohol, sex and women."

"Women!" interjected Dave, "where are they?"

From this I realized that the Americans did not have romantic relationships in their coed army.

"How is the morale of the Iraqi soldiers?" Jim continued.

"Their morale is very low. They don't want to be in this war. Most of them will surrender."

"How can we make it easier for them?"

"Show them the way. They can't go back because their commanders may shoot them and they can't go forward because the Americans will shoot."

I'm not sure if I can take any credit for this, but the Americans did drop leaflets later giving the Iraqis instructions on how to safely surrender.

Jim's trademark ending to each session was to empty out his pockets on the table and offer all the goodies that came out, an incredibly clever technique. This boyish gesture, of setting the lint aside from his candy and chewing gum, made me feel as if we were childhood friends; that I could trust him with my deepest secrets, if I had any to offer.

On the day that Chuck interrogated me, he tested my German. He was a typical blond and blue-eyed Minnesota guy, who had been stationed in Germany prior to Desert Storm. He asked how I spent the time alone in my tent all day long and I told him that I read the Bible. Upon hearing the few words of German that I spoke, he promised to mail me a German Bible whenever we were both back in the U.S. again. Dave asked Chuck if he wanted to ask me any other questions. Chuck, who was naturally calm and relaxed, was now obviously beginning to form another question. He asked what kind of music the Iraqis liked to listen to. I told him that different people liked different things and gave him a few examples. Overall, there were a lot of guest interrogators that day but only a few basic questions asked. The questions had no substance. I felt that Dave was showing me off, his trophy, to the less accomplished interrogators.

Genuine or not, at the end of each session the interrogators always asked if I needed anything before they dismissed me back to my solitary tent. For me, they were the only contact that I had with the outside world. Each time that they asked, I repeated the same request: I needed to be clean. I needed to shower and wash my clothes, and I needed to wash my face and brush my teeth every day. I offered up the best arguments that I could, saying that if I were to be kept at JIF, then I should have my basic needs met like any other Iraqi POW. But my requests continued to fall on deaf ears.

There was an American officer who visited me approximately once a week. Like any other interrogator, his name and rank were absent from his uniform, but the similarities stopped there. He was never there to interrogate me. The purpose of his visits, he said, was to check and see that I was OK. He looked like my uncle Sammy. Although he gave me his name, I could never think of him as anything other than Sammy.

Sammy said that he belonged to another unit and didn't know what was really going on at JIF, but he told me that I was not forgotten, that there were people working on my case to help bring me back to America.

I told him about my failed attempts in requesting permission to shower and wash my clothes. I explained that there was a dead man's blood on my uniform, oil from the oil-slick area in the gulf, and smoke, soot, and ashes from the burned boat. I had spent days and nights sitting and sleeping in the sand pits at the Marine camp. While at JIF, I spilled all kinds of food on my uniform before I learned how to eat in my dark tent at night.

Sammy was looking over his right shoulder and seemed very disturbed while he listened. "I don't know why they do these things," he replied. The disappointment in his voice was obvious. Our meeting came to an abrupt conclusion when he walked away with quick long strides, planting his heels in the desert sand. His body language assured me that he was going to do something to help improve my hygiene.

It was true; although I didn't see Sammy until the following week, JIF responded to my demands on the following morning; the guards brought me a bathrobe, bowl, detergent, and two five-gallon containers filled with hot and cold water. They told me that I could wear the bathrobe while I washed my uniform in the bowl. I washed it until I ran out of detergent and water. The wash water came out black every time.

I was also finally to be taken to a shower. One of the guards who was in his early forties blindfolded and handcuffed me using real handcuffs instead of the usual flex cuffs. In addition to his genuine steel handcuffs and his mirrorlike black sunglasses, his manner made me certain of his profession as a police officer back home. He twisted my arm behind my back and bent my wrist to the threshold of pain. I walked with one shoulder lower than the other in order to retain my balance and reduce the pain. Two armed guards walked in front of us, and two behind us. The wrestler was one of them. Blindfolded, I paraded with my miniskirt bathrobe—on a windy day—across the American camp to take a long-overdue shower.

After the cold shower, the wrestler and another guard blindfolded and handcuffed me, then they started to escort me back to my tent, where my damp uniform was waiting for me. While still in the shower, I noticed that they were hiding a camera. Although photographing POWs was against regulations, they asked if they could take a picture of themselves escorting me. I agreed but joked that with a smile my appearance could ruin the heroic atmosphere of war that they wanted to capture with their camera.

After taking the photo, the wrestler started to taunt me. "I bet you have no clue where you are right now." He said this halfway between the shower and my tent. From the left side I could smell the strong scent of food and heard the clattering of kitchen utensils and cafeteria trays. From the right side I heard the sound of a continuously running diesel engine and felt the hot exhaust blowing in my face. Although my tent was not electrified, the camp in general was lit and seemed to have electricity night and day. In the middle of a desert, the only source of electricity had to come from a generator.

"We are between the kitchen and the generator," I replied.

"What generator?"

"This one right here," I said pointing to the source of hot air.

"I don't know what you are talking about."

"This engine to my right, which runs day and night, is a generator."

"I meant you don't know where we are in the country."

From the scent of the air, I knew that we were not far from the coast. I also knew approximately how long the bus had driven from the Marine camp before it stopped at the 401st.

"We are probably a hundred and fifty kilometers from the Saudi-Kuwaiti boarder and not far from the coast."

"Do you know the name of the city we are in?"

"No, but was my estimate correct?"

"I don't know, probably, but I didn't say anything."

They took me back to my tent, where I lay down on my cot and relished the feeling of being clean.

29. The 403rd

After disappearing for quite a while, Dave visited my tent one
last time on February 28.

"Long time no see."

"Hi, Dave."

"I have good news and bad news for you, buddy. The good
news is that the war is over."

"When was that?"

"Yesterday."

I wasn't surprised that the war was so short. Indeed, the end
of the war was good news for the Iraqi people, who had seen more
than enough to convince them how powerful the American arsenal could be. The end of the war was good news for the Americans who had not seen their families for so long and could not
wait to go back home. But since I wanted to remain in American
custody until my case was resolved, I was not at all certain that
the end of the war was the best thing that could happen to me.

"What's the bad news?"

"We will have to transfer you to the Saudis."

I was extremely disappointed at the lack of effort the JIF ex-
pended in verifying my status and in helping me at least stay in
American custody.

"When will I be transferred?" I asked calmly.

"Right now; the Saudis will be nice to you."

"Tell me, Dave, do you guys still not believe a word I said?"

"We believe you. We checked on you and everything turned out to be accurate "

"So, knowing that I am a permanent resident of the United States and a green card holder, you decided to hand me over to the Saudis and expect them to treat me better than you did?"

"There are a lot of people working on your case, but we can't keep you here."

I packed Zimmerman's sleeping bag, the doctor's Italian-made blanket, and the chaplain's Bible. Dave gave the guards the plastic bag where my belongings were held and a care package containing travel-size toiletry items. The contents of the plastic bag were reduced to half the original size since most of my belongings were lost to souvenir hunters, including my gas mask and books. I was escorted to a pickup truck outside the seven-tent compound. The guards who watched over me during the last week of my stay at JIF took me without being blindfolded this time. They carried my belongings and helped me hop onto the back of the truck. During the week that we coexisted at JIF, these guards had rarely spoken to me. But before the truck drove away, they all wished me good luck and expressed their hopes that I would make it back to America and be reunited with my family again.

There were two high-ranking Iraqi POWs with me in the back of the truck. Apparently the three of us were the only occupants remaining within the closely watched seven-tent compound at JIF. Two guards were assigned to go with us. One sat in the driver's seat and the other in the back of the truck. At this point the three of us were handcuffed and blindfolded in the usual manner and, within minutes, the truck was going down a bumpy dirt road, winding through the individual POW "cities" that the Americans had constructed out of sand berm and barbed wire.

Luckily, the trip was short. After about fifteen minutes of breathing dust and bouncing between the metal walls of the truck, we came to a final stop at the 403rd MPPW Company. Someone approached the truck and addressed our driver and escort guard. He talked to them with a naturally loud voice and a slight Southern American accent, pronouncing each syllable very clearly so that there was no mistaking what he said. He greeted them and introduced himself all in one breath without waiting for a response.

"Hi, are you from JIF? How are you? I'm First Lieutenant Quinn. Nice meeting you." He gave the driver a small window of opportunity, in which the driver was able to slip in "Hi," before the first lieutenant began to talk again to the two guards.

"I want to talk to both of you, would you step aside for a minute?"

The first lieutenant paused a few seconds. The two guards began to walk away from the truck with him and he started to talk again.

"I don't want you to bring prisoners blindfolded again to this camp," he said.

Although, I heard it clearly, I had trouble believing it. During our six-day stay with the Marines, we were not allowed to see what was outside the pit. I spent all of February at JIF and was rarely allowed outside my tent without blindfolds. Now came this man, First Lieutenant Quinn, who was suggesting that we ought to be driven from one place to another with our eyes wide open. If this were true then my soul should have jumped with joy and popped right out of my body. I was eager to hear more, but the first lieutenant's voice faded as he walked with the guards farther away from the truck. I loved First Lieutenant Quinn even before I saw him. I made sure that I burned the sound of his distinguished voice in my memory so that I would recognize it whenever I might hear it again.

From the moment that I heard First Lieutenant Quinn's voice, I knew that my arrival at the 403rd marked the beginning of a new phase in my POW career.

After the talk, my hopes were confirmed when the guards came back and removed our handcuffs and blindfolds. They drove us inside a barbed-wire compound and seated us on the sand with our belongings in front of us. The guards at the 403rd quickly recognized my fluency in American English. I asked permission to stand up and told the guard, Chris Whitted, my story. I requested not to be handed over to the Saudis. He separated me from the other two POWs and asked me to wait near the processing tent while he went inside. Chris called his two friends, Abe Wooster and Johan Wik. While the two big guys stood outside and listened to my story, Chris went back to the tent and brought Cooper out. She was one of the soldiers who worked in, and was most knowledgeable about, the business of the processing tent.

Cooper listened for a few minutes and decided that she had heard enough. She seemed very concerned and sympathetic when she turned around and walked away with the same determination I saw on Sammy after I told him about my shower struggle. When the guys saw her reaction, they assured me that she was going to make things happen. I wasn't finished telling my story when she came back and interrupted with, "You will stay here with us. We will not send you to the Saudis. You can help us as an interpreter if you want." Just like that, she was able to do in five minutes what JIF failed to do in a month. I had known only one other person like her, Jwad, from the Engineering Department of the Iraqi Navy headquarters. Although Jwad and Cooper were small in stature, they both had an incredible amount of energy. They were hardworking, extremely humane, and highly ethical. But since his workday was a six-hour shift and hers was a twelve-hour shift, she outdid him by a factor of two. She was the little gear that spun the whole lifesaving engine.

Most of the other POWs found that their movements were tightly controlled and restricted, for logistical reasons—there were three great enclosures at the 403rd, with each enclosure composed of eight separate POW compounds of five hundred to six hundred POWs per compound. However, I spent most of my time in the second compound of Enclosure One, the Admin Compound, and never again was I handcuffed, blindfolded, interrogated, or confined to a solitary tent. I did not have to ask permission to speak, stand, or go to the bathroom. I was treated as an equal and walked freely within the Admin Compound. The only restriction was that I was not allowed outside without permission or a guard/escort.

Later in the day, just before my first dusk at the 403rd, I came out of the processing tent to watch a new batch of incoming POWs. They lined up in single file and marched away to their new compound. A very beautiful and energetic young female soldier with braided blond hair was leading the way, carrying her rifle on her shoulder. I didn't realize that Wik was behind me, watching me steal more than a glance at her.

"Beautiful, ain't she?"

"Yes," I answered, hoping to end the conversation there.

"You're probably wondering what a beautiful chick like her is doing in a place like this. Right?"

"I don't think she's even twenty, yet. What brought her here, anyway?"

"That's what we're all trying to figure out."

"You guys are lucky. I spent four years in the Iraqi Army. No matter where I turned my face, I saw nothing but burly guys with a lot of body hair."

Wik and I became friends. He was the first to employ my skills when he asked me to read the names and serial numbers from the POW cards of the incoming Iraqis. The Arabic names were written in English characters with more than one spelling variation for each name. Hussein, Husain, and Husein were different spellings of one name, for example. Furthermore, imposing the Western system of documenting the last name first, the middle name second, and first name last on the Middle Eastern system of documenting the first name first, father's first name second, and grandfather's first name last added chaos to confusion. Worse yet, the interpreters, depending on their background, were not consistent with the system they followed in filling out these cards. It was clear to me from that day that the Red Cross would not be able to identify a POW from his records with more than fifty percent certainty.

In all, my task was amusing. Wik wanted me to use the U.S. Army phonetic letters to spell out Arabic names, which made the names look and sound even stranger. I was reading the names one after the other when I stopped and said, "Oh, oh! This guy's name is bad." From the corner of his devilish eye, Wik looked over at Ellen, who was sitting next to him working quietly on her computer like a mouse.

Then he said to me with a wicked smile, "OK, shoot."

"Bravo, Alpha, Delta"

"You're learning fast."

"Actually, the name is misspelled. It's supposed to be Alpha, Bravo, Delta."

"We have to keep it like it is."

Toward the end of the day shift, Sergeant Kerwin brought me a cooked meal. The food was plentiful, so he had a little bite with me. While we chewed our overly cooked flank steak, he asked me if the Iraqis loved and supported Saddam like in the pictures he had seen of street demonstrations. I explained how people were forced into these demonstrations, as I myself had experienced during my college years.

I did my engineering studies at the University of Technology in Baghdad, which had a fifteen-thousand-student-strong campus. On many occasions, Ba'ath Party officials would lock all exits and sweep the university to drive everyone to the streets like a herd of sheep. They searched every classroom, bathroom, and hallway. My friends and I used to hide in the faculty club, from which students were generally forbidden during breakfast and lunch. Assuming it was empty, the faculty club was not searched by the Ba'athist. One day, they discovered our secret hiding place and drove us to the streets with the rest of the herd.

We were handed banners and Iraqi flags as we marched down the street. Military police marched along on the periphery to keep us contained and themselves outside the video and camera lenses. Nonstudent Ba'ath Party officials and student Ba'athists were among us. They shouted slogans, jumped up and down, and cheered for Saddam while TV station video cameras were recording. I was certain that we were denouncing something or sending a message to the U.S. or Europe. But no one explained this to me nor did I care to know. When the media finished recording, we were free to return to school and resume our classes. In all, it was quick and efficient. We were out no more than an hour.

When I explained this to Sergeant Kerwin, he said that he had always had a feeling that the people in the pictures were not demonstrating under their own free will. Our time together came to a natural conclusion after we finished the meal. Sergeant Kerwin loaded the food container onto his truck and drove away, just as the night shift began to arrive.

Before going off with the day shift, Chris asked me if I needed anything. I told him that I needed a new pair of underwear. When the night shift arrived, a very attractive woman was the first to walk into the processing tent. The guys from the day shift said to her, "Meg, you'll never believe this guy's story," but she turned to me and said, "I've heard about you already. Long before you got here. The first time was when my roommate woke me in the middle of the night, just to tell me about you." I hadn't quite achieved celebrity status, but my mental handcuffs were loosening.

I stayed up with the nightshift, silently celebrating my first wakeful night, falling asleep at around two in the morning. By six o'clock, despite having only four hours of sleep, I felt surprisingly rested. Part of the reason may have been that this was also my first uninterrupted four-hour sleep since joining the L-87 crew.

In the morning, Chris brought me a pair of underwear and, having noticed that my bootlaces were missing, brought a pair of bootlaces as well. He said, "Here, don't tell anyone." Not knowing about Chris, Wik and Abe each also brought me a pair of laces, instructing me not to tell anyone. Chris and Abe showed me the latrine and a table with mirrors for shaving in the far corner of the compound.

"Excuse me; I want to go and look at myself in the mirror. I haven't seen my face in more than a month."

"Don't worry, you're still ugly," said Chris, laughing.

Later in the day, Wik and Sergeant File suggested that I write a letter to my mother and offered to mail it for me. I gave them an open letter on the following day so that they might inspect its contents. Sergeant File shook his head and said, "This is not JIF." Wik wrote his return address so that my mother would know exactly where I was and would be able to write back and send any documentation that I might need in order to return to the United States.

During the same day, I met Jim and Chuck, who were both guest interrogators at JIF. They were both relieved about my partial freedom at the 403rd. Jim emptied his pocket and offered me a piece of chewing gum again. I smiled and thanked him, saying, "I have plenty of that now." Chuck took my mother's telephone number so that he could explain to her where I was and what supporting documents she needed to send to help my case. He asked me if I wanted him to say anything to her. "Ask her this: If the Americans couldn't hold on to me and decided to hand me over to the Saudis, would it be better for me to stay in Saudi custody or return to Iraq when they repatriate prisoners?" To my relief, the answer came back on the following day asserting that under no circumstances should I ever go back to Iraq. My mother gave him my uncle's address in the United Arab Emirates and Chuck gave her Meg's address so that my mother could send Meg all my supporting documents. Meg helped me send a letter to my uncle Sammy to seek his help.

Everyone was very friendly at the 403rd. I wanted to know what friendly city they all came from. "It's not like Chicago or Los Angeles," they said, "but Omaha is a beautiful city." They started to tell me all about Nebraska and were very excited when I promised to visit one day. Abe, Chris, and Loren Peterson gave me their addresses and offered their homes for me to stay. Chuck was from Minnesota while Lieutenant Quinn and a few others were from Kansas City.

Even though I was still in custody, still a prisoner of war from a defeated army, there had already been an invisible transformation in me. I was acutely aware of the power of that transformation in lifting me back up to a level of normal human relations, a place I had not inhabited for a long time. It's just that at that moment and in that place I could never have imagined how deep its effect would be, or guess at the beautiful possibility that was about to unfold.

30. The Truck Driver

It was perhaps the second day at the 403rd when the Americans asked if I could help unload some boxes of MREs from a truck that had just arrived. A couple of POWs who had been temporarily assigned to the Admin Compound came along with me to help. The truck driver happened to be an attractive young female soldier. She handed down the boxes from the truck bed while we stacked them in the supply tent nearby.

The two Iraqi POWs who were helping me found it highly strange to interact with a woman in this way.

"Do they do the same work as men?" asked one of them.

"It looks like it. See, this one is driving a truck," answered the other. (Women drove cars in Iraq, but it was unheard of to see one driving a truck.) "I don't think they send them to the front lines with the men though."

"The American guys don't seem to care that there are females among them," said the first.

The second one smiled, "I'm sure it's a different story at night."

The guys seemed baffled at how the male American soldiers interacted with the women in such a matter-of-fact way.

Since I had lived in the United States and my family was

Christian, not Muslim, I had enjoyed plenty of social interactions
with women. I wasn't inclined to fall in love just because a female soldier handed me a box of MREs. Still, I was hardly desen-
sitized to her presence, either. She was beautiful. She had red
hair. She smiled.

While we were working to unload the truck, I was aware that
the truck driver had noticed me, but she actually seemed to be
looking away from me a little more than one normally would in a
work-together situation. That served to focus my attention on
her. I felt sure that she must have heard about me through the
rumor mill.

But we had noticed each other, for better or worse, and although I took in her reddish hair right away, her beauty was
nearly submerged in her military uniform in the way that a uniform—any uniform—tends to dehumanize.

Within that miserable situation, I felt strongly drawn to the
appeal of her feminine energy, and perhaps hoped for a few caring words that could convince me that our world was still a good
world. In any case, to entertain the question of why she had noticed me was a luxury I didn't have. I continued unloading the
truck, reminding myself that I wasn't there to find myself a girlfriend in a POW camp. That was a concept for some Hollywood
production.

When we'd finally finished unloading the MREs, she came
over to talk. We introduced ourselves—Monica was her name. It
turned out she had heard about me and was curious to learn
about my journey from high school in the Chicago suburbs to
prisoner of war in Saudi Arabia. I told her about myself. I
couldn't tell what she was really thinking, but she listened in-
tently and only interrupted to ask more questions.

I was surprised by how good it felt to have this woman show

a genuine interest in me. The sense was that she was actually seeing me as an individual human being, and not just some enemy soldier. It wasn't really anything specific she said. She asked me the same questions I was asked every day during interrogation. The difference was in her body language, the way she leaned on her truck beside me, and the sound of her voice.

Over the next few days I watched Monica a lot. She had this breezy, warm, gentle air about her. Sometimes she hugged other soldiers when she greeted them. Other times it was just her smile and laugh, the way she brought a playful atmosphere into the processing tent—something I never would have expected in the military during wartime. She totally contrasted with this harsh and deadly place.

I began to get an idea of how deeply this simple, quiet exchange had affected me shortly afterward—perhaps the next day—when Monica entered the processing tent and proceeded to greet all the guys with a friendly hug. When Loren Peterson entered the tent, she opened her arms and called out, "Peterson!" as if she were surprised to see him and was inviting him into her arms.

I watched that California-style greeting with admiration and envy. What a strange and wonderful little ritual, I thought. What a simple way to bring a moment of softness to this arid place.

I had survived minefields, fires at sea, and explosions from Allied bombs. I had learned to recognize the smell of death at a distance and watched my commanding officer close up while he slowly died. In sleep, I was visited by Tahir's ghost against a background of violent nightmares. But even though I had built a strong wall to shield my emotions from these terrible surroundings, I now felt my internal fortress crumble at the simple sight of this California-style greeting.

And I think that this was the first time I realized that I was

carrying feelings for this woman, this truck driver, this soldier—
for the gentleness she represented.

Monica's curiosity was soft, not aggressive, but I had no recent experience with any woman who would look me in the face
and announce that she wanted to know more about me. I had no
idea how to react, so I just decided to be frank in my answers and
neutral in my expression. Nothing else felt safe.

She squinted a bit, remembering. "There's another prisoner
from Chicago with a similar story to yours."

"It's probably another version of my story."

"No. There's another POW," the truck driver asserted. Then,
as easily as she had approached me, she seemed to drop her interest and turned back to the work at hand. She gave me a little
wave while she drove away.

After so many years away from America, this was an unsettling
experience—a female soldier who (a) thinks nothing of going up to
a strange man, (b) a POW, to (c) express personal curiosity about
him, straight to his face, and (d) who then gets back into her military truck alone and drives away into the night. Not since I first
moved to the United States as a teenager had I felt such a full,
slap-in-the-face encounter with a fundamental difference between
American culture and the traditions of the Middle East.

Of course it was a shock, but surprisingly, not painful at all.

That same night, Sergeant Sheppard wanted me to speak to an
Iraqi POW who said he was an American citizen. Brian was born in
Chicago and lived in Ohio with his American mother and Iraqi father before returning to Iraq with his family when he was eight. He
and I shared a little tent in the Admin Compound, no more than
ten yards north of the processing tent. A few yards farther north,
there was a third tent where twenty-two senior Kurdish civilians
stayed. The youngest among them, about fifty-five years of age,

was the only one who spoke Arabic. He told me that his group had not eaten in almost two days. I told Lieutenant Cunningham, who handed them some of the boxes of MREs that I had helped the truck driver unload. Like many civilians, the Kurds were "volunteered" into the front lines and ended up in a POW camp with thousands of other Iraqi soldiers. The Kurds stayed temporarily in the Admin Compound and were referred to as interns while Brian and I were referred to as trustees. A few Iraqi doctors and medics stayed in a separate tent across the Admin Compound.

For a while, I did my best to ignore the fact that the female truck driver shined like a bright flame every time I saw her passing by with her pickups and deliveries among the other compounds. When she was around, everything else receded into a colorful blur, overwhelmed by the fascination that she represented. She was so familiar in my memories of American ways, but so utterly different from the realities of my last ten years.

For the next several days, the words "good morning" and "good night" were all that we said to each other. In the beginning, I was careful never to greet her first, since I had this little problem of being an enemy prisoner of war. And when I returned her greetings, I was careful to use the American custom of meeting a woman's gaze directly, but not staring at her.

Things began to change when Wik brought me up as a topic of conversation with Monica. "Do you know him already?" He asked Monica, gesturing with his head at me.

"Yes, he's my friend," she answered simply. Then she offered her hand to shake mine. "You are my friend, aren't you?" she asked.

I don't really know how much of Wik's prodding was deliberate, or whether I was just so self-conscious about the odd situation. But when Wik learned that Monica and her truck were free, he asked Lieutenant Cunningham's permission for all three of us to go to the 401st and retrieve my money and other belongings, which were still being held there.

With permission granted, Wik grabbed his M16 and sat with me in the truck bed while Monica drove a winding and bumpy dirt road. Once the novelty of riding in a truck driven by a female soldier began to wear off, I noticed that on Wik's rifle strap, the word BITCH was carefully drawn in bold letters. I was too curious not to ask about it.

"I named it after my girlfriend," Wik grinned. He thought about that for a bit, then laughed out loud. Then he thought about it again and laughed out loud a second time. Fifteen minutes later, Monica stopped the truck in front of the 401st.

I wanted to go with Wik and see Zimmerman, Brigadier Sabah, and the photographer, but he suggested that it might be better if I stayed in the truck. I was nervous about being left alone with Monica, especially when she stepped out and sat next to me on the truck bed. But then she began talking, openly and with no apparent awkwardness. It felt intoxicating. Here I was, alone with this lovely woman, in this improbable place. Normally, this would have been a perfect opportunity to ask her out. Which, I know, seems ridiculous. It was only Monica's matter-of-fact friendliness that kept the closeness from being overwhelming.

She wanted to learn more about the circumstances that led to my capture, so I began to tell her a little about my time on the L-87, the USS *Curts*, the Marines, and JIF. When Wik came back, he said that the guys at the 401st had a hard time recognizing my legal name, but quickly knew who I was when he referred to me as "Mr. Chicago." He broke the news that he was able to retrieve my money but none of my remaining belongings. To the best of my knowledge, none of the POWs were able to retrieve anything.

It was surprising that the one thing that was left untouched was the money, but I did not care about the money since I had no desire to return to Iraq. I was sad that I had lost my Misha bear.

When we returned to the 403rd, Sergeant File walked me to a nearby camp located about half a mile away. There, he took me to the supplies area and furnished me with new socks, underwear, jumpsuits, towels, soap, detergent, and many other basic items. I received my supplies with more excitement than a kid opening his Christmas presents. It was a thrill to realize that I could now dispose of my dirty uniform and that from now on, I could change my underwear and socks every day.

I was still folding up the towels when I heard a familiar voice calling out from somewhere behind me. "Cowboy!" I was very happy to see my old friend from JIF and immediately remembered that he had once asked me, "How can I get me one of them Iraqi uniforms for a souvenir?" I wasn't willing to wear my Iraqi uniform any longer than I had to. So, to our mutual delight, I took it off and changed into a tan jumpsuit—then handed him the dirty uniform over the fence.

One person's trash is another's treasure. It's true all over the world.

31. Conflicting Objectives

Every day a group of Kuwaiti interpreters spent a couple of hours in the Admin Compound, helping the Americans process the incoming Iraqi POWs. Naturally, the Kuwaitis were outraged by the Iraqi invasion. If they had had their way, they would have slaughtered the Iraqi soldiers, who were caught between Saddam's executioners' bullets, American guns, and the hatred of the Kuwaiti people. Thus, when the Kuwaiti interpreters came, they seemed more interested in watching the Iraqis in their defeat than in offering any help processing them. In the end—fortunately for me—their presence was more inconvenient than useful. The Americans began to rely on Brian and me whenever they needed the help of an interpreter.

The Kuwaiti interpreters resented our presence in the Admin Compound and channeled their energy into challenging the authenticity of our partial freedom. A Kuwaiti captain, the leader of the interpreters group, expressed his concerns to Lieutenant Cunningham saying that I might be KGB, his way of saying that I might be a spy. He told Lieutenant Cunningham that I should not be allowed to enter the processing tent. The young lieutenant, who did not like confrontations, decided to get me out of the way by asking me to go and help the American doctors who were seeing the sick POWs.

One of the Iraqi POW doctors, Doctor Bashar, was annoyed

by my invasion of his little world by being there to translate for the American doctors.

"This patient says he has kidney stone," I interpreted for the American doctor.

"Don't give diagnosis, just say what the symptoms are," Doctor Bashar snapped.

"I'm not giving diagnosis or symptoms; I'm only interpreting what the patient says."

"So the Iraqi patients come with their own diagnosis to the doctor. What's there left for the doctor to do?"

"I don't know. But I will interpret whatever he wants to say. It's my responsibility to do that. It is your job to make sense of it."

Doctor Bashar and I clashed three or four times in less than five minutes. I decided that I was better off with the Kuwaitis, so I left the doctor's tent and went back to the processing tent. The Americans were all inside the tent when the Kuwaiti captain forbade me from entering it. I walked away to avoid trouble. The captain entered the tent, then came out with Chris shortly after. Chris asked me to walk away with him.

"Where do you think you're going?" The Kuwaiti captain yelled in Arabic.

"The American soldier wants me to go with him."

"No, stay right here."

I told Chris what was happening with the Kuwaiti interpreter.

"I want him to come with me," Chris said to the Kuwaiti.

"Hurry up and go! Hurry up!" he yelled in Arabic again.

As we walked away, I told Chris what had just happened and asked him if the Kuwaiti interpreter had authority to treat me that way. Chris said that he doubted it, but that the Kuwaiti certainly had no authority to tell Chris whether or not to take me with him—or even to tell us to hurry up. While we were talking, a bearded, cross-eyed, heavyset Kuwaiti interpreter passed us by and figured out that we were talking about his captain. I saw him report his discovery immediately to the captain, who was still fuming near the entrance of the processing tent. Inevitably, it wasn't long before I found myself alone and confronted by the Kuwaiti captain.

"Why do you talk about me? I heard what you said."

"You didn't hear what I said. Your friend did. The worst thing that I said was that I didn't like you."

"Why do you talk to the Americans about me?"

"I told them what you did."

"I'll do whatever I want around here."

"So then, why do you care if I tell them? I'm only telling the truth."

"Are you implying that my friend is lying?"

"I don't even know what he told you."

The captain started yelling, "I can kick you out of this camp. I can torture you and kill you if I want."

"I am a prisoner of war. I'm sure you can do all of these things very easily."

"You are not a prisoner; you are a guest," he yelled at the top of his lungs. "King Fahd bin Abdul Aziz [of Saudi Arabia] has ordered us to treat you all like guests. But if I ever see you out on the street one day, I will surely kill you. I'm going to let you go this time because you are a brother Arab and a Muslim like us."

I did not have the courage to tell him that I was neither an Arab nor a Muslim, not for fear of losing my life but because I did not want to give him an invitation to insult my religion and ethnicity.

Two days later, another Kuwaiti tried to stop Brian from entering the processing tent, but Brian was more hot tempered than I. He pushed the Kuwaiti aside, entered the tent and immediately told First Lieutenant Quinn what happened. First Lieutenant Quinn was more proactive than Lieutenant Cunningham. He confronted the Kuwaiti interpreter.

"Is there a problem?" said the lieutenant, advancing toward the Kuwaiti interpreter with his hands on his belt and his head slightly tilted backward.

"Maybe he's KGB," said the Kuwaiti interpreter and took a step backward.

"That's all right, that's all right. I'll decide that."

"Maybe he's KGB," repeated the Kuwaiti, taking his argument as far as he could.

First Lieutenant Quinn kept his hands on his belt, nodded his head up and down and repeated everything twice, barely allowing the Kuwaiti interpreter to finish his sentences.

"This is my camp. This is my camp."

"Maybe . . ."

"That's my business. That's my business."

When I heard his naturally loud voice and slight Southern accent that I promised myself to never forget, I realized that it was First Lieutenant Quinn—the man who told the guards from JIF never to bring POWs blindfolded again. I finally had a name and face to put to that wonderful memory.

As for the Kuwaiti interpreters, during the next half hour, they only spoke in whispers. Shortly after, they sat in one big circle in the sand and listened to their captain who was explaining things to them. While passing by—quite inadvertently—I heard only one sentence. He was instructing the interpreters not to bother us anymore, no doubt courtesy of First Lieutenant Quinn.

Gradually, the presence of the Kuwaiti interpreters dwindled as they were replaced by Saudi interpreters. The Saudis were a little more available and less hostile than their Kuwaiti counterparts, who couldn't seem to get over their irritation at the Iraqis for overrunning their country and shattering their infrastructure.

32. Monica

Monica's work as a truck driver kept her away from my compound most of the time. When she came, she would only be in the processing tent for a short time, but she always made sure to say hello. To me, that small social courtesy was like cool water in a hot desert. From time to time, she would ask me for more details about the two sinking boats and about my miraculous survival story. She repeatedly inquired about the manner in which I was treated at the Marine camp and JIF. I explained to her the type of treatment that I had received. To me, the treatment was not as atrocious as she felt it was. After all, I had been hoping to get captured by the Americans—it seemed the only alternative to certain death. My extended stay in the interrogation camp did not bother me as long as I remained in American custody. I told her about my flashbacks and nightmares and about how the Bible helped me overcome my flashbacks, but that my nightmares were still haunting me. In my dreams, I would often see myself trapped again in Iraq. I'd also have the nightmare that Saddam had taken a liking to me and wanted me to always be near him, so I had to pretend that I liked him, too, or else he would kill me. But my most disturbing dream was when I saw the nineteen-year-old Tahir saying, "I wasn't dead when you left me."

I admitted that I procrastinated going to bed every night because I feared seeing Tahir in my dreams.

While Monica listened to my stories, at one point I felt her hand gently rub my back. I was afraid to comment on it, so I just kept going. "I don't know if I would ever be able to forget these things, to erase enough of it from my memory to be able to live a normal life again."

"You probably never will forget them, but eventually they won't be so painful anymore," she said. She paused for a moment, then changed the subject.

"Do you have a girlfriend in Iraq?"

I was afraid to even hope that this might mean she felt some special interest in me, so I gave her an answer that stuck to the facts. "The Iraqi society is more Westernized and open than most Arab countries, but still, couples have to date in secret with the intent to marry each other. Most marriages are still arranged. I was attracted to a few girls, some of whom had a mutual feeling toward me, but I never made any advances."

"Why not?"

"I didn't want to have a family—I never expected to survive the Iran-Iraq War. And if I did, I didn't want any ties to hinder my attempts in escaping Iraq and returning to America."

"Do you like children?"

"To tell you the truth, I usually don't give them any special attention, but they seem to like to play with me, anyway. The same thing is true with dogs."

"Children and dogs know a nice person when they see one."

"I wish JIF was run by children and dogs."

"Did they treat you badly?"

"They were polite enough when they spoke, but it didn't do much to humanize the process of being handcuffed, blindfolded, interrogated, deprived from my basic needs, or spending a month in a solitary tent while the other POWs could hang out together. But at least I believed them when they said that they would try to keep me in U.S. custody, and they did that much for a while. But then, even though they knew that I was a permanent resident of the U.S., they still sent me to you guys with the intent to ship me to the Saudis."

"I'm glad they sent you here, but I don't want to see you get sent off to Saudi Arabia. We like you here, you know? Everybody likes you."

"I like you, too. I—I like everybody here, too." It was probably my least articulate moment during the entire ordeal of captivity.

It was a huge thrill to feel some small degree of feminine outreach under these conditions. But as hard as it was to believe, it was even harder to give in to it; my recent experience at JIF made me suspicious of Monica's kindness. And because she was the one who initiated our friendship, I couldn't exclude the possibility that she might have been instructed to play the role of "good cop" to try to catch me off guard and extract some sort of information from me.

Nevertheless, as the days wore on, there was no denying to myself that I loved to be in her company. She was extremely open with me, and whether the Americans suspected me of spying or not, I knew that I had nothing to hide, so I decided that it didn't matter if she was playing a role or not. It felt so fine to have a female friend. It was intoxicating.

On the surface, we appeared to have little in common. Monica was a waitress from the Midwest, a people person who joined the Army Reserve to help make ends meet. Her life was tough in many ways, with her family crises and financial difficulty, yet simple in so many others, such as one would expect from a small-town life in a free country.

But it turned out that each of us was feeling lonely and vulnerable, far away from our families and normal lives, and in the middle of this surreal setting, we found genuine and mutual comfort in each other's company.

The stakes were very high, though. If we allowed our friendship to grow any deeper and were caught, Monica could be reprimanded. There's no telling how seriously. I could have easily been stripped of my special trustee status and transferred to the general population of Iraqi POWs. My interaction with the Americans would then diminish and with it, all my hopes of returning to the U.S. would vanish.

But the more we tried to stay away from each other, the more our feelings grew.

Given our circumstances, we both realized, of course, that it wasn't smart to have special feelings toward each other. Up to now, I had always thought that love should start from the head, and only later be allowed into the heart. I thought that logic had to prevail over irrational emotional impulses or forces that might attract us into relationships too difficult to maintain—Romeo and Juliet, for example, should have known never to fall in love. But my theories were of little help when it came to Monica.

In the meantime, we both acknowledged that it was unquestionably a very foolish idea for us to spend personal time together, even as harmless and chaste as it was. Although no one else had made any comments yet about our associating together, I was sure that back at their camp the guys had plenty to say. It was clear that people were noticing the attraction between Monica and me.

Soon, I decided that I needed to use my head and limit this

budding relationship with Monica—after all, she was one of my American captors. So I convinced myself that whatever time I spent with her should be no different than with the other female soldiers around the Admin Compound.

On the following day, Monica was mostly running errands somewhere outside the Admin Compound. During the few times that she was briefly present, I made it a point to walk away from the processing tent and not to return until her truck was gone. I felt miserable.

Later in the afternoon, I was sitting on a bench inside the processing tent, drawing on a sketch pad while waiting for another translation assignment. I was so intent on my drawing that I didn't notice that Monica had entered the tent until she sat next to me and simply asked, "What are you doing?"

"I'm trying to draw," I said. I didn't lift my eyes from the paper.

Monica stood up and walked away. For the rest of the day, she didn't come near me or even look my way. From that moment on, I didn't have to avoid her or pretend to go to the bathroom every time she entered the compound. She had taken the hint and was staying away from me.

But Monica was not the type who would leave things unsettled. Before she went home for the night, she asked me to sit with her in the truck, which was parked outside the processing tent. Inside the privacy of the truck cab, we started to talk.

"What's wrong? Why were you avoiding me all day?" she asked.

The directness of her question stabbed at me, but I was still sure that there could only be one answer. "Monica, you've been very kind to me. I just don't want to cause you any trouble. Your commanders could get all sorts of terrible ideas about this. They might think I am trying to use you. I think—Monica, I think that we should stop being friends."

She was quiet for a moment, but she appeared to feel relief at having the problem out in the open. "Listen, Shant, I know how to keep myself out of trouble. It's true that the guys have been talking about our friendship, but I also heard Sergeant Sheppard tell them that it's nobody's business what I do."

She waited for me to respond. I was lost for words. I could barely look at her. My throat tightened.

"The guys can talk all they want," she continued, "but I want to be your friend, Shant. I love you."

I held her hand and said, "I love you too, Monica." She kissed my hand and I kissed hers, and that simple gesture of affection was one of the most powerful emotional experiences that I had ever had.

She smiled and said, "You didn't expect to go to war and find yourself a girl, did ya?"

"This is crazy," I said, and I don't doubt that she felt the same way. "Monica, things can't get much worse for me—but I know that they could for you."

"It's funny how everyone preaches that we should love our enemy," she replied. Then she changed the subject. We talked for nearly an hour. I kept telling myself to leave, without success.

When I went back to the processing tent, Meg, who was sitting behind the main desk next to Jimmy, looked over at me in a peculiar way and sneered, "Are you *finished*, Shant?"

It felt like a roll of thunder moving over my head.

When I had revealed my feelings to Monica that afternoon, I realized that there might be a time when I would be confronted and ordered to speak the truth about the two of us; I just had no idea the moment would come so soon. After an awkward hesitation, I answered her with a simple "Yes." I hoped to end it there, but Meg would not stop.

"We saw what you did," she said. Then she continued after a brief pause, "Did you find you a girlfriend, Shant?"

I hesitated again, scrambling for some intelligent and short answer, but all I could say was, "Yes."

She seemed glad to hear the truth. Suddenly, her manner changed; she became friendlier. "There's nothing wrong with that," she said with a grin. Everyone should have a girlfriend. Jimmy here is my boyfriend."

I could tell that Jimmy did not want to be part of Meg's interrogation any more than I did. But since her last remark was not a question, I didn't respond. It was a relief to have some sense of tolerance from a couple of guards, though.

The conversation finally came to an end, not one word too soon. I walked away so that Meg would not start again. I retired for the night earlier than usual, just to avoid any further questioning regarding what my girlfriend and I did or didn't do in her truck.

The next morning, Monica asked me if I could help her carry some containers of liquid detergent from the supply tent to her truck. When we were alone inside the supply tent, she opened her arms and said, "Here, give me a hug." It was a long hug that we both needed. I let my guard down and forgot that I was a POW for a moment. We didn't kiss. We just hugged. But the next day she asked me into the supply tent again; she kissed me on the cheek and I kissed her back. It was not a passionate kiss. It could not have been. The processing tent with everybody in it was less than fifteen feet away. Anyone could have walked in on us any time. We decided not to be alone in the supply tent again, because we assumed that by that time, Meg had told everyone about our short-lived secret. Before anyone would notice that we were gone too long, we stepped back out.

"I wish that we were together," Monica said. "In civilian clothing, holding hands and walking down the streets of my hometown. People would see us but no one would care at all." Monica was wistful. She seemed a million miles away.

Even if Meg hadn't told anyone, any thought that we were fooling people was soon gone—when word came about an up-coming visit from General Schwarzkopf and Monica's influence over me became obvious to all.

All the Americans were getting ready. But as a POW, my hair and beard had grown long and it seemed ages since shoe polish had last touched my boots. Those boots had been through two wars, weathered by salty seawater, desert sand, and extreme temperatures. Their discoloration seemed to bother some people around the Admin Compound. A few offered shoe polish, but I always declined, trying to retain one of the very few privileges I had as a POW—not having to shine my boots.

At last a swarm of helicopters landed in the area and we were told that General Schwarzkopf was on board one of them. My American friends started to check their uniforms and get ready for the important visit. I would have done the same thing if I were a soldier expecting my supreme commander.

But while Monica was giving a last-minute polish to her boots, she asked if I wanted to polish mine. When I declined, she just grinned and quickly smeared some polish on the toe of my left boot, then continued polishing hers. When she was finished, I took her brush and polished just the toe of my left boot, then just the toe of the right boot for balance.

When I stood up to see how I looked with my half-polished boots, Monica said, "You look like a clown." Seeing that she was right, I compromised and completely polished my boots for the first and only time in my POW career.

To the delight of all who watched, I lost the battle to Monica and polished my boots in anticipation of the general's visit, revealing my desire to please her. That was the only purpose that the gesture served. In the end, the general never showed up.

33. Riots

It had been a couple of weeks since the end of the war, but tensions had not eased. The Americans were anxious to go home and the Iraqis were especially apprehensive, not knowing what would become of them. But the Americans had inherited the daunting task of caring for the tens of thousands of Iraqi POWs, while the Iraqis were frustrated with inefficient distribution of food and water.

Each compound had an Iraqi cook who selected a small staff from within the compound. The cooking staff received the compound's daily rations and then prepared and served the food for the whole compound. Apparently, they found it impossible to divide the food into five hundred or more equal portions. So the people in the beginning of the food line usually received fair portions but before the long line of hungry men ended, the food almost always ran out. The cooks were accused of favoritism and riots broke out every now and then. The Americans were the peacekeepers and caretakers, but the language barrier and cultural differences frequently made communications difficult. There were times when I was brought into one of the compounds of Enclosure One to break the language barrier and help diffuse tension.

On those occasions, the Americans wanted me to explain the rules and convey their promise that they would help the Iraqis as much as they could. The Iraqis complained about the limited access to the water containers located outside each compound, and about their unjust cooks.

Food wasn't always the problem with morale, though. Fights broke out between the anti-Saddam POW majority and the pro-Saddam minority, who had sometimes been inadvertently assigned to the same compound. Some were accused of being Saddam's agents, who had supposedly staged their surrender so they could spy on the remaining POWs and identify the anti-Saddamists upon their inevitable return to Iraq.

The sources of trouble were plentiful, but none as memorable as the night when I was called to help the guards in Compound Four. They took me to their tent outside the boundaries of the compound, to explain the problem.

"They refuse to come out for formation. I will call them out and have you explain to them the rules. They need to come out and stand in formation—twice a day—so that we can take their count. I want you to wait here until I make them line up, then I'll call you in."

"They're all soldiers; they should be able to do that without any trouble," I said.

"That's what I thought. But I kill myself every day screaming at the top of my lungs and they just stand there. Watch!"

The guard went to the compound and started to holler, "*Ma'lumat . . . Ma'lumat.*" I ran after him and asked, "What are you trying to say?"

"Isn't that the Arabic word for 'formation'?"

"Who taught you that?"

"Doctor Bashar. Why are you laughing?"

"Because, that's the word for 'information.' 'Formation' is *Ti' dad*."

"You mean I've been running around yelling 'information' twice a day for the past three days?"

"If you say so."

"So, that's why they've been looking at me like I've lost my mind."

I explained the rules to the Iraqi POWs, who were visibly relieved to learn that their compound guard might not be a linguist, but at least he wasn't a madman.

After I spent a month with the 403rd, the U.S. Army was beginning the dreaded transfer of POWs to Saudi camps. They were preparing to go back to America without me. At least with fewer POWs in the camp, the workload was relaxed and I found myself spending more time with Monica. By now our friendship was widely known, but no one seemed to mind. We sat on the bench and played cards in the processing tent. I won; she cheated. I stopped her from cheating, and she called on First Lieutenant Quinn. "Sir, he cheats, sir," she reported with an evil grin.

First Lieutenant Quinn shook his head and muttered, "Just like my kids, just like my kids."

Monica giggled and whispered in my ear, "He says just about everything twice."

"That's very unusual. That's very unusual," I replied. Childish jokes like that had the power to make us feel connected in a special way. The source of the humor didn't matter; its value was in the way it deepened our connection.

One night when Monica and I were standing outside the processing tent, she asked if I was ticklish. When I said yes, she asked Verkamp to hold me, then told me to prove that I trusted her by allowing Verkamp to restrain me. She swore that she wouldn't attempt to tickle me.

And so I stood willingly enough, wrapped in Verkamp's bear hug of a grip, but I started to doubt her when I saw her wicked smile.

"Remember, you swore that you wouldn't tickle," I cautioned her.

"Right. But I didn't say *when* I wouldn't tickle you," she replied.

I broke loose from Verkamp's grip, but Monica caught a piece of my jumpsuit from behind and pulled back on it so hard that the zipper suddenly broke from top to bottom.

"Uh-oh!" she said in shock. "What are you going to do now?"

"I have a couple of blue jumpsuits in my tent. If you give me a flashlight, I could go and find them."

"I don't have one."

"I'll go inside the processing tent and ask Cooper for a flashlight," I said, and started toward the tent, but Monica pulled me back.

"No, no, no! They'll say I ripped your clothes off! You stay right here. I'll go."

She borrowed a flashlight from Cooper, and I found my navy blue jumpsuit, and as soon as I put it on, I went directly to bed so nobody would notice the sudden change. The Iraqi POWs all had prison-style orange or light-blue jumpsuits. Of all the POWs whom I came across, I was the only one who had a tan jumpsuit, similar in color to the American uniforms. The Americans and I both liked this distinction, which suited my unusual status. In the morning, when the day shift arrived, they asked why I was not wearing my tan jumpsuit like I usually did. I tried to shrug it off, pretending that it was a casual decision I made in the morning. Monica was standing in the processing tent near me. Instead of helping me out, she focused the spotlight on me.

"Yeah, Shant, what happened to the tan jumpsuit?"

"It got torn," I said and looked at Monica in disbelief.

"How did that happen?" she continued to press.

"It was an accident."

"Tell them who did it."

"Uh, all right. It was—I mean, it was—all right, *you* did it. Actually, you ripped it off of my body."

They all started to laugh and explained that Monica had already told them about the tickling game and the bizarre consequences. In a POW camp, secrets are even harder to keep than a toothbrush.

34. Moving On

The 403rd promised to seek all legal avenues to help bring the two of us—Brian and me—back to the United States. To do that, they had to keep us in American custody as long as possible so as not to interrupt the flow of the process. However, Enclosure One was the first one scheduled to close down. Almost all of its Iraqi POWs had been transferred out, and now it was our turn. Besides the two of us and two Iraqi doctors, Enclosure One was also responsible for ten other POWs, all of whom were bedridden in the MASH unit. The Americans helped us to postpone being transferred to the Saudis by transferring the fourteen remaining POWs to Enclosure Two, scheduled to close down last, ten days later.

As expected of our gender, Brian and I did not talk too much or express our feelings toward the coming transfer. But that doesn't mean that we didn't talk at all. We both loved the 403rd, where we were surrounded by trusting friends who made us feel like free men. For each of us, our arrival at Enclosure One was the most refreshing development in our POW lives, after having experienced the fear and mistrust at JIF, not to mention my own intimidation at the Marine camp. Although we knew that one day we had to go, hopefully to the U.S., Brian and I were very apprehensive about moving on to another unit and making new friends. Based on my earlier experience, which was not necessarily pleasant, I couldn't be sure if my future captors would insist on handcuffing and blindfolding me, escorting me to the bathroom and twisting my arm while parading me to the showers. After all, I had no way of knowing whether they would care to continue the effort that the 403rd had invested in their pursuit of bringing us back home to the United States.

With burdened hearts, Brian and I gathered our belongings and piled them up in the corner of our tent. When Monica arrived, Brian loaded his belongings in her truck and tactfully waited outside. She walked into our tent and offered to help me with my stuff. Our hearts were crushed with the thought that we might never see each other again. Aside from the three of us, no one else was in the Admin Compound. I had more freedom than any other POW, yet I was still a powerless slave. Not only because I was unable to choose my destiny, but because every time I came close enough to touch Monica, my mind would focus on who was watching us from half a mile away, rather than allowing me to become lost in her sweet presence inches away from my body.

Just before I turned to go, I leaned over and kissed Monica lightly on the lips. Then we hugged and said "I love you" to each other. It was one of the sweetest moments in my life up to that point.

We joined the other twelve POWs and marched in a single file toward Enclosure Two. Monica led the procession with her truck carrying Brian's and my belongings plus two armed guards. Our friends from the 403rd all said good-bye and expressed discontent that they were unable to help us more. When we reached the gates of Enclosure Two, Monica pulled her truck to the side so that we were able to see each other, twenty yards apart. We looked at each other for a minute. Then she looked away, took off her glasses, and wiped her eyes. I had to press on my teeth to hold back my tears like I did the day I set foot on Qaro Island. Brian stood behind me; he didn't say a word.

The two doctors, along with Brian and myself, were escorted to the Admin Compound of Enclosure Two. The doctors were assigned to a tent where two other Iraqi doctors had been staying. The remaining ten POWs were assigned to one of the other compounds. Brian and I were standing alone when a truck stopped next to us and the driver asked Brian if he was from Wheeling, a suburb of Chicago. Brian didn't recognize the name of the city, but I overheard the question and couldn't stop myself from intruding.

"I'm from Wheeling," I said.

"I'm from Wheeling, too," said the driver. His face started to glow as he continued, "My sister told me that she heard about you in the news back home, but I didn't believe her. Where in Wheeling are you from?"

"I don't remember the name of the street anymore; it's been more than ten years. But pass Kmart, then make a left at the end of the street, and it's an apartment complex on your left-hand side."

"Oh my God! You mean Cedar Run?"

"No, it's the one next to it, on the same block. Then the name hit me, Fairway View."

"I have a friend who lives there! I go there myself, sometimes. It's like five minutes from our house."

"Did you go to Wheeling High School by any chance?"

"You mean we went to the same high school? This is wild! What are the odds of something like this?"

"That's warfare for you."

The soldier's name was Kurt Voight. He gave me his name

and address and told me to look him up when I returned to the United States. In turn, I gave him my mother's address. While we exchanged our addresses, Sergeant Kerwin suddenly stuck his head out of the window from the passenger seat and started to yell at Kurt to hurry up. I hadn't even noticed Kerwin's presence up until that moment. He pulled his head back in the truck and looked through the windshield, like a robot putting itself in standby position waiting for its next command. He seemed very irritated, although a few minutes earlier, he was ecstatically singing "Na na na na, na na na na, hey hey-ey, good-bye" as we marched from Enclosure One to Enclosure Two. I started to explain to Sergeant Kerwin how Kurt and I were practically neighbors. Sergeant Kerwin interrupted me saying, "Well, don't go flashing that around. It can be harmful for him, you know."

"Who's going to believe me anyway? I've said more credible things than this and people didn't believe me."

While the truck drove away, I heard Sergeant Kerwin starting to tell Kurt that he shouldn't have given me his home address. "He's one of us," answered Kurt, "he's not going to send me a bomb in the mail." I wish I could have heard the rest.

Brian and I were shown to our tent. Along with the doctors and the two of us, all the Iraqi cooks of Enclosure Two were assigned to the Admin Compound as well. Their system appeared to work better than that of Enclosure One. The cooks in Enclosure Two not only maintained all food supplies and cooked for all eight compounds, they also prepared daily feasts where the American and Iraqi residents of the Admin Compound sat side by side and ate dinner like one family.

How strange—and how indescribably welcome—to be treated in this way among captors.

35. An Unexpected Injury

That first day outside of my comfort zone back at Enclosure One was not as dreadful as I had feared. The American soldiers and Iraqi cooks were friendly. They welcomed us and made us feel at home. As for Monica, she came back to visit six or seven times that day. They had already begun tearing down the tents of Enclosure One, including the supply tent, where she and I had hugged for the first time. With the tent torn down, Monica made several trips and brought us its contents so that Brian and I were the most adequately supplied POWs in the Saudi desert.

She asked me for my mother's address and phone number, promising to call my mother and get an update from her to see when I was returning to the United States. I thanked Monica and asked how she was doing.

"I was upset when you guys marched in line."

"Were you crying in the truck, Monica?"

She sighed. "I was embarrassed when you guys saw me." She looked down at the ground and continued, "They shouldn't have made you march like a common prisoner."

"Thank you, Monica, but as long as I have this number on my wrist, that's what I will be." I raised my arm to show her my wristband. She nodded, then brightened, and said she could at least hang around long enough for us to have some dinner together.

In the kitchen, the Iraqi cooks were preparing a feast. They had three four-by-eight-foot rectangular pieces of plywood, each raised on a four-inch wooden frame. The cooks lined up the three pieces of raised plywood side by side and built a platform in the middle of the kitchen tent. The platform became our dinner table, where they served an assortment of Iraqi-prepared food on small plastic plates. The food was simple, but the cooks' spirits were always generous and festive. When dinner was ready, they opened the flaps of their tent and invited everyone in with broad smiles and brotherly love. Monica and I entered the kitchen tent and huddled with everyone else around the platform. The food was good, even though the way it was served reminded me of the Iraqi Army. As for the Americans, it was a great improvement over the dehydrated food that they often found in their MRE bags. They often made comments like, "Whoever thought that pita bread and fried tomatoes could taste so good?"

After we ate that evening, the cooks served tea and began to entertain the Americans with some Iraqi folk songs. Finally, the social event began to dwindle when it was time for the Americans to go back to work. Monica had to go, too, so I walked her to her truck. I held her hand and told her that I loved her and was grateful for knowing her. She said she loved me too, then took off her cross and gave it to me. I wore it and felt the crucifix close to my heart as I watched her drive away for the night. I walked alone in the dark and noticed the barbed wire for the first time during my stay at the 403rd. I felt weary and tired when I finally returned to my tent.

Brian and I expected to see Monica in the morning, but she

didn't show up. He watched the road looking out for her truck, no less than I did. To him, she was the spirit of Enclosure One, where we found comfort and made friends. To me, she was all that and more. Indeed, everyone was friendly to me in Enclosure One, but it was her playfulness that made every day a pleasant day behind the barbed wire. It was her that I looked forward to seeing every morning. Without her, the barbed wire became thicker, my days were longer, and even my POW wristband felt heavier. And once she promised to call my mother, I was anxious to learn what she said to her.

A truck finally came and parked in front of the processing tent. When a male driver stepped down, Brian and I were both disappointed. The American trucks all looked alike, not being identified by license plates or serial numbers. But luckily, I could distinguish Monica's truck from its little scratches on the side-view mirror. I realized that it was Monica's truck, but it was being driven by a stranger. I delivered the bad news to Brian, concerned that the truck had been taken away from her and that we might never see her again.

I walked away and stopped at the thorny barbed-wire boundaries of the Admin Compound. Looking in the distance ahead, I saw our old friends far away tearing down the barbed wire of Enclosure One. I had to marvel—the Americans were cleaning up the desert so that they could give it back to the Saudis the way they found it. I stood watching for a long time until I finally recognized Monica. She was too far away to notice me or hear my voice if I screamed. Although she had somehow lost possession of her truck, I was still hoping to be with her one more time.

I stood like a caged animal longing for his master.

With a life like mine, most people would have normally developed thick skin. I was no different, I thought. My life was like a jungle. I survived the beasts of the forest, but then, when least expected, I was captured by a dove.

How she penetrated my thick skin as easily as she did, I will never know for sure. But I can say with certainty that a broken heart was the one kind of injury that I never expected to suffer in war.

36. Acceptance

The friendliness of the American guards and Iraqi cooks at Enclosure Two made us feel welcome. By the third day, Brian and I had adjusted to our new environment well enough to let our guard down and make some new friends. This time, at least, we knew beforehand that we would have to say good-bye to them in seven more days.

One night, while breaking bread with the Americans, I met Lieutenant Magee, who was sitting on my right-hand side at our dinner platform. We came to talk about religion, and he was surprised to learn that I was a Christian, and one of the founding members of the first Bible Study and Youth Group of the Armenian Church in Iraq. Bishop Avak Asadourian had to obtain special permission from the Iraqi government for us to even be allowed to exist, because any regular meetings such as Bible studies (or even poker nights) were often confused with some sort of rebellious conspiracy.

Lieutenant Magee told me that he and fellow American Christians met once a week and held Bible studies in an adjacent tent in the Admin Compound. He extended an invitation and I readily accepted. Lieutenant Magee and his friends wanted to know if Christians were persecuted in Iraq. I told them that some of my best friends were Muslim, both Sunni and Shiite, and they respected me no less than their Muslim brothers. Although pockets of ignorance do exist in remote parts of the country where people might openly express prejudice. I gave my Bible study brothers partial comfort though when I explained to them that Saddam persecuted Christians as much as the rest of the Iraqi population. When it came to persecution, Saddam applied equal opportunity—that is, except for his kinsmen, the Tikritis, who always managed to live above the law.

Altogether, the Bible study lasted a little less than an hour. For the most part, we gave glory to Christ, who made us feel like brothers when we had come as enemies to the Saudi land, a place where Christians had very little freedom to practice their religion. "This is the universal concept of brotherhood in Christ," explained Lieutenant Magee.

Among my new friends at Enclosure Two, Hugh Grossman left one of the deepest impressions on me during my captivity, from beginning to end. I regret that my circumstances didn't allow me to know him for more than ten days. He was respected by all the Americans and was a great friend to the Iraqi cooks. He came with the night shift and met the day shift during dinner. His routine made him arrive with his truck a little late every night, so he entered the kitchen when everyone else was already dipping bread in the fried-tomato plates and eating the finely chopped salad appetizers that the cooks usually prepared. When he entered the big kitchen tent, the cooks cheered and applauded. Grossman bowed and raised his hands greeting his fans like a celebrity, then quickly sat down to join the feast.

Grossman often helped his Iraqi friends by bringing a pack of cigarettes for those who smoked. The Americans were astonished at the large number of heavy smokers that they encountered among the Iraqi POWs. On more than one occasion, the Americans felt compelled to ask if the Iraqis knew that smoking caused cancer. I explained to my American friends that during times of war, health concerns become secondary issues, at best. Most of the Iraqi soldiers were drafted unwillingly; they did not enlist by choice. They had been in the front lines of unjustified wars for a very long time; some more than a decade. Every day, they would die by the thousands, whether by enemy fire or Saddam's execution squads. An average Iraqi man would consider himself lucky if he lived long enough to die of cancer. Of course, the lack of Iraqi antismoking campaigns did not help discourage this self-destructive habit.

One day, Grossman carried a supply of sweat suits in his truck and distributed them to the cooks. When he noticed that Brian and I were hesitant to take some, he invited and encouraged us to take two suits each. We were happy to change out of our one-piece jumpsuits, which required us to completely strip whenever we had to go to the bathroom. Other times, when we were low spirited, he would tell jokes and take pictures of us while we were laughing. "This is how you should be remembered," he would say.

Grossman said that when the American officers learned that some of their soldiers had *Playboy* magazines with them in the Saudi desert, they feared that this might offend the highly conservative Saudis. The officers started to confiscate the magazines from the soldiers and encouraged all others to dispose of theirs. To rid himself of his, one of the American soldiers sold his magazine to an Iraqi POW for a twenty-five-dinar bill. This specific bill carried Saddam's picture and was a favorite souvenir among the Americans. The price was quite costly considering that the average monthly salary for Iraqis of all professions, at the time, was one hundred and fifty dinars. But to maximize the return on his investment, the Iraqi POW kept the centerfold for himself and sold the remaining pictures to his fellow POWs for five dinars each.

Another story told by Grossman was about three Iraqi POWs who escaped one night from their compound and then from their enclosure. They walked about a mile and reached the American camp. At the camp, they entered a tent not too far from the ammunition stack. They stole wood and carried it back to their compound. The thieves were caught by the guards while they were sneaking back into their POW compound. It was very cold that night and they wanted to burn wood for warmth. This and another incident where some Iraqi soldiers walked more than a hundred miles to find the POW camp and asked to be admitted, as if it were a hotel, left the Americans wondering why they had to stay up all night on their guard duties.

At first glance, Brian and I seemed to have a lot in common as POWs of American-Iraqi background with connections to Chicago. We shared the same tent, wore similar jumpsuits, and both lived in the Admin Compound. But other than that, we were totally different. Not only did his smoking habit and my allergies slow down the progress of our relationship, his personality was the opposite of mine. While I had to feign a temper to let others know that I was upset, he was naturally hot-tempered, explosive, and even more expressive when we received good news. When Chuck would come back with news from my mother, an outsider would probably think that it was Brian's mother Chuck was talking about judging from his reactions.

Yet, we shared the same troubles, worries, and hopes. We both longed for our days in Enclosure One and dreaded being transferred to the Saudis. We wanted to go back to America—he to his family in Ohio and I to my family in Los Angeles. We discussed our concerns with the officers in Enclosure Two at some point and told them that we preferred being shot rather than being handed over to the Saudis. We wanted to take our case to higher authorities, to the commanders of the camp, and to the U.S. embassy in Saudi Arabia.

At last, the efforts of many Americans started to bear fruit. A high-ranking military lawyer came to listen to our stories and raised our case to the U.S. State Department through the American embassy in Riyadh.

After our visit with the military lawyer, Brian and I were standing outside the processing tent, discussing the possibilities of our fate and expressing our worries to one of the American officers.

"Where do you want to go?" the officer asked Brian.

"I want to go to the United States, but my heart is still with my family and friends in Iraq."

"What about you?" the officer turned the question on me.

"I don't know where my heart is, but I want to go to the States and be reunited with my family. Only then can I resume my life."

Brian smiled and said, "But I know where your heart is."

I don't remember the conversation that followed, but from far away, a very pleasant evening breeze carried the lyrics of an old familiar song. The words were suddenly powerful, penetrating my heart, and given a completely new meaning in light of my circumstances. Without excusing myself, I walked away from Brian and the officer and drew nearer to the source of the music until I was stopped by the barbed wire. I stood there and focused all my attention and hearing on the song. I closed my eyes to block myself from my surroundings and inhaled the breeze so as to absorb the words and music directly into my soul, as if I were submerged in a dream. Before the second stanza began, the soft breeze died down and the music faded away. But the sweet moment that never came to completion was carved into my memory, along with the powerful words resonating in my head.

The song was "Time in a Bottle" by Jim Croce and the first line, "If I could save time in a bottle," struck a very sensitive chord in me. After being trapped in Iraq for more than ten years, I had no outlook for my future or any clue about how many years I might squander between here and wherever else they might send me next. I was being robbed of my twenties, the prime of my life. "If I could save time in a bottle" was my only consolation. I wanted so desperately to listen to the complete song. I waited by the barbed wire until the wind picked up again, but now it was carrying a different song. I dragged my heart and my feet and went to bed earlier than anyone else around me for the first time in a very long time.

Every day, I waited for Monica behind the barbed wire until I gave up hope that I would ever see her again. I had four more days before my transfer, one hundred miles north, deep into the Saudi desert.

I was particularly anxious to see Monica, because she'd asked for my mother's phone number in Los Angeles, and volunteered to call her for me. After three days of waiting miserably, I was sitting next to Lieutenant Magee in the kitchen tent one night when Monica suddenly appeared. She blurted out, "I want to talk to Shant, sir. I called his mom in the United States and I need to talk to him."

I jumped up to meet her, but waited until the lieutenant gave his permission for us to go outside. He granted it without difficulty.

"What happened to you, Monica?"

"They took my truck. I couldn't come to visit you anymore."

"I know about the truck. What happened to you? You look awful."

"I've been crying this whole time. I feel very helpless, I can't protect you anymore. They're going to transfer you to the Saudis in three days." Monica stopped talking. She bowed her head to hide her face from me.

"It's going to be a long way for you. You've been through so much. It's not fair."

I felt horrible, but all I wanted to do was reassure her. "Don't worry about me, Monica. This is how my life has been. I'll be fine." I took out three letters, handed them to her and said, "Here, I wrote you a letter for each day you didn't come."

She put the letters in her pocket, wiped her tears away and started to tell me about my mother. Ever since she learned of my safety, my mother had actually regained her strength and started to campaign to bring me back to America. When Monica told her about my upcoming transfer to the Saudi camps in Hafr Al-Batin, she started to cry on the phone. Ironically, it was my mother who then comforted her. After she composed herself, she had given my mother a fax number so she could send proof of my permanent residency in the United States and other supporting documents I would need to be released. She also promised my mother that she would call her again for a follow-up.

Monica and I talked for a long time. Seeing how upset she was, I tried not to talk much about my imminent transfer to the Saudis, and concentrate on the glimmer of hope that my documents would arrive and somehow save me.

Monica looked up at me. "Whenever you make it to the States, make sure you call me."

And with that, we both said our good-byes for the night.

She came back each evening for the following two nights and arrived with Loren Peterson on his water truck to say good-bye on what was supposed to be my last night at the 403rd. When I told her that there had been a change in plans and that Brian and I were to stay for another day, her happiness was radiant. She promised to meet and say good-bye on the following night, grateful for the reprieve.

After her brief visit, I watched the water truck disappear in the darkness and dust, not knowing that I would never see Monica again.

37. Last Days in the 403rd

Brian and I woke up before sunrise and helped the Americans line up eight hundred Iraqi POWs in groups of fifty. They had to be prepared for their designated buses, which would take them northbound to the Saudi-run camps in Hafr Al-Batin. By 7:00 A.M., all eight hundred prisoners were ready. They sat on the sand, still in groups of fifty, and waited for the buses that were supposed to be there by now. The POWs were relatively calm and quiet, lost in thought. Signs of concern were obvious on their faces. When they were under American custody, they were all quick to complain when food or water was short. Now, the big question facing them was, "Would their brother Arabs treat them as well as the Americans did?" They wanted to know about the living conditions that they would have to adjust to or endure in Hafr Al-Batin, and began to ask questions.

"Will we be living in tents or constructed structures?" they asked.

"Do they have good showers and facilities?" asked another.

Unfortunately, no one knew anything about the camps in Hafr Al-Batin, not even the Saudi interpreters themselves.

After more than half an hour of waiting, one POW started to sing very softly. The chatter quieted down so all could listen to the man who was obviously talented. Shortly after, the Americans gave him a megaphone and, in a matter of minutes, everyone was engaged in an eight-hundred-man good-bye party. The singer sang traditional Iraqi folk songs and replaced the original words with lyrics mocking the lifestyle of a POW. He was not only a great singer but also a great comedian who single-handedly alleviated the anxiety and worries of eight hundred men. The Americans couldn't appreciate his play on words but were happy to see cheerful Iraqis for a change and realized that, with the transfer of the men, they were one day closer to going home. The Americans participated by clapping their hands to the song while one of them danced with a broom and made silly moves to add to the laughter.

After singing for almost forty-five minutes, the singer stopped to rest his voice and sat down. But the American dancer was having too much fun and did not want to stop. He took the megaphone and started to search for a new talent. Several POWs tried but they were not nearly as talented as the first singer.

Finally, the buses were ready and the eight hundred POWs were quickly gone. It was suddenly as if they were ghosts, and had never really been there at all.

The Iraqi cooks, doctors, a few hundred remaining POWs, and Brian and I were the last remaining POWs at the 403rd. We were scheduled to be transferred the following morning. On our final night, the Iraqi cooks prepared a farewell party and cooked their last feast. The American soldiers and officers gathered as usual and brought with them high-ranking officers, including the commander of the 403rd. After we finished eating, the cooks collected the empty plates and started to dance on the raised platform where food would never be served again. Grossman and a female soldier, who was always quiet, got up and joined the cooks in a belly-dance lesson.

I sneaked out of the kitchen tent and paced the confines of the compound, waiting for Monica, who usually showed up immediately after dinner. Brian also came out of the tent and started to walk with me in the dark. We were both anxious about our transfer to the Saudis and disappointed that the Americans were not able to keep us in their custody. While we walked, the sound of cheers leaked through the kitchen tent. A glimpse of light escaped through the flap when two Iraqi doctors came out and started to pace the opposite side of the compound.

When the party was over, a major arranged for an ambulance to pick up the Iraqi doctors and me. They brought us to the MASH unit where the major met with us. For those of us who wanted to go to the United States, the major and his staff helped us draft a request to the American embassy.

One of the American soldiers was being extremely friendly and helpful. At first, I didn't notice his name tag but when he came closer, I recognized the Armenian trademark ending of his last name. With my eyes wide open, I said, "Koshkarian! That's an Armenian name." We were both excited to find an Armenian on the opposite side. In reality, he was a Greek adopted by an Armenian family in childhood. He was grieving the recent loss of his Armenian father. Koshkarian said that he had a list of fourteen Armenian-Iraqi POWs and that the U.S. East Coast archbishop of the Armenian diocese was planning to visit all Armenian POWs in the Saudi desert.

He said that the archbishop was planning to intervene to help them in any way he could. But I never saw the archbishop or heard anything about him again, either because of my constant moving from one camp to another, or because the archbishop was never able to obtain proper permissions from the American military or Saudi government.

I submitted my request to the major and waited for the ambulance to take me back to the Admin Compound in hopes of seeing Monica. There, I fixed my eyes on the road that led to the American camp, looking out for Monica's truck or Loren's water truck. From far away, I saw the headlights of a vehicle approaching the entrance from the American camp. The truck was Monica's, but the shadow of the person behind the wheel was too big to be her. The truck stopped a few yards behind the ambulance and the driver flashed his high beams at me. I ran toward the truck and found that it was my old friend Wik. I realized that since Monica was not with him, she was most likely forbidden to come see me.

Wik came down from the truck and said, "I'm glad I found you, man. These two letters just came in, from your mother, this evening. I was gonna kill myself if you left before I gave them to you."

I did not know whether to read the two letters first or spend my last few remaining minutes with Wik. In the end, I managed to read my mother's short letters intermittently while talking to Wik at the same time. Wik spent half an hour at the MASH unit and said good-bye to the Iraqi doctors. I walked him back to his truck. We said our good-byes, but he was avoiding eye contact. He was reaching for the door when I said, "I will visit Nebraska, you know, and I will look you up."

Wik turned around but was still avoiding eye contact. He said, "You better do that, man. You better do that. I've gotta go now. I'm not gonna be like one of those mushy guys who cry. You take good care of yourself now. Just keep a low profile, I know you will survive." Wik gave me his address in Omaha, then climbed into his truck and sped away.

38. Hafr Al-Batin

On the following morning, Enclosure Two was scheduled to close down and the last remaining POWs transferred to Hafr Al-Batin. It was our turn to say good-bye to the 403rd and to the new friends that we had made. The cooks, who used to greet us with a comforting smile every morning, came out of their tent looking dispirited. They were listless under the burden of their anxiety. They dragged their bags, which were nearly empty, and walked toward the buses as if they were being led to their slaughter.

A sad Grossman stood at the entrance of the processing tent. The quiet woman who had joined the belly-dance lesson with him the previous night was by his side. He wished that he could see a better solution for his Iraqi friends. With the departure of the Iraqi POWs, there was nothing more to do in the processing tent than prepare to tear it down, but Grossman was too hesitant to leave the shelter of the tent and mingle with the Iraqi cooks, the way we all knew he liked to do. The Vietnam veteran, who had seen horrors in his days, stayed back under the canvas so as not to succumb to his emotions.

Being the longest in captivity, I had the smallest POW serial number and was the first to be called. I boarded the first bus and Brian followed immediately after. One by one, the remaining numbers were called. It took a little more than half an hour before the 403rd was made POW-free and all eighteen buses were ready to go. Upon exiting the POW camp, the buses passed by the MASH unit, which meant that they would drive through the American camp next. I still hoped to see Monica one last time, and fixed my gaze through a small unobstructed part of a window on the right side of the bus. I saw people swimming, a male soldier wearing hot-pink sunglasses, field tents, and American-made wooden street signs, but I never saw her.

It was a bright and pleasant morning that day when the buses drove north across the Saudi desert. All seats were removed from the bus except for the one behind the wheel. Four guards sat on the floor behind the driver. They were separated by a net from the POWs who filled the bus. One of the four guards was a very quiet and attractive woman with short red hair and brown eyes. She did not show any expression on her face nor did she interact with the remaining guards or Iraqi POWs on the bus. She chewed tobacco and spat in a paper cup until she fell asleep from the rocking motion of the bus.

Luckily, the chewing tobacco spit collection cup didn't spill. The attractive woman guarded it with her hand even as she slept. But as the bus rocked from side to side, her pistol slipped out from its holster. It fell on the floor and slid under the net to the Iraqi side. Brian and I didn't dare to pick it up, fearing that the Americans might panic and go off on a shooting rampage before we could declare our intent. I was about to ask the guards permission to reach for the gun and hand it over to them, but another POW, who was either more courageous or less cautious than me, reached for the pistol and picked it up. Keeping the barrel pointed to the floor, he woke up the woman with short red hair and returned her pistol. By the time the remaining three guards noticed, the pistol was already back in her hands.

After three hours of driving, Hafr Al-Batin came upon us unannounced. It was located in the Saudi desert, west of Kuwait, near the southern border of Iraq. The name of the town means "The Bottom Pit" or "The Inner Pit." It reminded us of a maximum-security Iraqi prison called *Nugrat Salman*, meaning "Slomon's Pit." The prison was located in the middle of the Iraqi desert, where prisoners would have to battle the harsh climate of the desert upon escape. Absent of caves, vegetation and bodies of water, the desert provided the fugitives with no hide-outs whatsoever from search dogs or hovering aircraft. In many ways, it resembled San Francisco's Alcatraz. They were both self-contained maximum-security prison islands, one slightly more barren than the other.

We stopped at the 301st Company, an American unit similar to the 403rd. The 301st was to process all Iraqi POWs in the usual manner, then gradually transfer custody of the whole camp to the Saudis. We were again saved from being left alone with the Saudis for a little while longer. Based on a letter drafted by the 403rd, Brian and I were immediately isolated from the general POW population. Within an hour, we were assigned to a small tent. We were told to remain within the confines of the processing area, which was so large that we rarely felt like captives. The processing area served as a centralized Admin Compound for all the enclosures that comprised the 301st. In the meanwhile, the Iraqi doctors were assigned to the MASH unit and the remaining POWs were distributed among the large number of enclosures.

At night, Brian and I shared the tent with two guards who watched over a neighboring four-tent compound. The four-tent compound was vacant when we arrived but was later occupied by rebel leaders who participated in the temporary overthrow of the government in southern Iraq. One of them, Zack, recognized me

from the University of Technology in Baghdad. We had both graduated with a bachelor degree in engineering; his was in architec-
ture and mine was in production engineering and metallurgy.

Zack and one of his rebel friends, Hassan, told me stories of
their escape from imprisonment and the brutality of Saddam
Hussein's army. Saddam's army was ousted from the southern
Iraqi cities but eventually defeated the rebels and regained control. When Hassan was captured, he was tied to a tank. The tank
led the way in entering Hassan's hometown knowing that his
comrades would not fire at the tank. Other tanks and the army
followed. They bombarded homes at random, some with unsus-
pecting residents still inside, some at the dinner table. City after
city fell back into the brutal grip of Saddam Hussein, after having
tasted freedom for no more than three or four days.

The Ba'athists arrested thousand of males, with or without
knowledge of their identity. Their only crime was that they were
Shiites or that they co-existed with Shiite rebels. Tens of thousands were mass slaughtered outside their cities within days of
their capture. But Hassan was a rebel leader. His would be a formal execution. He was imprisoned, stripped naked, and tortured
daily. Before the day of his scheduled execution, his comrades
gathered a large sum of money and bribed his jailor to set him
loose one night. That night, Hassan escaped. He was still naked
and had nowhere to go without the risk of being caught again.
He stole some clothes he found on a clothesline from a nearby
house and escaped to Hafr Al-Batin, where prison life was safer
for him.

At the 301st, Brian and I roamed freely inside the processing
area with no restrictions imposed whatsoever. Aside from our
sweat suits and wristbands, we were virtually indistinguishable
from the American soldiers. The American-Iraqis was how Lieu-

tenant Jackson and Sergeant Pruitt liked to introduce us to the others. They managed the processing area and were assigned to take care of us. But the mess hall, located about a hundred yards behind the barbed wire, was off-limits.

Lieutenant Jackson suggested that one of the guys should bring two plates from the mess hall so that Brian and I could enjoy a warm meal once a day. The genuinely good-natured Sergeant Wisniewski took it upon himself to fulfill this daily task. Because no one could pronounce his name, he settled on what everyone else called him and introduced himself as Sergeant Ski. Every evening, Sergeant Ski carried our two plates and walked to the processing tent before going back to the mess hall to eat his dinner. After the third day, I could not bear to see him carry my food anymore so that I might enjoy my warm meal before he would enjoy his. I was very appreciative of his service, of course, but I was humbled by his humility. What made me even more self-conscious about the matter was that he was old enough to be my father.

"You don't have to do this. We can eat MREs or canned food," I told him.

"Yes, but it's nice if you can eat at least one hot meal a day."

"Why don't you eat first and then bring us our meal on your way back?"

"If I stay there a little too long, the food might run out before I get some for you. And if I take your plates up front, then your food will get cold by the time I finish eating.".

"Where is this mess hall anyway?"

"It's right there, behind the Saudi National Forest."

"Did you say forest?"

"Yes," he said and pointed to a little bush standing alone in the Saudi desert.

Many others at the 301st were extremely friendly and help-ful. Michael Rahilly, tall and thin with short black hair, who quickly made fun of himself before anyone else did, and Abdullah the Saudi interpreter soon became my good friends. Nothing spe-cific made them stand out, but their easy-going personalities went a long way in the harsh environment we were in. On one occasion, an American soldier gave me his denim jacket and told me to keep it. He had noticed that I was wrapped in my blanket while working through the night as I was helping the Americans fill out Red Cross cards and process incoming POWs. Another gave me a new pair of Reebok sneakers so that I did not have to wear my old boots day and night.

My mother's next-door neighbor, an American soldier from Glendale, was searching for me by name. Although the trail led him to Hafr Al-Batin, he was not able to find me because he fo-cused his search on the POW general population areas. In the meanwhile, Sergeant Pruitt, who was an attorney, received a par-cel from my mother containing my status documents. The parcel was originally sent to Meg at the 403rd, who received it one day after I was transferred. Meg redirected the parcel to the 301st that same day. Sergeant Pruitt contacted his American command-ers, the American embassy, and the State Department in DC. He was relentless in pursuing all avenues that might result in bring-ing us, Brian and me, back home to the United States.

There were times when I told my new American friends of the treatment that I had received during the early stages of my captivity. When I told them that I was suspected of being a spy, they were surprised at first, but then quickly realized that some-one with my background was a good candidate for one. They asked me, hypothetically, which country I preferred spying for. The ethics of a spy's world has always been a confusing issue to me. But in my mind, anyone who earned the trust of the people of one country, knowing that he or she would betray them later, was a highly dangerous person and no one to admire. So I told them that I wouldn't consider spying for any country, but if my ethics allowed me to consider such a job, they would probably not prevent me from choosing to spy for the highest bidder. My answer, "The one that pays more," seemed to strike them as acceptably American, from the capitalist point of view.

39. In Limbo

The American and Iraqi governments had negotiated the cease-fire agreement and began repatriating prisoners. All the Iraqi POWs who were traded to obtain the American POWs held in Iraq were taken from Hafr Al-Batin, also known as West Camp, which was one of the largest POW camps in Saudi. The majority of Iraqi POWs returned to the American camp in the following days and weeks. When Michael Rahilly, who took part in their repatriation, asked why they returned, they said that they were scared of what the Iraqi government might do to them and that they received such great treatment from the Americans. "Plus, the food is better here," they added. It wasn't necessary for the Iraqi government to involve itself in the negotiations. The actual negotiations needed to be held between the Americans, who wanted to rid themselves of the POW problem and go home, and the Iraqi POWs who were all too comfortable in their tent villages. In the meanwhile, new POWs continued to come in by the thousands.

After Saddam's invasion of Kuwait in 1990, President Bush, Sr., was heard on a foreign radio broadcast in Arabic encouraging the Iraqi people to rise against Saddam and topple his regime. Bush promised that the U.S. would help the Iraqis. When Desert

Storm broke out, the Shiites responded to Bush's appeal and cleansed their territories of Saddam and his shadow. For the first time in two generations, they opened their eyes to a foreign concept that they had heard other countries boast about—freedom. However, the promised help did not arrive and Saddam began to regain control over the southern territories of Iraq. The Shiites retreated under Saddam's brutal counterattack. They were driven out of their homes and sought refuge in POW camps in Saudi with the Americans, the lesser enemy, who would protect them from the cruelty of Saddam's Republican Guards, the lesser friend.

The Shiites were expecting the Americans to arm them and send them back to Iraq, so as to help them reclaim their territories from Saddam's army. But Bush had had a change of heart and decided not to interfere with Iraq's internal affairs.

Knowing that they had betrayed the Shiites, the American forces decided to protect them this time and put an end to Saddam's advances and massacring campaigns in the south. In March of 1991, they managed to seal off the Shiite territory from Saddam by controlling southern Iraq. They stopped at the outskirts of Baghdad and manned roadblocks on the two highways that connected Baghdad to the south. The Americans stopped all vehicles on the road and took into custody anyone who was in uniform or whom they suspected was a soldier. The ones who were detained were brought to Hafr Al-Batin to join the multitudes of captured POWs, fleeing civilians, Saddamists, and anti-Saddamists.

Among those whom I helped to process was a ten-year-old kid. I never asked him why he wore khakis, which were undoubtedly the reason why he was apprehended. Many kids wore an army or special forces uniform because they thought it was stylish or were too poor to buy their own clothing. Others wore it in memory of a family member whom they had lost. When I asked him his name, the kid broke down in tears and started to cry uncontrollably. He said that he had an important exam tomorrow and if he missed school, he would fail. I did not know how to break the bad news to him. The only thing that I could guarantee him was that he would miss school tomorrow. The Americans were sending POWs back to Iraq, upon request. But the quickest return to Iraq would take at least two days. I could not spend too much time with him; there were hundreds in line behind him. I told him that school was the least of his concerns. The country was at war, the government was collapsing, and hundreds of thousands were either dead or captured. "Look around," I said, "you might find your teacher here."

While processing another POW, he asked me if I was on the L-87 the day it was sent to its demise. I didn't recognize him but realized that he must have been from Ra's Al-Qulay'ah. He said that all the boats in Ra's Al-Qulay'ah were destroyed and that the commander of the Red Crescent boat was publicly executed upon his return to the base after abandoning us. I received the news with neither delight nor surprise. However, I did make a comment to the effect that what the commander of the Red Crescent boat had done to us was nothing short of cowardly.

POWs were brought to our desk in groups of twenty. They were seated on the sand while Brian and I called them one by one. We gathered some basic information and filled out their Red Cross and POW cards. After we were done with them, they were sent to the next station where more information was entered on a laptop computer. The process culminated when a wristband with a six-digit POW serial number was placed around their wrists. Every now and then, the process was halted for ten minutes. We were not sure exactly why, but we were told that the computers were not to be used during consolidation.

Once, we were delayed a little longer than the usual ten minutes. To entertain them while they were waiting, the American guards taught the Iraqis a new song. The people of the two nations, who were once enemies, sang in unison with uplifted spirits appropriate for the End-Of-Hostilities statement that they were greeted with before being sent to the wristband station. For the Americans, the song was very familiar, although for the Iraqis, the music and lyrics were utterly foreign. The POWs didn't know what they were singing, but they seemed to enjoy it nonetheless. It turns out that the words to "Itsy Bitsy Spider" sound funny in any language. Before it was over, the Iraqis had perfected the song, complete with the hand gestures.

With the absence of the Kuwaiti interpreters and merely an intermittent presence of the Saudis, the demand for interpreters was always pressing. Brian and I worked extended hours, driven by the urgency of the moment and our will to help the Americans bring the weary Iraqis to their tent-and-barbed-wire homes at Hafr Al-Batin. We both thought that the job was interesting. Because our contribution was completely voluntary, we didn't feel exhaustion or have any realistic concern over time. On two consecutive days, we were overtaken by fatigue after spending nearly twenty hours behind the desk, and still went to bed feeling guilty for abandoning the others who needed us.

When a group of English-speaking Iraqi POWs came—mainly doctors and engineers—I asked them if they were willing to volunteer as interpreters. They readily accepted. I taught them some military terms, which were unlikely to have been included in their medical- and engineering-school curricula. Of course, Lieutenant Jackson thought it was a great idea to increase the number of interpreters until there were enough of them to be available upon request, day or night. Instead of sending the doctors and engineers to one of the main POW enclosures, they were kept in the four-tent compound, the same one where Zack, Hassan, and their rebel friends once stayed. The four-tent compound was already vacant because the rebels had been transferred to one of the regular enclosures. They joined other rebels and anti-Saddamists and were kept in compounds as far as possible from the Saddamist groups. Yet another group, the moderates, blamed both the Saddamists and anti-Saddamists for destroying the country with their fanaticism. Those too were kept in separate compounds, as far as possible from the other two groups.

From the doctor and engineer interpreters-in-training, I learned that the Voice of America radio station had broadcast my story in Arabic to the people of Iraq. Although my name was never mentioned, the story was so unique that those who knew me easily identified me. Before long, many who had never crossed roads with me were familiar with my strange Armenian name, "Shant." Among them was Ziad, a dentist, who was one of the interpreters-in-training. That's how small this planet had become.

I felt relieved that my relatives were informed by the Voice of America radio broadcasts that I was alive and that they had learned something of my condition. Until then, I had often dreamed that I was knocking on the doors of my aunts or stepmother in Baghdad to tell them that I was alive. But I never went past the front door because I always felt eager to return to my POW camp in Saudi. In the dream, I was simply paying a courtesy visit and always turned down invitations to go inside and rest. The best excuse that I could come up with was, "I have to

go back and finish my term as a POW." But before they said anything, I usually woke up.

For my aunt Alice, the radio broadcast brought no consolation; her neighbor was a nurse in the naval hospital, and he led
aunt Alice to believe that I was certainly dead. "All our boats and
ships were destroyed," he told her. "There were no prisoners.
He's either dead or injured—and he's not among the patients in
the hospital." And so for my aunt Anahid, my newfound fame on
the Voice of America eased her fears about me, but at the same
time amplified them for herself—it brought the Iraqi government
to her front door, and more than once. Ba'ath Party officials
wanted to know why I hadn't returned with the other repatriated
prisoners.

"I'm waiting for him, too," she told them. "But you know
something? You took him away from me—*you* bring him back."

All the POWs at the 301st had access to a shower, one way or another. Brian and I, however, due to our limbo status as semi-
POWs, still didn't have shower access during our confinement to
the processing area. Although two shower stalls had been erected
near the spot where Americans and POWs once sang "Itsy Bitsy
Spider" together, their water tanks were empty and for some reason were never filled.

Easter came a little early in 1991—March 31. Lieutenant
Jackson obtained special permission to allow us entry into the
American camp and enjoy a hot shower on this holiest and most
celebrated Sunday in the Christian calendar. A guard escorted us
to the shower area, a five-minute walk from the Saudi National
Forest. Brian and I were very excited about the blessing that was
bestowed upon us on this festive day. We each entered a shower

stall, got undressed and started to bathe while our escort guard waited in the shower room. A couple of other stalls were also occupied. While rinsing his body, one of the Americans barraged our escort guard with questions and comments. He made very clear his resentment toward the fact that Brian and I were treated as equals and were allowed in the shower room with him. I couldn't tell his rank, since he was naked, but he talked like an officer.

"They're American-Iraqis," explained our escort guard.

"Oh yeah, then why do you have to escort them? For all I care, they are POWs and shouldn't be here. Who told you to bring them here?"

"Lieutenant Jackson did."

"I'll make sure this won't happen again. The females use these showers too. I don't want them to see these POWs when you take them outta here."

Having heard the insults, Brian and I finished our showers very quickly and got out as soon as possible. I was wet less than two minutes, while Brian took an additional minute to finish up. We asked the guard to take us back to the processing area and did not speak a word until he broke the silence midway along the route.

"Hey guys, I'm sorry about that. I'll report it to Lieutenant Jackson and he'll make sure it won't happen again."

"Oh, it won't happen again," I retorted, knowing that I spoke for the both of us.

I felt bad for Lieutenant Jackson who went out of his way to provide us with a simple luxury that the naked officer ruined. I took advantage of the five-minute walk to calm myself so as not to appear unappreciative when Lieutenant Jackson asked how we liked the showers. Brian, on the other hand, was steaming with

anger and rage was radiating from his eyes. I knew that he was
going to do all the talking once we were back in the processing
area. Lieutenant Jackson met us with a smile.

"How was it?" the lieutenant asked.

"It was terrible!" Brian exploded. He went on, furiously explaining the whole incident, barely allowing the guard to throw
in a word. The guard verified Brian's account and revealed the
identity of the naked officer. The disappointed lieutenant called
the commander of the 301st, who had originally granted us permission to use the showers. Lieutenant Jackson reported the incident to the colonel, and even though he worded it a little more
moderately than Brian would have preferred, Lieutenant Jackson
came back in less than half an hour and told us that the colonel
said that we were allowed to use the showers every day, if we
liked.

He also said that this had just been made clear to the entire
staff, and especially to the naked officer, who turned out to be a
captain. We thanked Lieutenant Jackson and told him that we
preferred taking cold showers to being subjected to such unwar-
ranted insults and humiliation. Based on our request, Lieutenant
Jackson arranged to refill the water tanks of the abandoned
showers in the processing area where Brian and I henceforth took
our showers.

40. Access

On the morning of April 7, Sergeant Pruitt took me aside and told me in a whisper that the American embassy had just requested a meeting with Brian and me. The embassy was located in the diplomatic quarters, a neighborhood of foreign embassies, in Riyadh, the capital of Saudi Arabia. He said that we probably had to leave Hafr Al-Batin around 8:00 A.M. to make the interview at around 3:00 P.M.

"Don't say anything 'til you've been officially notified," he warned us.

"Why are you telling me this, then?"

"Because . . . Do you know your mother's phone number by heart?"

"Yes, why?"

"Prince Bandar is here. The Saudi King who I believe is either his father or uncle, gave him the responsibility of overseeing the operations here in Hafr Al-Batin. I asked him if you could use his car phone to call your mother in the United States. He agreed! It is 10:00 P.M. in California right now. Call her and tell her to contact the American embassy in Riyadh. Today is Sunday. Tell her to call them first thing in the morning, tomorrow. It would be preferable if she talked to them before your interview. She needs to understand what course of action the embassy suggests to help bring you back to the States. At the same time, the embassy will be reassured that your family is waiting for you and that they are willing to support you. All of that will have a positive influence on the interview."

I was impressed with Sergeant Pruitt's attention to detail and his meticulous planning. To keep things secret, he suggested that I hide while talking to my mother in Prince Bandar's SUV. She and I hadn't spoken in a very long time—a son who was lost in war, presumed dead, and a mother who nearly died mourning him. Nevertheless, under such constrained circumstances, I had to keep the conversation short and to the point. I did not want to talk about anything that would cause her to express any emotions. Emotions are very unpredictable. There was a great chance that we might both emerge teary-eyed from this conversation, and I had to return to my world of POWs. I knew she would be shocked to hear my voice. I decided that while still in her shock, I would tell her all I needed to say and then end the conversation quickly. First, I asked how she was, then assured her that I was fine. I told her that I was calling from a Saudi prince's car phone inside of my POW camp. While she was still digesting that one, I asked her to call the American embassy in Riyadh in the morning, and to convey Sergeant Pruitt's advice. I reminded her about the eleven-hour time difference between Saudi and California. Again, I assured her that I was fine and physically uninjured, that I'd been praying, and had been treated well by the Americans. "They are trying to help me but they might not be able to do anything after they're gone. That's why I need you to contact the embassy." And as quickly as that, it was time to say good-bye.

There was a sickly feeling in the pit of my stomach as soon as

I hung up. I convinced myself that the true reason for the emotionally subdued phone conversation was not my reluctance to emerge teary-eyed from the prince's SUV into a world where men were not allowed to cry. I didn't want to be the boy who cried in camp upon hearing his mother's voice, when everyone else around me seemed to be as emotionally solid as a rock. I concealed my feelings and insisted to myself and to the world that the conversation with my mother had to remain short to avoid abusing the prince's generosity. But no matter how I looked at it, in the end I emerged as having robbed my mother of her chance to shed tears of joy with me.

My perfectly good excuses were useless. For the rest of the night, I lived with the fact that guilt makes loneliness worse.

In the morning, Brian and I were accompanied by two officers on a five-hour drive to the capital city. Once in Riyadh, we helped the officers navigate by reading the Arabic street signs, so we found the diplomatic quarters with no trouble. I would like to suggest to the Saudi government that at least that sign, which is intended more for foreigners than locals, be written in English. From there, the American embassy was easy to locate, with its prominent flag piercing the sky. After an extensive security check at the gate, we were allowed entry. I was disheveled and dust-covered, with long hair, a two-month-old beard, and dirty clothes. I followed the two American officers through the large halls, proceeding with timid reluctance. I felt as if I were upsetting the janitors, defiling the sanctity of the embassy every time my dirty old boots touched the mirror-polished marble floor. I felt like a Van Gogh's potato eater entering the Taj Mahal.

We were asked to wait in a conference room, and eventually a woman in civilian clothing came in and introduced herself as a colonel. Then she immediately turned her attention to me and told me that she had spoken with my mother, only a few minutes before our arrival.

"The reason why you're here," she said with a little grin, "is because we wanted to see if you were a real person." Then she unloaded a three-inch-thick file on the table. "Tell me something," she said, "just how many people do you know? A lot of people called us, wrote us letters, and came knocking at our door to tell us about your strange story. Take a look at your file."

She dropped her hand on my file, which stood in obvious contrast with Brian's thin one. I could offer no answer, but I remember feeling a contented smile spread across my face, all by itself.

In my file, I caught a glimpse of my Wheeling High School report card and a congratulatory letter informing my parents that I had achieved a GPA better than 4.5. Then the colonel spoke up again and told me that she had knowledge of my exhibition in the American Cultural Center in Baghdad. She also told me that before closing down the American embassy in Baghdad, the staff destroyed all their documents. However, before destroying all pending applications, the staff had compiled a list with the names of the applicants and the type of application they were processing. The female colonel had checked the list and found that my name was there under green card renewal.

"Your case looks good," she said.

The embassy petitioned the State Department in Washington, DC, for an indefinite humanitarian parole as a quick way to bring me back to the U.S. Once in the U.S., I would have to contact the local Immigration and Naturalization Service (INS) office and reinstate my permanent residency status. However, she did not promise when and if the State Department would approve.

In fact, the American embassy was very careful not to mislead us to optimism or build our hope high. The colonel turned to Brian and said, "We tracked your birth record in Chicago. You are a citizen by birth. But do you know that we can revoke your citizenship because you bore arms and fought against the U.S.?"

"I had to go to the army," said Brian with obvious frustration in his voice. "If I didn't, they would have taken my family away and done what they liked with my sister."

She turned the question to me. "What about you?"

"I had to go, too. All males eighteen to fifty-five years of age had to go. All Iraqi residents are subject to Saddam's laws, whether you are a citizen or not."

The colonel took me to a separate room while a lieutenant colonel took Brian away. They asked us some questions—mainly focused on whether we knew any other Americans who were being held captive in Iraq. We both answered in the negative.

The embassy was ready to send Brian to the United States as soon as they could establish contact with his uncle in Ohio. Brian knew that his uncle lived in Cleveland but did not have his phone number or address. Of course, he was unable to call his mother in Baghdad and ask for her brother's contact information. Among the first things that the American bombing campaign took out were all communications systems in Iraq. Not to mention that if the embassy did manage to put a call through, the Iraqi government would be listening and recording. All foreign calls are monitored and can result in serious problems for the Iraqi household. The female colonel suggested that the lieutenant colonel interviewing Brian should call the operator in Cleveland and ask for the phone number for Brian's uncle.

"It's not listed," said the Cleveland operator.

"Did you find his name though?" asked the lieutenant colonel.

"Yes, sir, but I'm not allowed to give out the number."

"This is very important. I am a lieutenant colonel in the American embassy in Saudi Arabia. This man's nephew is an American-born Iraqi POW who's been captured and we need—"

The lieutenant colonel stopped talking. He placed the phone down and said, "She didn't believe me; she hung up."

"I don't blame her, honey," said the female colonel.

41. Moving Out

Brian and I explained to Lieutenant Jackson and Sergeant Pruitt what went on during our meeting at the embassy. Their faces glowed with excitement and they began to analyze the situation and project optimistic views. As for Brian and me, we went about our usual daily routines. The meeting in the American embassy was in the past, and we were both determined to protect ourselves from disappointment. We didn't allow any false hopes, or discuss the possibility that we might be free in the foreseeable future. Personally, I didn't want to even think of the word "free" until I safely set foot on American soil.

As the Americans began to wrap up business at the 301st, they gradually transferred ownership of the camp to the Saudis. Within days, all POWs would be under Saudi custody. However, the processing area where Brian and I were confined remained under American control. We were glad for that—the Saudis proved to be less tolerant toward unruly POWs than their American counterparts had been. On the first day, the Saudis shot and killed an Iraqi prisoner who refused to back away from the gates of his compound.

The Americans were intoxicated with the thought that soon they would go back home. There were talks of family, girlfriends and boyfriends, eating pizza or steak, and going to the movies and to local pubs. But, of course, going back home did not include Brian and me. While everyone talked about the first thing that they would do when they arrived home, Brian and I tried not to spoil the moment by bringing up our worries. We dreaded the possibility that we might be left behind under Saudi mercy in the absence of our American big brothers. Seeing that we were worn with anxiety, Sergeant Pruitt gave us some reassuring thoughts. He said that now that the embassy was involved, the Americans were not going to abandon us. They were more likely to take us home to the U.S. with them. "Even if as prisoners," he said.

As the workload shifted to the Saudis, the Americans were able to relax during their daily duties. On the night of April 13, I saw the colonel commander of the 301st strolling about the processing area, chatting briefly with his soldiers. Prior to this, I had not seen him before. He had a pleasant smile and seemed much more approachable than the sadistic Iraqi colonel, who was the commander of the Second Naval Brigade in Umm Qasr.

"Did he talk to you?" asked Brian.

"No, did he talk to you?"

"Yes, he thought I was you and congratulated me on going home tomorrow."

"Are you sure he said tomorrow or did he mean that the embassy visit will bring good results soon?"

"No, he said tomorrow. Go ask him!"

"I'm not ready for an emotional roller coaster. If what you say is true, then they should have informed me by now."

"Go ask him, I say! If I were you, I'd be all over him."

"If he says tomorrow, I won't be able to wait another day. What if they delayed it another week?"

I lingered around and saw the colonel pass by me a couple of times, but he went back to his quarters without saying anything. I stayed with Brian trying to act calm and cool but the suspense was killing me. I decided to go to bed a little early that night. About an hour later, an officer came to my tent and woke me up.

"Are you Shant?"

"Yes."

"Get your things together. Early in the morning you will be going home."

I was still not quite ready to let my guard down yet. "What do you mean by home?" I asked.

"The United States," he said.

Those were exactly the words I wanted to hear. I laughed and shouted, "This is the best news I've heard in eleven years!"

He congratulated me and said that he would come to pick me up in the morning, then he walked away—without realizing that he had just been linked to a major milestone in my life and that he was part of a moment that I will never forget.

I ran off and told Brian, who cried, "See, I told you!" Then he laughed out loud, as if the suspense had weighed just as heavily on him as it had on me.

"I'll go and pack so I don't waste any time in the morning. Do you want any of my stuff?" I asked.

"No, give it to the new doctors."

I packed everything in a small duffel bag that Monica gave me when I was transferred out of her compound. I took the chaplain's Bible, Zimmerman's sleeping bag, and the American doctor's blanket. Regretfully, I had to leave my old boots behind, breaking an old promise to myself that I would carry them wherever I went, in appreciation for carrying me through two wars.

I was unfaithful to them, giving in to the temptation of the new pair of Reeboks which were just too comfortable for me to revert to the old boots. I decided to wear Grossman's black sweat suit and give the blue one and my other jumpsuits to the new doctors and engineers—the interpreters-in-training. Upon hearing the news, these interpreters expressed excitement and congratulated me. My news brought hope to them, since they all wanted to go to other countries—anyplace other than Iraq.

I was surprised that my green card had been processed so soon after my visit to the American embassy. I finally learned why in February of 2007. While I was still a POW in Saudi, my case was assigned to a lady who worked in the Refugee Affairs office at the State Department in Washington, D.C. While carpooling to work, she expressed her frustration with the case she had at hand. She said that she was hitting a brick wall trying to find out whether a particular Iraqi POW "really" had a green card. Dan, one of her fellow riders, asked if this particular POW happened to be Shant Kenderian. Astonished, she inquired how he knew my name. Dan said that he was processing my green card during his assignment to the American embassy in Baghdad. When Iraq invaded Kuwait, the American embassy was shut down, and its staff returned to the States. All pending applications and other paper trails were destroyed, including my file. This information allowed the lady to verify my story, and she ended up being among those officers who cleared me for reentry into the United States.

I knew that I needed to save my energy and get ready for a very long journey in the morning. A six-hour sleep would have been ideal but I could not manage to pin myself to my bed for more than five seconds. I wanted to share the good news with the whole world. I wanted to shout jubilantly, dance with the stars all night, and thank God in heaven.

By 3:00 A.M., I had to force myself to lie in bed. I had no clue about the process that I would have to go through between Hafr Al-Batin and Los Angeles. No doubt the journey would be exhausting. My vision of the future was dark and blurry, but at the end of the tunnel, I saw my family greeting me with plenty of hugs and kisses under the bright sun. From photos that she used to send, I had seen my mother's gold-colored Chevy and yellowish stucco house. Her garden overflowed with flowers and ceramic penguins, ducks, cats, and birds. I had seen the interior of the house from her photos, too. One specific photo that I remember well was of my brother eating a juicy mango in her kitchen. He seemed bothered by the camera a little, but didn't allow it to interrupt his appetite. There was an empty chair beside him. Oh, how I wished I were there.

My eyes were still wide open when the officer came back for me in the morning. Another officer and an escort guard were in his company. He told me that I had thirty minutes to get ready.

"I'm ready now."

"We have to wait until eight o'clock anyway. Go say good-bye to your friends."

Like the night shift, the day shift was reduced in staff. On that morning, very few people were present in the processing area. I thanked Lieutenant Jackson and Sergeant Ski for all their hard work and asked them to thank Sergeant Pruitt and all those who were absent. Then I said good-bye. Brian walked with me to the truck. After spending every minute of the day together for the past two months, we had bonded and become friends, despite our different personalities.

Although he expressed nothing but happiness for me, I was sure that my departure was hard on Brian. When the truck was fully loaded and ready to go, Brian and I shook hands and hugged. I told him that his day would come soon. He just laughed and told me to hurry up and go, before they changed their minds and kept me there.

I got in and we began to drive away. I looked back and saw Brian standing alone in the Saudi desert. He waved once, and I never saw him again.

For breakfast, we stopped along the way at an American military unit, which seemed entirely dedicated to serving food. One of my escort officers noticed that I was still wearing my POW wristband. He took out his Swiss Army knife, cut the wristband off, and gave it to me as a souvenir. After breakfast, we continued our drive toward the capital city, Riyadh. We arrived six hours after saying good-bye to the 301st and entered an American military complex there. A captain at the complex had been expecting us. He gave my escort officers three envelopes. The contents of the first envelope allowed me to board a plane, the second requested a signature confirming my departure, and the third granted me humanitarian parole to the United States. The captain instructed the two officers to take good care of me and make me "feel like a soldier." In military terms, this was the best way to describe dignified freedom. The captain also instructed us to be at the airport by 11:00 P.M. Since we had several hours to kill, we decided to have dinner at the American complex, drive to see the beautiful city of Riyadh, then head toward the airport before eight o'clock.

We found our way to the main commercial airport in Riyadh. While the place was busy, as expected, no one seemed to know anything about flights for American troops. The Saudi Royal Airport was only a few minutes away. There was obviously no flight activity, but we decided to ask the guards since the word "Royal" made them look very authoritative. The guards knew nothing about the American flights but said that their supervisor might. All eyes turned toward the supervisor who was in the middle of his evening prayer in the guard booth. After he finished, he told us that there was an American base on the other side of the royal airport and that American flights used to be scheduled there. He went to his car and told us to follow him. He drove like a madman, on and off the road, and at times, on the royal runway. We could barely keep up with him. Nevertheless, fifteen minutes later, we were at the American base.

Saudi soldiers guarded the gate.

They knew that I was an Iraqi POW, or at least they suspected something. My cheap sweat suit, disheveled hair, long beard, and being accompanied by American guards and officers led them to want to see my papers. We told them that my plane was leaving at 11:00 P.M., but that made them enjoy my torture even more. Thinking that he had an ace in his pocket, the American officer pulled out the three embassy documents that we were given and waved them in front of their faces. But, of course, the Saudi guards couldn't read English. At this moment, I had a feeling that they knew they would lose the argument in the end, but they were determined to inflict the maximum damage.

"It's an American plane, and we want him on it," said my escort officer forcefully. The Saudi guards called their supervising officer, who was home sleeping, and explained the situation to him. They told us that their supervisor was on his way to see us. Trying to be subtle, the Saudi guards were whispering to one another and stealing glances at me. While waiting for the Saudi officer, our hopes were thwarted when we heard the takeoff of a plane at 11:00 P.M. I sat on the curb and put my head between my hands.

"Don't worry," said the American guard, "everything will be OK."

This time self-pity got the best of me. "It's just another page in my book," I said without looking up. He didn't reply.

When the Saudi officer showed up, we explained the story to him and showed him all the documents. Still, he was not convinced. "This is an international incident," said the American officer, "I will report it to the embassy and make sure it won't happen again." The Saudi officer did not know what to do; he did what his subordinate guards did to him. He called his supervising officer and woke him up. Twenty minutes later, the supervisor of the supervisor came and at 11:30 P.M. we were granted permission to enter the American-operated air base. Once inside the gates, the American officer said, "If it weren't for us protecting their country, it would have been an Iraqi guard standing at this gate."

Much to our delight, aside from the three guards and their supervising officer at the gate, there was no Saudi presence inside the base. When we were told to be at the base by 11:00 P.M., no reference was made to the actual flight. We understood this as an 11:00 P.M. departure time. We were extremely relieved to learn that my flight was actually scheduled to depart at 4:00 A.M., April 15. My escort officer exchanged one of my three letters for a boarding pass, then we got in line for customs. By now my heart was hammering so hard that I could almost hear it.

Everyone had to fill out a little customs card declaring the amount of cash and monetary value of any gifts that they were bringing into the country—beyond a minimum limit, that is. For me, the answer to both questions was unambiguously zero. However, I did not know exactly how to answer the last question, which inquired about the purpose of my visit. The questionnaire expected the traveler to select one of only two options that were made available—"Business" or "Pleasure." The American soldiers all marked "Business," for liberating Kuwait, of course. But neither option described how and why I ended up in the country. I decided to be on the cautious side and leave that part of the questionnaire unanswered rather than checking the wrong box. At first, my escort officers agreed with me. When we came closer to the building, we saw that an officer was checking all the customs cards before allowing anyone entry. My escort officers suggested that I complete the questionnaire so as not to attract any unnecessary attention.

"I don't know what to select. I didn't go to liberate Kuwait like you guys," I said.

"Why did you go back to Iraq then?" one of the officers asked.

"I went back to visit my father."

We conferred with one another and all agreed that if it were not "Business," then it must have been "Pleasure." Ten minutes later, I entered the building and handed my card to the officer who stood at the entrance. The officer crossed out "Pleasure" and marked "Business" instead. With no expression on his face he gave me back my card and said, "We know your story, it certainly was no pleasure."

42. *Flight to Freedom*

While we waited for the plane, the lieutenant colonel who interviewed Brian at the American embassy came to make sure that everything was OK.

"I want to verify that we're sending the right person," he said.

"What about Brian?" I asked.

"He'll be on his way to Cleveland in one week."

The lieutenant colonel didn't stay long. I thanked him, he congratulated me, and we said good-bye.

At 3:00 A.M., we were told to line up and get ready for boarding. The gate was opened, and a large TWA airplane stood waiting. The air was vibrant with excitement while everyone waited in line for their turn to ascend the stairs to the aircraft.

My escort officer had to obtain a signature confirming that I boarded the plane. First, he asked the person who stood behind me in line but then he decided to ask the pilot and turned away. But the person behind me was curious now, and asked what the signature was all about. He quickly recognized my story from articles he had read. He shook my hand and congratulated me on my freedom, then turned around and told my story to the person behind him.

The escort officer came back with the pilot's signature. Before ascending the steps to the plane, I thanked the three Americans who'd been my companions during the last twenty hours. They were my deliverers from captivity to freedom.

The plane was on schedule, taking off at 4:00 A.M. to the sound of cheers and applause from everybody on board.

During a thirty-minute stop in Ireland, my story became popular in the airport bar; many came back to the plane, congratulating me on my freedom and treating me like a hero. They took pictures with me, some asked for my autograph, and a military reporter conducted an interview for one of their publications.

The plane landed at a Navy base in Norfolk, Virginia. I heard the pilot say "Norfolk" several times but I never heard him say "Virginia." I wasn't sure where Norfolk was, but because we landed in the morning, I knew that we were somewhere on the East Coast, still far away from Los Angeles. I was hoping that the embassy's plan of taking me home would not stop there.

Many families and loved ones were gathered at the Norfolk base. They greeted their heroes with waving flags, flowers, and open arms. I descended the plane with the soldiers and walked through the crowd, then continued on until I found myself on the street. There were no people watching me, no barbed wire, or tents. Considering the months that I spent in the Saudi desert, the green grass, trees, paved streets, and even the humid air around me felt like a great luxury. It was the smell and feel of freedom. I was so excited to be on American soil that the daunting task still remaining ahead of me, to find my way to Los Angeles, did not seem to trouble me at the moment. But, I didn't know what to do.

I went back inside the base and asked the most basic of questions, "Where am I?" A lady behind a desk told me where Norfolk was and showed me to a little room where two immigration officers were present. I handed the letter from the American embassy in Riyadh to the two officers, who filled out and stamped an I-94 card for "Indefinite Humanitarian Parole." They instructed me to see the immigration office as soon as I arrived in Los Angeles. The lady informed me that the base had no flights to Los Angeles, and that the embassy had not specified what they should do with me; I was on my own. She arranged for someone to give me a ride to the international airport so that I might manage to go to Los Angeles somehow. I was still intoxicated with my freedom and numb. I had no concept of what to do next, so I decided to absorb it all in one moment at a time.

The lush vegetation I saw on the side of the road between the Navy base and the international airport was one of most spectacular sights to my eyes. In retrospect, it was nothing out of the norm for the season, but coming from the desert, my retina was almost burned by the color green. I rolled down the window and breathed in free air.

Inside the airport, I approached the first ticketing agent who was available. Briefly, I explained my story and told her that I had no identification or money but wanted to go to Los Angeles. Baffled by my request, she directed me to the upper level where there was a uniformed soldier inside a military booth who might be able to assist me. I found the booth, allowed two older ladies to go before me, and stood at the end of the line so that I could gather my thoughts while they were being helped. The ladies were done so quickly that I still didn't know how to begin.

"I need help," was my best opening line.

"What can I do for you?" said the soldier pleasantly.

"It's a long story."

"Does it start Once Upon a Time?"

"Yes, it does. I am an Iraqi POW, I just came from Saudi Arabia, I have no ID, no money, and I want to go to LA."

"That should be easy. Do you have anyone in LA?"

"Yes, my mother."

I gave him my mother's phone number. He called her collect and told her where I was. Ten minutes later, she called back and instructed me to pick up my ticket and boarding pass from the TWA ticketing agents. As simple as that.

I picked up my boarding pass and checked back with the soldier. His shift ended shortly after and he took me to a little art exhibition that school kids had organized inside one of the waiting rooms in the airport. The purpose of the exhibit was not totally clear to me, but it seemed to be centered on the Desert Storm theme. The soldier introduced me to the girls in charge of the exhibit and directed me to some free cookies and juice that were made available for the visitors. He then showed me to my gate and said good-bye.

Norfolk was hit with a quick weather change, unlike any I had seen in Iraq or Chicago or will ever see in California. The storm was so severe that boarding was delayed until the rain subsided. To make things more complicated, I had a connection in St. Louis. There was not enough time for me to hop from one plane to the next. Once again, I had to explain my circumstances, this time to the TWA agents in St. Louis.

"It's not our fault, we waited until your plane landed but you were late."

"I'm not saying it's your fault but I need to fly to LA; I have no money and no place to go."

"The next flight is in the morning."

"That's OK. I have a sleeping bag; I'll just sleep right here next to your booth."

The agents arranged for a hotel, courtesy of TWA, and showed me how to get to the shuttle. I called home from the airport and told my stepfather that I was spending the night in St.

Louis, thus ruining the Armenian Church Youth Group airport reception that my brother had organized. In a way, I was not ready for a big reception nor was I comfortable with attracting every living being's attention in the Los Angeles airport. I took my first real shower in the hotel, instead of in my mother's house as I had hoped. Although I had not slept in three days, I was both too excited to sleep and afraid that I might not be able to wake up in time for my 8:00 A.M. flight. I watched the news and weather channels, in all their variations.

When the sun started to rise, I took another shower, ate a package of MRE that I brought with me from Hafr Al-Batin, hoping it would be the last, and then caught the shuttle to the airport.

April 16 was a glorious day. At LAX, I followed the signs to baggage claim. As I descended a flight of stairs, I passed under a banner that showed Mayor Bradley welcoming visitors to the "City of the XXIII Olympics." With every step that I took, the joy in my heart grew bigger and more difficult to restrain. I was also full of anticipation, wondering what the moment would be like when I first met my family. After descending the stairs, I followed the exit signs and walked through a long tunnel. A bright light came through the glass doors at the end of the tunnel, where I saw my mother, brother, stepfather, and some friends to whom I had not yet been introduced. My mother searched me with her eyes to see if I was missing a limb. The others waved balloons and flowers. My spirit was jubilant, even though my body was too exhausted to express excitement.

"Could the end be this simple?" I thought to myself. The closer I came to the glass doors, the bigger I smiled. I walked with that broad smile on my face until I was tackled by hugs and covered with kisses.

Epilogue

During the first night that I slept in my mother's house, I woke up in the middle of the night not remembering exactly where I was. For a moment, I thought that leaving the POW camp and going to Los Angeles was nothing but a dream. With my hand, I felt the wall in the dark and realized that it was not canvas.

On the second morning, my brother drove me so I could have my hair cut. The hairdresser covered me with a black sheet and then was about to wrap a strip of white fabric around my neck. I flinched, certain that she was going to blindfold me. I looked in the mirror and saw my brother with his big smile, which had not left his face since I first saw him at the airport. Later that night, he drove me to a friend's house. As we drove East on the 134 from Glendale to Pasadena, I began to sweat. My hands felt damp and sticky like they did when I held the smashed ribs of First Lieutenant Mahdi before he died. My eyes blurred; the brake and signal lights of the cars crowding the freeway in front of me flared like the fire that was burning on the deck of the L-87. I smelled the smell of death and insisted frantically that my brother check the engine. He tried to calm me down, but when all his attempts failed, he obliged. He pulled over, opened and closed the hood, and we were back on our way to the party. Little did we know that the friend whom we visited in Pasadena would later become my wife. These flashbacks persisted for about a year, but luckily they've dwindled, and I now only occasionally have nightmares about the experience.

A week later, I called the American embassy in Riyadh and asked about Brian. They said that he was flown home to Cleveland the night before. Although we have not seen each other since Hafr Al-Batin, once or twice a year we talk and follow up on each other's lives. For that, all credit goes to Hugh Grossman, who was the connecting link in providing the two of us with each other's contact information.

On the fiftieth anniversary of the founding of the American Red Cross, May 8, 1991, I was invited to Washington, DC, to talk about my experience. One Saturday afternoon in June, I visited Kurt Voight in Chicago, and we drove by our high school in Wheeling. I looked nostalgically at the soccer fields where I used to practice after school, and the vending machines where we all used to get our daily shots of caffeine and sugar. I also visited Glenbrook South, the high school I attended during my first year in Chicago. The grass behind the gym was still wet. This is where I played my first softball game and immediately fell in love with it. What wasn't to love? In the middle, where second base used to be, I slid once and had one of the most beautiful girls in school fall in my lap.

From Chicago, I flew to Connecticut and visited my aunts, then drove to New York and visited Father Vahan and Michael Rahilly, one of the soldiers I befriended at the 301st. From New York, I fulfilled my promise to visit Nebraska and stayed with Abe Wooster, Chris Whitted, and Loren Peterson. I saw Cooper, Meg, Ellen, and many others. I never saw Wik, since he was out of town during my stay in Nebraska.

In Los Angeles, Todd, the gunner on the helicopter, visited me several times. I also visited him in San Diego and joined Corey and the other SEALs from the USS *Curts* at a barbeque pool party. Chuck, who was a guest interrogator at JIF, visited me from Minnesota and brought the German Bible he had promised when we first met. We saw each other on a more regular basis when he accepted a new job with the State Department in Washington, DC, when I was finishing my PhD program at Johns Hopkins University in Baltimore.

I spent the first few Christmases with my family in Los Angeles, but in 1994, I visited Father Vahan again. Our beer glasses touched on Christmas Eve at a restaurant in New York and brought a very long and strange journey to an end.

As for Monica, thanks to her help, and the help of many other soldiers, I made it from Saudi Arabia to the United States just two weeks after I said good-bye to her. Monica came back from the army two or three months after that. When I called her, she was cold to me. Then she said she was engaged. The guys from her unit told me later that after I left, she cried all the time. Then she met someone else. I never saw her again.

In a way, we were doomed from the start. But all the hardest things in our relationship—the fact that I was Iraqi and she was an American, the fact that our countries were at war and I was her enemy, that I was a prisoner and she was one of my guards— we were able to overcome. What ended up dooming it in the end was the most ordinary thing of all: She couldn't wait for me.

We didn't have control over the war or the politics in our countries, we didn't have control over where we were born, where we came from or were going to. But the one thing we had control over—being able to wait for each other, being patient—that's the thing that broke us up. She didn't love me enough for that. I guess our love never had deep roots. Like I said, love should start from the head, and only later be allowed into the heart.

Upon my return to the U.S., I began reading the *Los Angeles Times* searching for employment ads in engineering. I sent out hundreds of résumés but to no avail. Having a degree from Iraq and no experience or references in the U.S. provided plenty of reasons why I never landed a job interview. I decided to continue my education toward a master's degree at an American university and establish more contacts here. I was turned down by every university I applied to. My unofficial and uncertified Iraqi transcripts did not stand a chance against the fierce competition in the admissions offices, despite my high scores on the GRE and TOEFL exams. In Iraq, we were not given an official diploma or transcripts. All schools and universities and nearly all jobs were government controlled.

To prove my authenticity as an engineer in America, I took the Engineer-in-Training (EIT) exam. This is an eight-hour comprehensive exam covering all engineering disciplines. It is not easy for engineers to pass, let alone non-engineers. It is the first step toward earning a certification of Professional Engineering (PE). Only a small percentage of American engineers attain PE certification. Some report this number to be as low as 5 percent. After passing my EIT exam, I made an appointment with the dean of graduate studies at California State University, Los Angeles. I explained my long story to him and presented my GRE, TOEFL, and EIT scores. He decided to admit me under what they call a Special Action of Admission, which meant that I did not really meet the qualification criteria but that they have reason to believe that I am qualified.

I decided to complete my master's degree in manufacturing engineering, but because such a department did not exist in the university, I was allowed to create a special major by combining classes from the Technology Department, chaired by Dr. Ethan Lipton, and the Mechanical Engineering Department, chaired by Dr. Neda Fabris. As soon as I started the master's program in January of 1993, Dr. Fabris noticed that I was an exceptional student. In June, when she was approached by a baseball cap manufacturing company, Cali-Fame of Los Angeles, seeking to hire a young engineer, she immediately suggested my name. That was my breakthrough into the American job market.

I finished my master's degree while working at Cali-Fame, topping the score in almost every test I took and every homework set I submitted throughout the program. Looking at my 4.0 GPA score, Dr. Lipton said, "It's people like you who encourage us to grant the Special Action of Admission more often." From Cali-Fame, I moved on to a jewelry manufacturing company and then to a cosmetics manufacturing company. As a manufacturing engineer, I was able to improve their processes, reduce defects, increase production, and improve their quality. From there, I accepted a job in Palo Alto, in Silicon Valley, with Space Systems/ Loral. I worked on the assembly floor for satellites and later in the program office of the International Space Station.

On more than one occasion, my coworkers complimented my work as I stood in the Mechanical Test and Assembly building of the satellite division.

"Shant, you're doing a great job as a new guy. Where did you come from?"

"I came from a place much tougher than here."

"What is that? . . . Hughes? . . . Lockheed Martin?"

"No, I was a lipstick engineer."

To this day, I consider making lipstick one of the hardest jobs I had to do. There were four temperature settings on the machine; all had to be set precisely to within one degree. The temperature settings varied with production batch and lipstick color and we had to arrive at the proper temperature settings through trial and error. When either one of the four temperatures was not optimized to the desired value, the lipstick either did not come out of the mold or left a gooey mess. The machine then had to be shut down. More than two hundred molds had to be delicately cleaned with Q-tips before resuming the operation with an adjusted temperature setting. If the mold was too cold, flow lines were observed on the lipstick when it came out. Flow lines were not desirable. When all of these obstacles have been conquered and production is successful, the lipstick had to pass one more test—it had to look sexy, a quality not very well defined in my engineering text books. I went home covered in lipstick every day. Luckily, my fiancée was not the suspicious type.

I was married in 1997, and my wife, Ani, moved to Palo Alto from Pasadena to live with me. After about a year, I applied for a PhD program in the Materials Science and Engineering Department at Johns Hopkins University. Four of my first cousins were already students at the university. I was fortunate to be accepted under the advisory of Dr. Robert E. Green, Jr., who is one of the most respected names in the field of Nondestructive Evaluation (NDE) for the characterization and inspection of materials. His accomplishments would humble any man, yet he was as humble and genuinely good natured as they come. "There is nothing I can do that would add to your résumé, Dr. Green," I used to say to him. He always responded with a smile, "I don't have a Nobel Prize. Why don't you get me one?" I did not win the Nobel Prize but I was granted two precious gifts from heaven. Both my

daughters were born in Baltimore during my PhD program—
Nairy in 1999 and Talar in 2001. I took the second part of the
Professional Engineering license exam and became a PE in 2000.
In January 2003, I defended my dissertation in front of a commit-
tee and completed the requirements for my PhD. In May, I gradu-
ated with a second master's degree and a PhD from the Materials
Science and Engineering Department.

I was appointed as a research scientist with the Center for
Nondestructive Evaluation at Johns Hopkins University, where I
continued my research and developed a prototype for a laser in-
duced ultrasonic inspection technique for the railroad industry. I
am the lead inventor on two patents and coinventor on two others in this field. I have also published more than twenty-five articles in scientific journals; some have been translated into Italian
and Chinese.

In the aftermath of the space shuttle *Columbia* disaster in
2003, NASA approached Dr. Green, who recommended that I
join their team of experts in the fields of materials science and
nondestructive evaluation. The team, in general, was assigned
with several challenging tasks aimed at developing new nondestructive evaluation techniques that would evaluate the struc-
tural integrity of critical parts of the space shuttle. Mainly, I was
tasked with developing airborne ultrasonic methods for the inspection of sprayed-on foam insulation, which covers the exter-
nal tank and was the leading cause of the space shuttle *Columbia*
disaster. I brought this task with me to the Jet Propulsion Labora-
tory, a NASA center in Pasadena, my wife's hometown in the Los
Angeles area. Then I moved on to The Aerospace Corporation,
also in the Los Angeles area, where I think I have found a home
for my career. At The Aerospace Corporation, I continue to work
on NASA projects as well as support other programs of launch

vehicles. God continues to bestow his blessings on me. My son, Aram, was born in 2006 to adorn our happy family with another shining star.

Like many things in my life, earning my U.S. citizenship was not as easy as expected. I visited the Immigration and Naturalization Services (INS) building in Los Angeles shortly after my arrival back in the United States. I filled out an application to reinstate my U.S. residency status and had to wait for hours to receive a number. Then, I had to wait at one of several windows until my number was called. When I finally approached the window and explained my story to the INS officer, she was not sure how to process my unusual request. The officer suggested that I try the window next to her. This meant that I had to receive a new number and wait for hours again before I was called. This confusion repeated for the next three days until I completed visiting all six windows on the first floor of the INS in Los Angeles. Finally, they suggested I visit the INS officers on the second floor.

On the second floor, I stood in line and explained my story. Here, the people in line stood behind me, unlike on the first floor, where we sat in a waiting area until our numbers were called. After the people in line heard my story, they applauded. The officer checked the computer and said that my green card had not expired. I had no need to renew the card, but she wanted me to provide her with new photos so that she could reissue the old card with a more recent photo. In the years that followed, I lost my green card and was issued another. I also applied for a reentry permit, which is a passport given to permanent residents. When that expired, I renewed it, but I never used either because I never left the country. In 1995, I submitted the application to become a naturalized U.S. citizen. In 1996, I was called for the interview and passed the test. I was told to wait a few months until I was called for the oath.

In 1997, Ani and I were making plans to honeymoon in Europe. I had not yet been called for the citizenship oath. Therefore, I visited the INS to inquire about my citizenship application. They discovered that I should have had a new green card issued to me in 1991 rather than a reissued one that retained the old number. They took my green card away and offered to give me a new one based on the letters I had from the American embassy in Saudi or my impending marriage to a U.S. citizen. I insisted that I should not be punished for an error that the INS made and wanted to go to court. "The only court you can go to is deportation court," they said. It wasn't the first time I took the road less traveled. I made a request they never heard an immigrant make, "Let's go to deportation court."

Ani and I went to Hawaii for our honeymoon.

For the next two years, I would fly back to Los Angeles from Baltimore on short notice to appear in court. Sometimes, the judge called in sick. Other times, my file was missing from the courtroom, so we had to reschedule. Although the INS had two or three sets of my fingerprints taken at different times, I made at least two additional flights from Baltimore specifically to be fingerprinted again. In the end, more than nine years after my return to America, I finally became a U.S. citizen.

Back in 1978 and 1979, in Chicago, I used to stand on the soccer field with my teammates while they fixed their right hands on their hearts and their eyes on the flag while the "Star Spangled Banner" played. I used to look at the flag admirably but kept my hands to my side, not in defiance, but because I had not yet earned that privilege.

Twenty-one years later, on September 8, 2000, I took my citizenship oath and paid my due respect to the flag that I have always wanted to represent me.

Two years later, I visited Armenia for the first time. For a long while, I couldn't lift my eyes from its national symbol, Mount Ararat, on the Turkish side of the border. From base to peak, they say it is the tallest mountain in the world. Although I knew every little feature from photographs, its majestic beauty was far greater than I could have ever imagined.

Like the story of Job in the Bible, the early misfortune in my life has been compensated many times over, and for me that has taken the forms of my beautiful wife and children. They fill my world with heavenly blessings and make me feel richer than the richest.

Acknowledgments

On April 9, 2003, I stood in the conference room of the Center for Nondestructive Evaluation (CNDE) at Johns Hopkins University, watching the TV monitor as the U.S. forces brought Saddam's statue down. They were surrounded by Iraqi civilians celebrating their freedom on Ferdous Square in Baghdad. Boro Djordjevic, the director of the CNDE then, turned around and told me it was time to write my book. Months later, I gave my manuscript to Dr. Green, my PhD program advisor. He had been looking at thesis and dissertation manuscripts for more than forty years and was happy to review something else for a change.

When I returned to Los Angeles, Sharlene Martin introduced me to Anthony Flacco who edited my manuscript. The timeliness of my story led me to publish the book myself through Booksurge.com, an Amazon.com self-publishing program. Before the book was released, my first cousin Nadia Sarkis contacted me about pitching my story to public radio's *This American Life* with Ira Glass, Julie Snyder, and Jane Feltes. On February 10, 2006, and again in 2007, *This American Life* aired a segment with my voice reading excerpts from the book. Prior to my story being aired on *This American Life*, producer Jay Burns approached me about a movie project. He teamed up with Robert Cort and Scarlett Lacey from Robert Cort Productions and Director Scott Burns. They were all eager to tell my story.

Amy Tannenbaum, an editor from Atria Books, heard the story on *This American Life*. After a few e-mails and phone calls, she and Johanna Castillo presented me with an offer and a contract was in place. Liz Balmaseda edited the opening chapters of the book and Amy oversaw the entire editing process until the book was ready for publication.

I would like to thank all of those mentioned above who found inspiration in my story and helped share it with the public. I am fortunate for the constant support I receive from my immediate and extended family. But most of all, I would like to thank our Heavenly Father for the life I was given, Christ for walking with me throughout my difficult journey, and the Holy Spirit for always giving me hope. I especially want to thank my wife and children, my true guardian angels and my gifts from God, who brought stability and sunshine back into my life. There were times when I thought nothing could bring my life up to par with others who have not experienced such a traumatic event, but with my wife and children, I now feel that I am overly blessed.